TRUTH OR TREATY?

TRUTH or TREATY?

Commonsense questions about the Treaty of Waitangi

DAVID ROUND

CANTERBURY UNIVERSITY PRESS

First published in 1998 by
CANTERBURY UNIVERSITY PRESS
Private Bag 4800, Christchurch, New Zealand

ISBN 0-908812-72-8

Designed and typeset at Canterbury University Press
Printed by Rainbow Print, Christchurch

To my countrymen
of both sexes and all races

CONTENTS

All the world may see to what a point we are come, that we are not like to have a good end when the divisions at the beginning are such.

– Charles II, at the dissolution of the Oxford Parliament

INTRODUCTION

My claims for this book are modest. It does not claim to say much that is startlingly new: it merely hopes to put into ordered form the good sense most of us already possess and express. It cannot even claim to be particularly courageous, since, in the south anyway, these ideas are ones which nearly all of us hold – including many Maoris, who often take as cynical a view of their leaders as anyone else. Indeed, it is a mystery to me why more people have not written such books earlier. I despair that the points I make need to be made at all. But nature abhors a vacuum, and if men and women of sense do not state their position, we will be abandoning the state to the angry and greedy.

It is not a history book. It cannot, of course, escape referring to historical events; but anyone who wishes to study the Treaty of Waitangi, and relations between the races, in our history, must look elsewhere. Nor is it a work of law, although it contains one chapter on that useful topic. It is instead – so I would like to think – a book of common sense; a book of simple and obvious home truths that somehow few people seem inclined to want to put into print. It is a political book, as all books on race relations and our country's future must be, regardless of their academic disguises. It will doubtless be praised or condemned on political grounds, not on the quality of its writing or research. Almost certainly there lurks, somewhere in these pages, some unnoticed error of fact with which my opponents will attempt to belabour me, but which will make little if any difference to my argument as a whole. I write this book out of love for my country, out of my increasing depression at the mire – notably, but not only, the racial mire – in which daily we seem to sink deeper – and out of the belief that it still is not too late to make things better.

We live in an age of experts. Even such plain, homely questions as the running of our own families and the education and care of our children are now to be answered by highly paid experts. Consultants and counsellors lurk everywhere. We are in no better position than the humble medieval peasant who watched uncomprehendingly as the priest muttered the words of the mass in Latin. Scientists, lawyers, and experts of all kinds are our priests. They, too, speak an incomprehensible language – and since they claim to have the answers, all we can do is listen and obey. The best we can hope for is to find some expert who has come to a conclusion we like, and whom we can then cheer on, uncomprehendingly, from the sidelines.

Nothing is simple any longer. Even last century, a pioneer of native wit and fortitude could, given favourable circumstances, turn his hand to agriculture, science, politics and art. He could make a good and valuable contribution in a number of fields. It is more difficult now. Now, if one ventures to attempt anything, or offer an opinion, outside one's own narrow sphere of expertise, one is immediately condemned by the expensive experts in that field as not knowing what one is talking about.

To some extent this tendency may be inevitable as the amount of detailed scientific knowledge grows. No-one would claim to know more about nuclear physics than a nuclear physicist. But in many cases it is not inevitable. We all have and are entitled to have valid views on, say, the raising and education of children, the appearance and quality of our cities, the general purposes which our economic structures should serve, and the place which the Treaty and Maori claims should have in our society. These questions involve moral and political judgments, where 'experts' are in no better position than anyone else to come to a proper conclusion. We should realise that, under the disguise of 'rational and neutral science', experts often carry a huge amount of moral baggage and political agendas of their own, which they attempt to pass off on the public as 'science'. If they succeed in this deception, of course, then they have won the war, for none of us would dream of questioning any decision emanating from science, our new god. This is a profoundly anti-democratic tendency. We pay lip-service to democracy, but at the same time the areas where ordinary people are held entitled to have a valid serious opinion are shrinking daily.

If we are not careful, the Treaty of Waitangi will be one of these areas. We see the process beginning already. Everyone who pontificates on the matter informs us that the subject is immensely complicated – and clearly, therefore, something no layperson could hope to understand.

Although the merest handful of legal cases have anything to say about the Treaty, and a barely larger number of statutes refer in passing to the 'principles' of the Treaty, university law schools establish whole courses to teach – and propagandise – the subject. Whole books are written that in half-mystical tones expound its 'principles' in such a way as to make it seem that the most bizarre ideas of Maori sovereignty or independence flow naturally and inevitably from that tiny, vaguely phrased scrap of paper signed by a handful of men so long ago. But the facts, law and issues are really very simple.

In writing this book I have of course been worried that I may be revealing myself as paranoid. Perhaps the Treaty radicals I disagree with are but a small handful who simply receive a disproportionate amount of attention from news media always hungry for sensation. Perhaps we should think more on the words of a famous revolutionary: that if ordinary comfortably-off people knew how difficult it was to start a revolution, they would sleep much more easily in their beds.

But ideas, even stupid ones, have lives of their own – and if someone does not raise a voice to point out the absurdities and injustices inherent in the Treaty mania, those stupid ideas will live unmolested. Bad ideas do not die off automatically: they have to be killed by good ones. We can, surely, think of plenty of times in human history when bad ideas have prevailed. Such times may come again. And revolutions, ultimately, are made not by guns, but by the ideas that fill the minds of those who carry the guns. For stupidity, as well as evil, to triumph, it is enough that good people do nothing.

The Treaty mania, then, must be rooted out – if that is still possible – before it becomes a full-grown tree. In the last decade or so, New Zealanders have, more than ever before, made real efforts to remedy past injustices, real or supposed, done to Maoris. What has happened? Has the level of Maori agitation diminished as wrongs have been righted? On the contrary. The more we give, the more they want. The policy of appeasement is fatal. We have been throwing petrol on the flames. It is time for a powerful fire-extinguisher.

This book is the distillation of some years of thought and argument on the subject. The alert reader will notice various places where the author refers to actual incidents and arguments – often, arguments wearily repeated on many occasions. Inevitably, too, it contains generalisations, for it would be tedious to hedge about every statement with cautious legalistic provisos and exceptions. Nor does it always give chapter and verse for every statement it makes. Certain chapters, especially those on the law, do contain more references; but this is chiefly a book of argument and principle, not a historical handbook. Besides, the general background outline of most of the statements made and facts and incidents referred to will be known to most New Zealanders, even if they, like I, have not always dated their newspaper clippings most scrupulously.

Just as so many of these arguments may be familiar, so too may be some of the words. I have, I hope, acknowledged all my quotations; but I fear that some words of other people may have lodged in my mind and crept into my writing. If so, I apologise.

It has been difficult, in writing this slim volume, to think of suitable labels for the parties involved in the argument. One cannot, obviously, speak of 'Maori' and 'Pakeha', for, quite apart from any doubt as to whether a true 'Maori race' still exists members of both races hold the full diversity of views on the matter.

I object, in any case, to being referred to as a 'Pakeha'. The origins of this term are obscure; and, even if it is not a Maori corruption of a common English expletive, it is still, for the non-Maori inhabitants of this country, a word from another language and culture, not from their own. I am a New Zealander, or a European New Zealander. I know some sympathetic readers may object to my use of the term 'European New Zealander'. They may insist they are just plain 'New Zealanders', and not 'Europeans'. I see what they mean, and am sympathetic. But it is difficult to find another word that will do. To refer to the small but vocal collection of my opponents I have invented the nasty but serviceable word 'Treatyists'. I apologise for its ugliness. Such are the times.

Readers will notice also that I refer to 'Maoris', not 'Maori'. I do so not to be old-fashioned or derogatory, but for a sound practical reason. To speak of 'Maori' implies that all those of Maori descent are one coherent body, with a more or less agreed set of philosophies, attitudes, beliefs and politics, when this is simply not the case. I know, for example, that there are some, at least, of Maori descent who agree with everything I have written here. No-one is entitled to claim that those sensible people are therefore somehow less authentically 'Maori' than more radical people. I use 'Maoris' to remind us that those of Maori descent have all the differences and diversity of other human beings. They are people, not just a useful category for manipulation, like 'the masses' or 'the proletariat'. The Treaty itself recognised that there was no 'Maori people' before 1840: the Treaty was with tribes, not a state or a race.

I must thank many people for their help; my family, and so many strangers who have offered their support for previous things I have written on this subject. Racial arguments easily become unpleasant, and without that support my natural desire to avoid unpleasantness and avoid the usual accusations of spiritual corruption would probably have meant this book would not have been written. I thank my friends for discussing these questions, raising new points and tolerating my occasional monologue. I thank those friends who have disagreed with me, for helping to refine and hone my arguments, and for remaining friends. I thank those who examined and improved parts of my manuscript. The improvements and corrections are theirs; the errors remain my own. I thank in particular David Garrett for his contribution (pages 89–92) on the latest full and final settlements, and Maxine Marriott of the University of Canterbury Faculty of Law for her cheerfulness and patience with my handwriting. I must also thank Mike Bradstock of Canterbury University Press for his unobtrusive wisdom, helpfulness and gift for conviviality. Finally, I thank my readers. Let us go out and make this country better.

D.J.R.

August 1998

ONE
The World

Things fall apart; the centre cannot hold;
Mere anarchy is loosed upon the world,
The blood-dimmed tide is loosed, and everywhere
The ceremony of innocence is drowned;
The best lack all conviction, while the worst
Are full of passionate intensity.

– W. B. Yeats, 'The Second Coming'

The best lack all conviction. They have so little confidence in their own beliefs and the virtues of their civilisation that they stand by – not idly, perhaps, but wringing their hands, and full of vague concerns – while barbarians take over. Very often they invoke the principle of tolerance as a reason for not condemning cruelty, stupidity and ignorance.

Civilisation is suffering from a failure of nerve. The totalitarianism of Soviet Russia and Nazi Germany, the inhumanity of unbridled capitalism, the injustices of colonialism and the environmental crisis which science and materialism have led us to, have led many to conclude that Western civilisation is worthless, and better abandoned. Instead, some new tribal deity – of some particular race, sex or sexual orientation, religion or political cause – is found to embody our highest desires and longings.

The worship of early nineteenth-century Maori culture as some ideal of what human society and civilisation should be is only one symptom of a far more widespread spiritual sickness. Many of our cultural leaders have some sense of self-hatred for their own civilisation. No-one expects them to say that it is perfect; but they seem to maintain that the very opposite is true.

Notice the way in which certain teachers or activists inform us that, let us say, much of Greek literature first came to the attention of medieval Europe through the Arabs – or that the Chinese, and not Europeans, invented gunpowder and printing with movable type – or that in some other way, Europe had feet of clay, and did something beastly, or did not do something good or clever first. It is, of course, fair enough to say these things – if they be true – but notice the *glee* with which the teacher announces this fact – a fact probably well known in any case, to someone whose education is better than his. How much pleasure the teacher derives from this blow against a civilisation that is clearly the enemy. How many of our intellectuals and would-be intellectuals are, to paraphrase W. S. Gilbert,

> *The idiot who praises, with enthusiastic tone,*
> *All cultures but this, and every race but his own.*

New Internationalist magazine, highminded and commendable in many ways, may serve as a convenient example of this devotion to

> *falling out with that or this*
> *and finding somewhat still amiss.*[1]

It even complains that multiculturalism does not go far enough, and has 'directly contributed to the resurgence of racial violence in Britain'. It invents a distinction between 'racial prejudice' – 'wild notions about people who looked so obviously different and came from a world away' (which everyone has, and which is presumably all right) – and 'racism' – an ideology which bundles up prejudices to prove that [people of other races] are inferior' – which evidently only Western Europeans have. This distinction is absurd: all groups have a natural and inevitable tendency to suppose that they are better than anyone else. But Europe is said to be the only home of this belief.

This self-hatred may spring from admirable motives. Those who possess it might prefer to describe it as 'humility', and as a necessary and inevitable reaction against an over-weening confidence and arrogance which saw everything Western as good and superior. There is some grain of truth in this point of view, but it is not the whole story.

Many historians and philosophers have observed that, in J. W.

Krutch's words, 'societies are most admirable just before they collapse'.[2] In the search for human values we neglect the natural virtues and animal principles which serve to keep the anthill sound. Civilisation, humanity and tolerance contain the seeds of their own end; and in history's great cycle, barbarians are always inevitably appearing – from beyond the borders, or merely from the despised lower orders – to bring in necessary infusions of fresh blood, vigour and common sense.

Tolerance is indeed a civilised virtue. Yet it contains the seed of its own downfall. Civilisations, like empires, are made by the vigorous and self-confident, who are not afraid to impose their own views and visions on others. (This is, of course, also the way that unpleasant dictatorships are made, which is a great problem.) The foundations of a civilisation are laid by those lacking large amounts of tolerance; and when their more refined and sophisticated descendants express contempt for the brisk and straightforward ways of their pioneering ancestors, one knows that that particular civilisation is in trouble. When a civilisation falls, then tolerance will fall with it.

It is, in some ways, unfair to lay the blame at civilisation's door for the crimes of Communism and Nazism, capitalism and colonialism. Space does not permit us to consider the arguments here. But one cannot condemn a civilisation thousands of years old on the basis of several very recent aberrations. Nor has any civilisation anywhere been without its faults. Silly

The philosophical movement that embodies the spirit of extreme tolerance, and the attack on accepted Western ways of doing things, is the philosophy of 'post-modernism', which, believing it is making a completely fresh start, denies the existence of any order or objective moral standards in the universe or in human life. There is only individual judgment, and no idea is better or worse than another. In art, post-modernism refuses to accept the existence of any external principles and glorifies the ugly and bizarre. Self-indulgent or offensive behaviour is defended in the name of self-expression and tolerance. Standards are claimed to be inherently oppressive, in that they discriminate against oppressed minorities, who are forced, unfairly, it is said, to observe standards unknown in their own culture.

It is uncertain whether a successful, coherent, stable human society can survive without agreement on common standards of thought, skills, behaviour and morality. Perhaps if a society is a stratified hierarchy, then such common standards are not necessary, but in a democracy they may well be. It may, however, in the long run, be just as necessary for any sustainable society to believe in objective principles of personal morality and commonly agreed standards of spelling and grammar, as it is to adhere to standards of political, business and environmental morality.

Post-modernists would be horrified by the accusation, but their attitudes are merely the philosophical expression of extreme free-market capitalism. There is also the claim that 'society' does not exist; there are only individuals, and individual interests, all equally see p. 23 valid. No-one – God or State – has any right to arbitrate between them, and say that some interests and beliefs are better than others, or that such a thing as the common good exists. Without any widely accepted binding ideals, the belief that self-interest leads to the greater good, as if guided by an invisible hand, means that no-one is entitled any longer to view any other point of view, however squalid or absurd, as invalid.

This is moral relativism. It is a denial that any permanent and objective standards of moral behaviour exist at all. It is, ultimately, a recipe for anarchy and self-indulgence, and it is one of the most popular beliefs of our age. But so many of its adherents also subscribe to a completely contradictory belief. They believe, very often, that racism, sexism and heterosexism are completely wrong. They condemn those who practise them – or allegedly practise them – as evil. But how are they entitled to do so? If one denies the existence of any objective standards of right and wrong, then one cannot condemn anyone else. I condemn racism, but then I am old-fashioned enough to believe in right and wrong. Modern people who deny right and wrong cannot condemn anything or anyone.

A lecturer in law at the University of Waikato claims, during lectures, that people who purport to have 'objective knowledge' are on a 'God trip'. No arguments (except her own, presumably) have objective validity. 'Knowledge' is plural; there are 'knowledges' which are 'located' in the individual's 'social reality'. The same university's Psychology Department defines racism as a white person prejudging a person of another race. Discrimination *against* whites is not, therefore, racist. A professor of law claims that 'reason' is a 'peculiar fetish'. 'Reality' is a 'social construct'. White students are passed over for entry into specific courses in favour of less qualified

Maori applicants, who are said to possess their own, equally valid, 'knowledge'. [3]

We see these contradictions when staunch feminists remain silent and sit at the back on a marae because traditionally, in most Maori tribes, women behaved in this manner. They remain silent because a logical consequence of this moral relativism is the view that no culture (with its set of moral values) can judge another. There are no universal principles. This leads, of course, to absurdities, such as accepting cannibalism, human sacrifice, female circumcision and incest. But even Judge Durie, of the Waitangi Tribunal, has maintained that 'one culture should not be judged by the standards of another; each must be appreciated on its own terms'.[4]

This attitude does no service to Maoridom. It demands freedom from criticism, and it requires that no-one form a judgment about any other culture. It assumes, in effect, that Maori culture, if it were to change, would somehow cease to be Maori. Instead, it is to be fossilised, as it existed in some uncertain time in the past – a time after cannibalism had ended, but before women's liberation. This is absurd. We cannot stop people from forming judgments. All cultures change; some make a virtue of it, and many benefit from it.

This is one aspect of an eternal human problem: how can we, at one and the same time, sympathetically understand other people – see things through their eyes, walk in their shoes – and, at the same time, retain our own sense of judgment and proportion? It is a problem that faces those involved in history, anthropology, all of the social sciences – that entering into the minds and hearts of those one observes can easily lead to a loss of ones own moral sense.

The present crisis of confidence also arises in part, simply from that sense of inferiority which over-civilised people often feel in the presence of vigorous and confident barbarians. Professor Toynbee, in his *Study of History*[5] observes that when a civilisation grows weary and begins to disintegrate, there is often 'a process of proletarianisation along . . . two parallel lines – vulgarisation by contact with the internal proletariat, and barbarisation by contact with the external proletariat'. He writes of the barbarising effect of the American frontier, and how a European can be transformed into something very like an Indian. The same spiritual malady may well be at work here.

Professor Toynbee also observes that other societies deal with a

[margin handwritten note:] does "barbarian" mean one of another culture or of no culture at all?

changing world by what he calls 'archaism' – a deliberate and conscious return to the past. We see this in Rousseau's 'noble savage', and we see it in the nineteenth-century Teutonic romanticism which later developed unpleasant teeth and claws in Nazi Germany. We see it also, perhaps, in the way in which many Maori activists announce, sometimes in these very words, that 'in the past lies our future'.

Admiration of the noble savage has been assisted by the refinement of Marxism. As it gradually became clear that Marx's explanation of history, in terms of class conflict and the struggles of the proletariat, was difficult to reconcile with reality, various intellectuals, reluctant to abandon Marxism entirely, tried to adapt the philosophy by discovering new 'proletariats'. Any oppressed group would do; so women, and people of other races, became the two favoured quasi-proletariats. And indeed, in South Africa, the United States and here in New Zealand, dark-skinned people often do, for one reason or another, form a significant part of the lower working – or non-working – classes. Enthusiasm for them arises in part from the desire not to forsake Marx completely, but rather to revise and refine him.

Our societies seem to be in danger, not just of changing (for that is inevitable, and may well be healthy), but of disintegrating into a new tribalism. Tribalism is not just another word for diversity. Tribalism – be it racial, sexual, based on class or religion – has a <u>closed mind</u>. It is the enemy of rational discussion. It is a new dogmatism. It is, by its very nature, anti-social, for it can only define itself by its separation from the rest of the community, and by the assertion of its 'interests and rights'. It is all too often run by self-appointed spokesmen who profit through antagonism and ill-feeling, and who are as ready to be dictators and demagogues as any of their supposed enemies. The double standard has not disappeared.

This double standard exists overseas as well as in New Zealand. We must tolerate the Virgin in the Condom – but the outrage when the Iranian clergy imposed their fatwa on Salman Rushdie was very muted. What *we* do is 'oppress'; what *others* do is 'their culture'. And very often, indeed, history is rewritten so that nothing oppressive was ever done by anyone except the 'pale, patriarchal, penis people'. The noble savage lives. The Ngai Tahu Maori Law Centre in Dunedin has declared that before Columbus 'the native peoples of America governed themselves by consensus. There was no conquest involved.' No human sacrifice, evidently, no wars, no torture, no slavery. The Centre's statements reveal an ignorance of history almost as profound as its ignorance of human nature.

(handwritten margin note: some were Nubian)

Robert Hughes notes that black Americans, claiming that the Ancient Egyptians were negroid – even such Greek Egyptians as Euclid and Cleopatra – also claim that black Africans created all the ideas out of which arose 'Judaism, Christianity, Islam, dialectics . . . arithmetic, geometry, mechanical engineering, astronomy, drama, architecture and the arts'. There are even claims that these black Egyptians invented the aeroplane. The fundamental role played by black Africans and Arabs in the slave trade – a trade in which Europeans were only buyers, albeit willing ones – is written out of existence. (The African slave trade had, in fact, existed long before Europeans bought black slaves, and it lasted well after Europe and America abolished slavery.[6]) Some black American leaders, including Jesse Jackson, have even proposed that America and Europe should make financial reparation to African states. None of them have suggested that any Arab states should provide contributions, which, by all rights, should be rather larger.

Some see the end of the nation-state in this dissolution of society into sects and tribes. That may be too pessimistic, but even if it is true, its decline would not be, in every way, a disaster. We have not always had such units of sovereignty: they arose only out of the destruction of feudal power, and for much of human history we have not known them. Many of the problems facing us today are ones where either specific local solutions are needed or, at the other extreme, international co-operation is required. 'Think globally, act locally', runs the sound environmental maxim; yet the nation-state does neither.

But if we are to replace the nation-state with other organs of government, let us do it properly and consistently. Let us delegate power to organs that actually have vital force, not to tribes, which most of Maori descent have very little, in practice, to do with, and by which most Maori very possibly do not want to be ruled. Let us delegate power in ways that will serve the common good, not just one or two currently fashionable sectional interests. If we are going to recognise minorities, why not be consistent and recognise all of them? There are, after all, hundreds of minorities.

We are all members of quite a few minority groups. Roman

Catholics, Anglicans, Methodists and Baptists are all minorities. And consider racial ancestry – Irish, Scottish, Dalmatian, Dutch, Chinese – most of us will belong to a racial minority group. The province we live in will be a minority in New Zealand. Every occupation and class is a minority, as is every political party, age group and interest group. Yet we know that Roman Catholics, or the Irish, for example, do not enjoy the favour which women and Maoris do. It is entirely arbitrary and unjust that society and the law should favour just a handful of minorities, and ignore all the others. *precious – ignores who has power*

Nation-states have, in many ways, served us well. They have eliminated feudal violence and the oppression of class and religion. They have given us public administration of integrity, and democracy of a sort. A nation is also, in part, a community, with a common history and culture. It is part of the betrayal of us by our rulers that, in many parts of the world, those rulers have so little loyalty to their own nation and national identity, but regard themselves instead as part of a global society – inevitably, a society of the rich and comfortable. They consider their first loyalty to the global economy, and not to their own nations. They accept none of the obligations of citizenship of a nation, and they often object to paying taxes even in principle. As this small, privileged elite appears, and as more and more of the population becomes part of an under-paid, precariously employed lumpen mass, so the middle class – always rising, in our history books, as the incorruptible and astute allies of kings against feudalism, and republics against kings – so often maligned, yet with its solid virtues, whose security and decency so many of us have relied on, and whose comfort we have sought – the middle class is declining. Whether the virtues and attitudes of millionaires and an urban proletariat will be any better for civilisation remains to be seen.

This disloyalty to one's political community may, of course, be defended on high-minded grounds. One's own fellow citizens may not be sufficiently morally worthy. Overseas, as well as here in New Zealand, intellectuals and anti-racism activists smugly believe that they alone are not racist. This is absurd: in Europe, America and in New Zealand – perhaps not in Asia or Africa – the worst of us are far more racially aware and tolerant than we were fifty years ago. What is often called 'racism' is very often, in fact, the opposite: it is, like this book, an objection to the offensive double standards, hypocrisies, and ignorance of the smug and politically correct.

Western civilisation, as Mario Vargas Llosa has said, differs from other civilisations in offering a secure place for people who do not originate from it. No Asian country treats its ethnic minorities with as much respect as New Zealand does. Neither were tribal Maori racially and culturally tolerant.

There exists worldwide what Robert Hughes has called a 'culture of complaint'. It has become almost obligatory, not merely to regret past iniquities – which is entirely good and proper – but to apologise for them, which is absurd. The Prime Minister of the United Kingdom apologises for Britain's actions in Ireland last century, even though no-one alive now was responsible for those actions. Robert Hughes recognises that our most fashionable religion is the 'cult of the victim'; victims alone can be heroes; hence the child abuse mania which reveals how so many of us were victims as children. As victims we all look for someone else to blame, never ourselves; we have rights, but never duties or obligations. Standards and measurements of quality are condemned, for they will be 'oppressive'; instead, the emphasis is on what we *feel* (however mistakenly), not on what we actually think or know or can do.

why?

institution, alive & responsible

How eagerly and uncritically we believe an alleged 'victim'. When grown men and women suddenly claim that they have 'recovered' the memory of sexual abuse they suffered as children, but had 're-pressed' for years, people are convicted and sent to prison without even any corroboration of the charges. Claims of injustice to Maori which are unsupported by evidence, and even on the face of it highly unlikely, are uncritically believed. *like…?*

It is remarkable that an age so ready to condemn guilt as a destructive and unhealthy force (at least, if it be that perpetual bogeyman, the Catholic Church, who is responsible for it) is also so keen to embrace it. Thirty years ago, someone in the United States, observing white breast-beating for racial beastliness, and referring to Stokeley Carmichael, leader of the Black Panthers, spoke of the 'Please-Stokeley-rape-my-sister' syndrome. No seminar on the Treaty of Waitangi can begin without a thorough guilt-inducing session. Indeed, that is all that most 'educational' seminars on the Treaty are – partial, and usually highly coloured and inaccurate, accounts of Maori virtue and European perfidy, leading to some unsurprising political conclusions.

→ labor policy in early 19thc.

The welfare state's commitment to decency, and its belief in the dignity of all human beings, are fine ideals. Nevertheless, it cannot be denied that in practice it has assisted the cult of the victim. It has led to some blunting of our self-reliance and initiative. The welfare state's ideology of compassion, also, subverts democracy, which 'depends not so much on compassion as on mutual respect. A misplaced compassion degrades both the victims, who are reduced to objects of pity, and their would-be benefactors, who find it easier to pity their fellow-citizens than to hold them up to impersonal standards, the attainment of which would entitle them to respect.'[7]

In the United States, many former supporters of the whole 'affirmative action' programme – the policy of discriminating *in favour* of certain minorities – are now reluctantly turning to the view that it has been an enormous failure. Its motivations may be generous, but it teaches those who take advantage of it that their future success lies in their status as 'victims'. It says that society is formed of groups – black and white, male and female, gay and straight – rather than people. Individuals are merely branch offices of the group. But there is more to human diversity than race. It is absurd that President Clinton could fill his Cabinet with high-powered lawyers of various colours, and then claim that the resulting group

→ post-modern see p. 17

23

[Handwritten marginalia top: "He assumes qualified on basis on 1 test for example merit by numbers — police exams."]

[Handwritten marginalia left margin: "No pool of qualified view PREFER the underrepresented or under utilised"]

was 'diverse'. Affirmative action is certainly unjust at an individual level, as it prefers less qualified people belonging to a minority group to better qualified people unfortunate enough to be of the majority. It favours and advances the less competent – and, even in this country, we all know of cases of lazy or incompetent people who are kept in their jobs simply because they are not white. There is also plenty of evidence that affirmative action does little, if anything, to help the people who need it most. It is more likely to be already well-educated and prosperous children of well-established parents who benefit from these scholarships and quotas, rather than desperately poor members of the underclass. *[Handwritten: "with means test af. act is ok?"]*

It is true that racial distinctions will not disappear just because governments refuse to recognise them. But it is also true that racial distinctions will not disappear while governments not only recognise them, but also enforce them.

Well-meaning, but foolish, anti-racists play with forces which they do not understand. They are fools if they do not see, in themselves and in others, the dark and destructive, angry and hateful aspects of our human nature. We are not all sweetness and light.

Rousseau's rhapsodic accounts of the 'noble savage' led to the atrocities of Robespierre and the Reign of Terror. And, as Professor Toynbee observes 'the harmless professorial cranks who spent the nineteenth century . . . in idealising the primitive pagan "Nordic" race cannot entirely disclaim responsibility for the Nazi terror of our own day'.[8] Who knows where the unthinking glorification of traditional Maori culture will lead us?

[Handwritten: "I don't think so or does he mean excess of Romanticism? I don't know what caused R. of Terror."]

24

TWO

Our Own Country

A blight lies on our country. It destroys conversations and friendships, sours all political discourse and disrupts dinner parties. It obsesses us all; we neglect other pressing issues and tear ourselves apart on this one. It encourages divisiveness, bitterness and hatred. One side labels the other reactionaries and racists; the other replies with the labels of weaklings, dupes and fools. It is the Treaty – once, long ago, a sign of hope and a harmonious future, but now, if we are not careful, a recipe for anarchy and civil war.

The worship of the Treaty is to some extent doubtless one of fashion, and that will subside. But what damage may have been done in the meantime? Small boys throw stones at frogs in jest; but the frogs die not in jest but in earnest.

But it is not all fashion; and in any case political fashions can cause harm to the body politic. There are already influential vested interests supporting the Treaty mania.

There is a lucrative Treaty industry. The Waitangi Tribunal funds researchers and consultants, and claimants before the Tribunal employ their own consultants and lawyers. Many government departments have their own Maori sections; universities and polytechnics shelter activists ready to present their political opinions as established wisdom. Most, if not all, law schools now run courses on 'Treaty law', and it would be surprising indeed if the political views of the teachers did not colour their lectures. Some Treaty law courses devote a quarter or a third of their time to the future – an occasion, doubtless, for much wishful thinking. Some wealthy tribes are becoming economic forces in their regions, and businessmen hasten to court those who may soon acquire substantial assets.

The ridiculous spectacle

We know no spectacle so ridiculous, Lord Macaulay observed, as the British public in one of its periodical fits of morality. What absurdities we accept in the name of cultural justice. Female politicians who would sternly object to European sexism are rather more meek when Maori tell them to sit at the back of a meeting hall.

Eminent persons make expensive overseas pilgrimages to recover Maori heads, which, last century, were freely sold by Maoris, along with shipbuilding materials, provisions and sexual favours. Some of the heads that were sold were those of enemies, and the sale was the selling tribe's method of insulting its enemy further. It could surely be argued that to bring the head back is an insult to the selling tribe's mana. Slaves were sometimes tattooed to order and then killed. It was not unknown for the bearer of a fine tattoo to be killed for his head if a European buyer had admired him. One even hears claims that many, if not all, heads held overseas were looted from burial grounds. This is an obvious attempt to rewrite history and surely reveals a desire to mask the actions of Maori ancestors. Some Maoris, however, have called the repatriation of these heads a waste of time

and money, and have urged MPs to worry about more important issues.

Polytechnics and colleges of education have done their bit for bad race relations and cultural misunderstanding in recent years by conducting large sections of their ceremonies in the Maori language – totally incomprehensible to nearly all of their audience. They justify this by the legalistic claim that Maori is an official language, although in other cases they would not necessarily conclude that whatever is legal is just or sensible.

Nelson Polytechnic has been found in breach of various human rights laws by reserving places on a fishing cadet course for Maori and Pacific Island students. Many university departments have quotas for Maori students – quotas which, by definition, offer places to people who would not be able to obtain them by merit. Some advertise their job vacancies in Maori as well as English.

Now Victoria University is considering making all its students sit 'compulsory courses in Asian culture, Maori culture and research skills'. The Vice-Chancellor describes this proposal as 'courageous', and explains that it is what employers want. There is no mention of compulsory English, say, or mathematics – are we to believe that employers do not want literacy or numeracy? *students don't HAVE to take English or math?*

Other examples include a government agency which pays a 'fishing school' $450 for every Maori trainee it places in work. A student at Lincoln University discovers that out of forty-four scholarships offered, his European ancestry disqualifies him from twenty-five. Not one scholarship, however, was offered to students of European *POWER again* descent only. Taieri High School announced that, although all its schoolboys must have short hair, Maori pupils who 'substantiate a case on cultural grounds' may wear their hair long.

Long hair has, of course, at various times, been fashionable in Europe. We all know, for example, of the long-haired cavaliers of Charles I – as well as the genuine cultural movement of the 1960s. Was the headmaster ignorant of this? Or is Maori historical 'culture' to have special rights, and European history to be condemned?

Mr Tau Henare wants the official status of the Maori language to be entrenched, so that later parliaments cannot alter the law. It is interesting that he is worried that this might happen.

Compulsory Maori language education is suggested, from time to time, for all schoolchildren. This would, surely, be just as coercive and pointless as compulsory Latin. One form of oppression would merely be replacing another. Yet the Christchurch College of Education will require all its teacher-trainees to graduate as 'speakers' of Maori by the turn of the century. (To be a 'speaker' is, it seems, less than to be a 'competent or able speaker' – that earlier proposal was abandoned.) But teachers will still be expected, for example, to 'address the Maori dimension of the maths curriculum'.

Europeans cannot win. If, for example, European artists do not paint Maoris, then they are accused of denying their existence. If they do paint them, they are then 'colonising them'. If Europeans do not study Maori, they are ignoring it; if they do learn the language, they are attempting, in the words of one well-known Maori educator, to 'take it over', and they merely become 'informed racists'. It is a similar scenario with Maori history, which some Maori activists claim should be taught and studied only by Maori. How are Europeans, then, to *learn* of their alleged past wickedness?

If Maoris do not appear on television, they are being marginalised. When Telecom put a Maori girl on one of its advertisements, a Maori Anglican bishop and former Governor-General complained that this was 'tokenism'. (The girl's mother objected to the bishop talking about her daughter in public, and said that he was 'the last person to be speaking about Maori tokenism. He's done nothing for us.'[3])

Maoris, it seems, if we may believe some of their spokesmen, regard knowledge as special and sacred and reserved for certain privileged – and therefore more powerful – ears only, usually the ears of people 'entitled' to it by birth. Even Sir Paul Reeves evidently sympathises with the concerns of Maori elders that 'information they had given to New Zealand historians had been put into books which were being sold in shops for money'.[4] It is, as Professor Munz says, a return to the Dark Ages when certain knowledge is private, and common people are not allowed to share it.

Maori students have criticised university curriculums because they make knowledge available to everyone, and allow everyone to discuss and question it. It has even been suggested that Maori monitors should be stationed in every university department to prevent knowledge from being bandied round. Professor Munz says that the atmosphere of the marae (respect for elders and tradition) and that of a university (open inquiry) are mutually exclusive, and that it would be unfortunate if universities, gradually freed from domination by the Church, should now surrender themselves to the bondage of maraes. One might say, surely, that if Maori secret knowledge is actually secret, the answer is for Maori to keep it that way; and if it is not secret, but rather public knowledge, then it cannot become secret again.

Professor Claudia Scott, of the Creative New Zealand Arts Board, states that Creative New Zealand should recognise Maori arts 'independent of the requirements of the [legislation]'.[5] In other words, the Arts Board chooses in this matter to set itself above the law. Suppose, Professor Scott was asked in the same interview, five artists applied for the same grant from Creative New Zealand; four were sensitive, bicultural and mediocre; the fifth was culturally insensitive and brilliant. Who would get the funding? Professor Scott replied that an application 'doing something to promote New Zealand and its bicultural society' would receive 'special attention'.

subjective

Creative New Zealand has a special funding system for Maori arts; under it, it has made a grant to a band, one of whose singles has celebrated the eventual overthrow of the white man in New Zealand. But they do not mind receiving his money. Creative New Zealand has also, so *North and South* reports, made grants to Maori planning huis (but none to non-Maori planning conventions) and gave $3000 to *Brown Pages,* a directory of non-European creative types.

Mr Haydn Rawstron observed in 1995 that the new Arts Council of New Zealand did not possess, among its leading nine councillors, a single South Island European or Ngai Tahu. It was, he considered, a Polynesian/North Island administration. Its strategic plan spoke of 'Maori and other New Zealanders'.

Judges dabble in politics and launch themselves on irresponsible political adventures. The Court of Appeal (see Chapter 5) has led the way. In Northland, District Court judges have on various occasions discharged Maori, even second offenders, charged with poaching native pigeons, without penalty. One judge, who had earlier asked the Department of Conservation to meet with Maori to discuss the possibility of a legal taking of pigeon for 'cultural purposes', declared that he did not regard the defendant as a criminal.[6] So much for the laws made by parliament: a judge announces in effect that he – and Maori – may ignore them.

some laws wrongly criminalize

A Maori sovereignty group in the far north urged Maoris not to pay their rates. Incredibly, the Mayor's response was to say that the 'council would need time to consider' the group's ideas. But the mayor had 'no problems going into a hui with them'. A local body which, in a dry summer, imposed a total fire ban, nevertheless granted an exemption for a hangi for cultural reasons – even though the application for an exemption did not mention any such cultural reason – as if the elements themselves would behave differently in Maori circumstances.

The Presbyterian Church – itself a major landowner – wants local and regional authority land to be available for settling Treaty claims. A spokesman has said that it was such incidents as at Moutua Gardens that led to the recommendation. No local bodies were consulted before the General Assembly of the Church made the recommendation.

Anglican Maori clergymen 'lift tapus' everywhere – at an accident at the Christchurch Central Police Station; at Cave Creek after the accident there; in a Christchurch hotel where a murder had been committed. One wonders how exactly this fits into Christian theology. A Christian minister of religion has warned the unknown thieves who stole a greenstone cross from his church that bad luck would befall them if the cross was not returned. This is superstition, not religion.

The Anglican Church has always had a proprietorial attitude to the Treaty, and in its increasingly frantic attempts to prove itself relevant to the times, has produced a constitutional arrangement of three 'cultural streams' – Maori, European and Polynesian. In a fine burst of legalism, each is given its own constitutional organ. Anglicans evidently cannot be trusted to listen to each other within the same assembly. Even clergymen such as the Dean of Christchurch claim that European New Zealanders are 'a treaty people'. Exactly where that leaves Polynesians and other later immigrants is unclear. There is no home, it seems, for Asian New Zealanders – or even for just plain New Zealanders.

The other mainstream Protestant churches also desperately pursue the Treaty. It is no longer necessary, it seems, for Protestant clergy to subscribe to the most basic truths of the Christian faith – even the bodily resurrection of Jesus, even His divinity, is optional – but the Treaty is compulsory. These sects, however, will soon discover that the church that weds itself to the spirit of one age usually finds itself a widow in the next. 'Render unto Caesar the things that are Caesars,' said Christ; but the Protestants, having essentially lost belief in any heavenly kingdom, can think only of the kingdoms of *this* world, and seem in danger of identifying their dreamed-of new Treatyist constitutional structures with the Promised Land.

A group of prominent Maori have demanded that the Rugby Union stop negotiating professional contracts until a (non-rugby-playing) Maori Sport and Recreation Committee is consulted as a Treaty partner. Matiu Rata advocated a separate, race-chosen organisation to control Maori rugby and sport.[7]

Racial sensitivity has reached the stage that the simple statement by a Hamilton road safety consultant that a disproportionate number of Maoris are involved in road accidents is investigated by the Race Relations Office.

Maori growers of kiwifruit claim that trade is a 'taonga' guaranteed by the Treaty and therefore the Kiwifruit Board's export monopoly is a breach of the Treaty. Presumably, therefore, Maoris would be exempt from international trading agreements the Crown has concluded, and not entitled to their benefits.

A Maori leader proposes that Maoris should receive superannuation at a lower age than Europeans, because their life expectancy is slightly lower.

The Maori Council claims that to refuse an elderly Northland Maori man dialysis treatment was a breach of a Treaty right. The man was a 'taonga', and not to treat him was to 'sacrifice treaty rights to financially driven policies' and a 'clear sign of a lack of faith on the part of the Crown treaty partner'. The Maori Council – not the most radical of groups, surely – proposes, then, that normal clinical rules about who is to receive treatment should not apply to Maoris, and so, in effect, non-Maori New Zealanders may receive medical treatment only after all Maoris have been satisfied – for it would be surprising if all other Maori people were not 'taonga' as well.

The Lottery Grants Board allocates $6 million for 'marae heritage' – such spending being part of the National and New Zealand First coalition agreement – and consequently cuts grants to the disabled.

Ngai Tahu have recently announced that it would be an offence against their religious beliefs for mountaineers to stand on the summit of Mt Cook – or, very possibly, several other peaks – because Mt Cook is their ancestor, and its summit the head – the most sacred part – of their ancestor. So far, anyway, they have not asked the Department of Conservation to enforce this attitude, but merely to provide educational material on Ngai Tahu beliefs. We live, of course – at present – in a society without a state religion, and one where freedom of religion, and movement, are guaranteed by law.[8] One wonders what the reaction would be if, say, a group of Christians were to announce that no-one should set foot on a certain public place because someone had received a vision there. (In fact, of course, the Christian tradition is to encourage pilgrims and worshippers; Christianity is welcoming: it is tribalism which is exclusive.)

Are we seriously expected to believe that any human beings actually have a mountain as their recent ancestor? By their own admission – in their more rational moments – Ngai Tahu are northern invaders who only completed their conquests shortly before Captain Cook's arrival. They have been in the south not much longer than Europeans. They enslaved or ate the previous inhabitants.

If Mt Cook is their ancestor, then, they have only recently been adopted. Before they arrived in the south they were, presumably, orphans. Ngai Tahu claimed first that the top of the mountain was 'tapu', although they later amended this to say merely that they requested 'respect' for the top by not standing on it. The desired result seems to be much the same.

Pre-European Maoridom had few, if any, 'universal tapus': many outsiders were enemies who would delight in desecrating the tapus of their enemies. One wonders, too, if Ngai Tahu observe *all* their ancient tapus, or only some. Do they still cook their food outside? Indeed, before European times there was no 'Maoridom' at all, only a multitude of tribes; and this is, of course, what most of Maori descent going to the Tribunal want to continue.

The Ngati Whatua tribe is paid $80 an hour (by Transit Consultants Serco Group) to 'frequently bless land where a new motorway interchange is being built'. Maori regard the blessing as an important way of protecting construction workers as well as motorists. (In the event of a car crash will they refund the money, since in that case they will not have provided the service they were paid for?)

It has even been claimed that a land free of pornography is a 'taonga', and so the presence of pornography in New Zealand is a breach of the Treaty.

Maori occupations of public land are allowed to drag on for months. Maori protesters intimidate locals and tourists and, while still breaking the law, negotiate with Ministers of the Crown. Would a European trespasser be treated so indulgently?

The Treaty of Waitangi Fisheries Commission suggests that Maori are entitled to use whales for commercial purposes, even for hunting.

The kiore, or Polynesian rat, a pest actually introduced before Maori settlement by ocean-wandering voyagers (not necessarily the ancestors of later Maori settlers), and which can eat rare insects, lizards, and birds' eggs and chicks, is claimed as a 'taonga'.

Scientists hoping to isolate the moa's gene for size have been made to stop this research (which might assist our emu and ostrich breeders) because Ngai Tahu claim that moa are a taonga – 'part of the family that makes up our whole environment'. A Ngai Tahu spokesman denied that Maoris were responsible for moa extinction, although he conceded that 'humans were a factor'.

In 1996, many European and Maori New Zealanders greeted the visiting replica of Captain Cook's *Endeavour* with enthusiasm. Certain activists, however – the ubiquitous Ken Mair and the Reverend Eru Potaka-Dewes, for example – opposed the visit because it was 'offensive' to Maoris. Other protestors spoke of sinking the vessel. In Poverty Bay, local elders objected because Captain Cook's killing of three Maoris (in self-defence) was an 'atrocity . . . still very much in [their] minds'. One wonders, of course, if oral tradition really recorded the incident, or if it was only a more recent study of Cook's log that reminded them.

The most bizarre racial masochism, however, came from the *non*-Maori group Action for an Independent Aotearoa. Their poster, after referring to the rape and pillage of Maori land and resources, stated: 'Cook was just a crook. He came here to "case the joint" for his colonial masters. The Hawaiians stopped him dead at Kealakekua Bay. Let's stop those who want to glorify his crimes at Lyttelton.' The same group has asked the Christchurch City Council to cancel its plans to celebrate the year 2000, which is the 150th anniversary of European settlement, because it would be 'downright offensive' to Ngai Tahu. (Sir Tipene O'Regan has replied that this group does not speak for Ngai Tahu, who do not wish to be mean-spirited and ruin any celebration or commemoration of any group's coming to New Zealand. Other Ngai Tahu, however, such as the Reverend Maurice Gray, think that there will be 'little to celebrate' – unless a reconciliation between Maoris and the 'Crown' has been completed by then.)

A Maori MP proposes that prisons should be run by Maoris, which would not, he says, be a soft option, because they would have their 'aunties and uncles sorting them out'. Another MP – who has, presumably, taken an oath of allegiance to the Crown – has labelled non-Maori New Zealanders as 'visitors' – who, by definition, have no *right* to be here.

And as for claims before the Waitangi Tribunal, these lost touch with reality a long time ago. They are no longer claims for lands of which tribes were dispossessed, or for which proper payment was not, allegedly, made. They are no longer claims about pollution of coastal areas from which food is taken. Instead, we hear of claims made, or proposed, for pests such as the Kaimanawa wild horses and the Polynesian rat. A claim has been lodged for all native plants and animals – and that claim also covers Maori 'intellectual property' and place-names. It seems that, even though there was no Maori name for the whole of New Zealand,[9] this claim alleges that Maori are entitled to have our country renamed as Aotearoa – and every other place also renamed in Maori.

Maori music is claimed as a treasure and property; will we be expected to pay royalties every time we sing 'Now Is the Hour'; and if so, to whom? Certain North Island Maoris claim exemption from dog-licensing fees because dogs have always been part of their heritage; others claim an exemption from putting money in parking meters, because a car is a sort of conveyance, like a canoe. (Indeed, one recent decision from the Court of Appeal favours this argument by analogy – see p. 155.) It would only be a small step to demand exemption from firearms licences, because Maoris are warriors. Coal, offshore oil, and radio frequencies have been claimed; a claim of 'genocide' has been lodged, because the Crown allowed tobacco (which evidently Maoris did not want, but had forced on them). It seems very possible that deer will soon be claimed; already some people in the Department of Conservation have suggested that Maoris should be given them as 'compensation' for the loss of the moa, even though European New Zealanders had no part in that.

The Treaty is now merely the disguise of any and every wish, however preposterous, of Maoris. But if they want law changes in their favour, they should ask Parliament, like everyone else, and not hide behind the increasingly frail excuse of the Treaty.

New Zealanders are reasonable people, as their patience and generosity in the past prove. But the more we offer to Maoris, it seems, the greedier some become. Our reasonableness is mistaken for weakness and folly; and, to judge by the craven and ignorant attitudes of our rulers, it is correctly judged.

Appearing gradually from behind all these claims is a denial of the Crown's right to govern, and of the right of those not of Maori descent to live here. It is a wonder that the Queen's Ministers choose to ignore this.

Some of this, doubtless, is no more than theatre. It never hurts to have extreme demands, so that 'final' compromises later will seem more reasonable. But it is all claimed to be serious, and much of it no doubt is. This assumption that all Maori claims and grievances are valid has the corollary that to be Maori is, by definition, to be aggrieved. This is, as the Public Access NZ researcher Bruce Mason says, 'not a very rewarding position for anyone to be in'.[10] It is a difficult position to get out of. Collective grievances have a kind of immortality. The Irish have made the injustices of history a way of life. It is demeaning to Maoris to class them as victims; it is demeaning also to offer 'affirmative action' programmes, for this implies that Maoris can succeed only if they receive special treatment. *Not*

Views of history

History – apart from, of course, the tale of wicked European intrusion into the blissful innocent Maori idyll – is a subject hardly taught in our schools. This is a great pity, for, as is often tediously but accurately observed, those who do not learn from the past are doomed to repeat it. So many of us – and the young in particular – also live in a state of blissful ignorance. We assume that the state of mankind has always been one of democracy, plenty and content. We assume that democracy and open, impartial government appeared without any effort on anyone's part and will continue regardless of any attacks made on them, and even if no-one makes an effort to defend them. This faith in perpetual, automatic political progress is groundless. Only by long struggles did England attain that comparatively democratic constitution which, even last century, was the envy of most countries of the world. And, like any ancient building, our constitutional structure will last only as long as we repair and maintain it. There is nothing in New Zealand's air, water or soil, nothing in the order of the universe which will prevent our constitution and government from becoming less democratic. Indeed, if we look around us we can see the trend already. Somehow the myth has become established that pre-European Maoris lived by love and were committed to aroha and sharing. Yet how can this be reconciled with savage tribal wars for territory? How can it be reconciled with vigorous inter-tribal arguments today – about the distribution of the income from the Treaty Fisheries Commission, for example?

To be Maori is to be spiritually and environmentally sensitive and full of love, supporting each other, secure in the knowledge of where one stands. It is to be that lucky thing in our age: a victim, with someone else to blame. It is remarkable that loving aroha-filled support is so often claimed to be available to Maori offenders when they come before the courts, but does not seem to have prevented them from coming to court in the first place.

History – our interpretation of the past – changes from age to age. Some of the former glowing encomiums of our perfect racial harmony may well have been over the top. But neither has our history been one simply of exploitation and grievance. Ours is not a history of resented invasion, or of an imposition of an unwanted religion. Europe and its culture and religion offered an escape from a way of life dominated by war, slavery and cannibalism.

As Dr Robert Mann writes: 'This very recently settled land had, in only half a dozen generations, so little racism that the Maori Battalion volunteered and died magnificently to defend it from the Axis. Were they duped?'

Maori-worship is connected with the dissatisfaction many of us have with the way we live today. Our society is environmentally destructive, increasingly mercenary and uninterested in its citizens' welfare. It spurns religion and denies that such a thing as 'society' even exists. It is not surprising, then, that many people should turn to something close at hand which seems to be the opposite of all these things.

But Maori society was environmentally destructive. It was never democratic, just as modern tribalism is still exclusive and hierarchical. The lives of slaves were worth very little, and the lives of enemies even less. One can admire it as a model for the future only if one completely misunderstands it. Moreover, even if it had been like that at one time, that is the past. Maoris are no longer like this, and we cannot reach environmental and social redemption simply by yielding our place.

The problems that face us are the problems of a society to which we all belong, regardless of our ancestry. We may not be able to solve them at all. But if we do solve them, we will do so by using the ideas and precedents offered to us by all cultures, not by returning to the past of one of them.

The Maori were a stone-age people. They used no metal. Although they may have experimented with clay briefly after their arrival here, they did not even have pottery. Their religion was a simple matter of departmental gods (of the forest, the sea, the wind and so on) and of spells and charms. Although some scholars mention the concept of a supreme being, known as Io, it is unclear whether this shadowy being was the Maoris' own invention, or whether he was invented by some tohunga after Christian missionaries appeared, in order that the Maori religion might be able to stand on more of an equal footing with the sophisticated theology of Christianity.

Maori made superb stone weapons, but made no use of stone when building. They were a proud, handsome people, courageous but cruel, hospitable to their friends (who is not?), with a love of poetry and music. But theirs was not a 'civilisation' at all: it was a simple, primitive, superstitious society. For all its poetry and song, it was a less sophisticated society than that even of our Germanic ancestors, as described in such poems as *Beowulf*.

One and many cultures

Maoris fret about the erosion of their culture. True, it changes, but then so does every other culture that is still alive. Only the dead, and fossils, do not change. Erosion and change are hardly the same thing.

Interesting things happen when cultures meet, for they enrich each other, and out of that healthy cross-fertilisation they rise to new vigour. To deny change and evolution is to condemn a culture to death.

However, it is true that what we see may in some respects be an erosion, or destruction, rather than merely evolution and change. But Maori culture is hardly alone in this predicament. The potent forces of capital, a money economy, an international free market, American television and popular culture, are eroding cultures everywhere. The old literate, settled, land-based hospitable cultures of Europe suffer just as much as Maori or Eskimo. I am greatly concerned by the erosion of those European traditions, which would be a far greater loss to humankind than the loss of Maori ones. But there is little that any of us can do about it. We cannot stop change, and protect culture, by an Act of parliament. Maoris must fight for their culture as we all must, not simply expect this protection as another gift from the generous European.

Moreover, all this talk of biculturalism and multi-culturalism indicates a confusion as to what 'culture' actually is. One's culture is how one lives: how we see and think, speak and listen; how we feed and clothe ourselves and make food and clothing; how we work and play: it is everything about us. It is not simply going to the art gallery, the opera or the marae – activities that few of us do daily. The culture of some of us may still be substantially Scottish, let us say; but not because we occasionally wear a kilt and listen to bagpipes. Those are simply the outward signs of something more solid. In the same way, 'Maori culture', too, is a whole way of life, more than occasionally visiting a marae or uttering a greeting in Maori. Maori songs and dress may, like Scottish ones, be charming remembrances of days long past, but they do not make a culture. The plain fact is that the culture of most of us in New Zealand is neither Maori nor English nor Scottish. Our culture arises out of our own circumstances of history and geography, time, place and situation. It is a New Zealand culture. It contains, in different proportions in different parts of the country, elements of our ancestry. But is also arises from the historical development of this country since 1840 – its agriculture, industry and recreation, its climate and landforms. It is significantly affected by the international culture which television and radio, America and capitalism are spreading everywhere. Most

[handwritten margin notes: language, poverty, ritual customs, neighbourhood — they DO]

Maoris do not, in any significant way, *think* or *live* in distinctly Maori ways; just as most New Zealanders of Scottish descent do not think or live as did an eighteenth-century Highland clansman.

The world is becoming a global village, and a separatism which rejects other cultures is doomed to fail. Maoris can enrich New Zealand culture, but European culture can enrich Maoris much more. Learning about another culture does not make one's own culture invisible. Yet we now see this separatism. We hear some Maoris insist that only Maoris may teach and write about Maori history. Certain sorts of knowledge are sacred, and only for privileged ears. Does this mean only Maoris may study Maori history? If so, where to draw the line between Maori and European history?

The history of Maoris is not for Maori alone, any more than that of Europeans is for them alone. As Terence said, 'I am a man; I count nothing human foreign to me.'

Would those who favour Maori cultural sovereignty here accept that the English inhabitants of England are entitled to a superior status for their indigenous culture, and may impose it on West Indians, Pakistanis, and other more recent arrivals?

Exposure to other cultures does not necessarily lead to the loss of one's own culture. It is important for the common good that we all participate in various ways in the common endeavour of society. This is not necessarily assimilation, and it is vital to a sense of community.

The allegation is still occasionally made that Maori children were forbidden to speak Maori at school as part of some Anglo-Saxon campaign to stamp out the Maori language. Yet there is abundant evidence that this rule was the desire of Maoris themselves, who recognised that the past was gone, and wanted to have their children taught the things which would offer hope for the future.

I object to a lot of teaching of Maori history and culture in schools because it gives a false depiction of Maori life as one of innocent brotherly love, happy and peaceful, with environmental harmony, disturbed only by wicked Europeans. But I object to it perhaps even more because of the belief, widespread amongst our educationalists, that children's brains are so small that not a lot can be taught them at all. If they are to be taught about Maori culture, there is not a lot of brain capacity left for a study of any other culture, and so we are raising generations of children who are ignorant of everything that happened before they were born. Some literate, intellectually minded university students have never even heard of Homer. Some students of art, and even some born-again Christian students, are ignorant of the simplest Bible stories. How ignorant of history – and how gullible – these trusting simple minds will be. They will be prey to every would-be demagogue. At best, they will spend their lives reinventing the wheel.

Children's minds are not so small. But if there is room inside them for only one culture, let it be European – more valuable by far, and also, in most cases, their own. Europeans here may be accused of being 'Eurocentric', but given the immense wealth of civilisation that we brought with us from Europe, it is not unreasonable to remember our roots; and is that memory any less reprehensible than for Maoris to speak of their ancestral homeland of Hawaiki?

Some years ago the novelist C. P. Snow spoke of the 'two cultures' that co-existed in the United Kingdom. One of the cultures was that of science – of reasoned, dispassionate, high-minded investigation; the other was the old lingering humanistic literate culture of Europe, versed in poetry and painting, history and the classics, and all those attributes of the 'civilised man'. But a man cannot serve two masters: he must hate one and love the other. As Theodore Roszak states, 'There are never two cultures; only one – though that one culture may be schizoid.'[11] Professor Roszak concludes that our age is one where the culture of science – or, often pseudoscience – rules, for better or for worse, and the old humanistic culture is, at best, a mere ornament.

But this principle applies here in New Zealand, too. Any coherent society must, at base, be 'monocultural'. Unless we share certain essential, basic values, then peace and civil order will have to be maintained by force of arms. We must accept democracy, the rule of law and the value of tolerance before we go any further. It is impossible for our society to co-exist peacefully with any group that denies these principles by claiming, for example, that its own racial privileges are beyond democratic debate, or that it is exempt from particular laws, let alone the entire legal system.

All diversity of bi- and multi-culturalism must arise from the universal acceptance of these basic principles. Arthur Schlesinger, in *The Disuniting of America*,[12] says that the United States experiment of creating a common identity for people of many different languages, cultures, races and religions can succeed only while Americans continue to believe in a common goal. If that ideal of transcending those old divisions falters, then, he fears, the American community could disintegrate into forms of apartheid, tribalisation and Balkanisation.

This is not necessarily to condemn, say, Maori parliamentary seats. That institution was a necessary historical compromise, although its importance may be disappearing as proportional representation offers another way of guaranteeing a Maori presence in parliament. But the present arrangement of separate Maori seats and electoral roll is voluntary; it is not an enforced separation. Individual New Zealanders are not forced into one ethnic group or another, and thereby somehow limited in their rights as citizens. There is no place for a separate Maori parliament or separate Maori laws. That would be the complete end of democracy; the companion to the partition of our country, if not worse. The proponents of these things are the enemies not only of good race relations, but of the state.

Double standards

Before the English Civil War, John Milton was among those who hoped that the overthrow of the royal power by parliament would lead to religious freedom, and an end not only to Anglican persecution of Puritans and Presbyterians, but to all religious persecution. He was soon disillusioned: the Presbyterians were just as keen on persecuting those who did not agree with them as any High Churchman had been. Observing this, Milton, in his sonnet 'On the New Forcers of Conscience in the Long Parliament', made his famous observation that 'New Presbyter is but old priest writ large.' New oppressors are just as bad as, if not worse than, the old ones.

One thing that outrages those genuinely concerned about justice is the blatant use of double standards by Treatyists. There is one law for Maoris, and one for everyone else. Maoris may, on certain occasions anyway, dance and sing in the public galleries of parliament; anyone else who made the slightest murmur would at once be removed. It is gravely improper to offer any disrespect for Maori culture, even if one is simply telling the truth. A Crown witness during the hearing of the Ngai Tahu claim was informed by Ngai Tahu's counsel that he had insulted the tribe simply because he had given an accurate account of the environmental damage done by Maori in the South Island. What was he expected to do? Perjure himself?

In early 1998, the Waikato Museum of Art and History refused to show an entire exhibition of paintings by an Auckland artist, Dick Frizzell, after one Maori elder took objection to one or two paintings within it. At different times the Museum/Art Gallery gave two quite different reasons to Mr Frizzell for the withdrawal. Yet shortly after that, the new Museum of New Zealand revealed that it was not 'our place' at all when it refused to remove from display two creations grossly offensive to Christians – one, a statue of the Virgin Mary, covered in a condom; the other, a copy of Da Vinci's *Last Supper* with Christ replaced by a half-naked woman. *NEA debate*

We may agree or disagree about censorship in art. Some of us think it should never be allowed; others think that in some cases it is permissible. But we should surely agree that whatever rule we decide on should be applied in all cases. If censorship of offensive things is allowed, then let us censor things offensive to any interest group. If censorship is not allowed, let us censor nothing.

What did New Zealand's vigorous anti-racism movement say and do at the time of Colonel Rabuka's coup in Fiji? That coup was a racist one, with its aim of perpetual domination by Fijians and the subjugation of Indian Fijians. It was also, perhaps, motivated by the desire of the old Fijian ruling class to preserve its distinctness and superiority in the face of lower-class Fijian support for the Indian political party. On both counts one might have thought that freedom-loving anti-racists would condemn the coup. But instead, from our anti-racism campaigners there was a deafening silence. This silence must be evidence that the anti-racism movement is motivated in part by the racist belief that brown people – <u>Polynesian brown people</u>, anyway – are always right, and people of other races always wrong.

It is worth noting in passing that various Maori activists loudly praised the Fijian coup as a model for Maori action in New Zealand. Non-Maori New Zealanders were to be a subjugated people like the Fijian Indians. No sentimental, liberal nonsense of freedom and democracy here.

Race-relations legislation

Harmony between races is a good thing, just as harmony between cultures and between classes is good too. The objectives of the Human Rights Act and its predecessor, the Race Relations Act, are commendable and good. Let us bear in mind, though, that they are the enforcement of a particular morality. The phrase 'the enforcement of morals' is usually associated with the attempts of conservative and Christian moralists to reassert 'traditional values'. Liberals and free spirits often condemn them for this, even though a shared morality is necessary for any decent society. Liberals who support race-relations legislation are supporting the enforcement of a morality of tolerance. Tolerance of human diversity is not a bad thing in itself, as long as one does not move from there to a tolerance of every perversity and wickedness, a denial of the existence of objective standards of good and bad, and a refusal to condemn anything at all as being beyond the bounds of civilised behaviour. But let us

Labour party politicians agonise over the correct moral reponse to Colonel Rabuka's coup.

No

recognise that <u>human rights legislation</u>, however commendable its aims, <u>is social engineering and moral enforcement just as much as</u> attempts to prevent the Hero parade and denigrate homosexuals are.

When, several years ago, there were claims that oppressed Maoris had the right to destroy statues and other symbols of colonial occupation, the Race Relations Conciliator did not condemn this, but suggested that this simply reflected an impatience at the delay in settling claims. In other words, we should avert the threat of violence by speeding up the transfer of assets to Maori. But, as David Lange has said, 'The threat of violence in pursuit of a political agenda is simply terrorism . . . [The Conciliator's silence about the threats] might have given rise to doubts about his office. His statement confirmed them.'[13]

Where was the Conciliator when someone spoke of a 'Kill a White' campaign, or when Maoris called European New Zealanders 'unwanted guests'?

The Race Relations office is going beyond its commendable statutory aims and into far more questionable approaches. There has always been the danger that such a thing would happen. Since its establishment, the office of Race Relations Conciliator has almost always been held by someone not of the predominant cultural strand of New Zealand, and when that person was not a Maori (as in the case of Mr Wally Hirsch, who is of Jewish descent, or the present Conciliator, Dr Prasad, who is Indian), Maoris criticised the appointment, clearly expecting that the Conciliator should be Maori, defending and extending Maori interests.

The present Race Relations Conciliator has recently stated that people are concerned about Treaty rights and settlements only 'because they do not properly understand the issues'. With this argument he places himself on a slippery slope, for it suggests that those people speak from ignorance, so their views can be dismissed without argument or further thought. 'Diversity', one of his own movement's favourite words, does not appear to apply to views on the Treaty. But in pushing the radical Maori view that good race relations necessarily mean accepting radical Maori views, he discredits his office.

Several years ago in Christchurch, a Japanese company sought planning permission to build a hotel on the bare, brown hills above Sumner, a picturesque seaside suburb. This was opposed, not on racial grounds, but on aesthetic and environmental ones, by local residents and by several environmental groups concerned about the erosion of Christchurch's surrounding green belt. Rumour had it, however, that the hotel would be for Japanese guests only; that New Zealanders would be refused admission; and indeed this rumour was not denied at the town planning hearing. In defence of the green belt, and in seeking support from all quarters, I telephoned the Race Relations Office in the innocent hope that it would disapprove of this racial discrimination. An officer informed me not only that such an exclusive arrangement as this hotel would be perfectly lawful, but that I was racist for opposing it; and moreover, that any objection to foreign ownership of New Zealand was racist in origin and probably unlawful.

One cannot help but notice this unpleasant conclusion in many discussions on the race question. We are being manoeuvred into the situation where any opposition to immigration or foreign control can be labelled, and instantly dismissed, as racist. It is not, of course, racist to oppose foreign ownership and control of our country. It is surely a basic principle of liberty and independence that we own our own country, so that we, and not landlords and employers – foreign, or, for that matter, local – can decide how we are to run our lives. Some minimum of private property for all is necessary for freedom.[14]

Nor is it necessarily racist to oppose immigration. To oppose the entry of a certain race or races would be racist; to oppose immigration generally is not. The world is, after all, overpopulated; in many places human populations exist which those places cannot sustain for ever. We do not know what a sustainable population is for New Zealand. If we wish to have wide open spaces and to retain the easygoing spaciousness which is so central to our own culture, we must keep our population at a level below the maximum number we can support. We need a population policy; but an immigration policy must be part of that, and immigration is of course the aspect of population growth that is easiest to control. The government assures us that 20,000 or 30,000 migrants a year is negligible; but a mere 30,000 a year is still a population the size of Dunedin every three years; the size of Christchurch every ten or twelve years, and a city the size of Auckland every generation.

There is, it should be added, a curious contradiction in the attitude of the anti-racism movement to immigration. On several occasions, when white South Africans suspected of holding racist views expressed the desire to live here, the anti-racist movement objected, and suggested that all potential immigrants should have to pass an examination on race and Treaty issues as a condition of being granted entry to New Zealand. (The possibility that potential immigrants might simply memorise the 'correct' answers to the questions does not seem to have occurred to those honest souls.) It is perfectly reasonable to object, as the anti-racism movement does, to the presence of an immigrant whose ideas are not compatible with our existing culture. Immigrants should be prepared to accommodate themselves, by and large, to the customs and style of their new homeland. But of course our culture involves much more than just an absence of racism. (Indeed, judging by the remarks of numerous people, including the Race Relations Conciliator, our culture may not actually involve an absence of racism at all). If all immigrants are to be examined on their racial attitudes (for after all, racism is not confined to South Africa), should they not be also examined on their environmental attitudes, their views on sexual equality, on 'a fair day's pay for a fair day's work', and on many other things we accept as part of our culture? This is not, of course, what the anti-racist movement had in mind. But their call for cultural compatibility – not an unreasonable idea – has wide implications.

To rely on immigration for overseas funds is a desperate and very shortsighted policy. It is remarkable that certain Asian countries indicate that any restrictions on immigration would be interpreted as a sign that we were 'unfriendly' to Asia. Yet their immigration laws would prevent us from living there – not that we would want to. Our acceptance of continued significant immigration is another part of our 'cultural cringe'. Why else would we feel an obligation to give our country away?

Personal motivations

On the playing-field, or in the classroom, we have all learnt the importance of playing the ball, and not the man, and of the impropriety of the *ad hominem* argument. It is no argument at all simply to attack the speaker and ignore the speaker's arguments. Even stupid and bad people can still have sensible and good arguments.

46

Simply to attack a party to an argument for his or her supposed failings is irrelevant.

We all know, however, that not everyone abides by this sensible rule. Some are only too ready to accuse anyone holding any opinion but their own of being racist. One prominent Maori leader has referred to conservationists as 'eco-Nazis' and 'eco-fascists' simply for doubting the wisdom of handing our conservation lands over to Maoris. It is surprising, in one way, that Maori spokesmen do so, given that they also tell us often enough that 'Maoridom has many voices' and has just as much diversity of views as any other society. We know this perfectly well already, since there are certainly Maori voices agreeing with us. Nevertheless, they continue to use abuse instead of rational argument, and trot out the weary old cry of racism. Fortunately the claim is not widely believed, and has grown stale by repetition. The Treatyists have not succeeded in their attempt to claim the moral high ground. Nevertheless, the cry of racism is still hurtful, and (often) as unfair as it is unthinking.

New Zealand does, of course, have its racists, just like every other country, although we have fewer than most countries. In Japan, for example, Cabinet Ministers can still maintain that their country did nothing wrong in their invasion of China and during the Second World War; and school textbooks, if they mention these events at all, do so with no sense of wrongdoing. Japan, both officially and unofficially, still regards Koreans who have lived in Japan for several generations as inferior beings, and subjects them to various humiliating legal and social constraints. Japan's pre-Japanese 'indigenous' people, the Ainu, also suffer from prejudice and discrimination. Nor do Japanese approve any more of Westerners, for all that they do business with them. But the anti-racism movement does not seem to have noticed this racism in such an important trading partner.

However, we, too, have racists. Not, of course, that they all believe in the inherent superiority of the white race. At least as many evidently believe in the superiority of the Maori race.

Nevertheless, we concede that racists exist, and that they agree with us on some points. That does not, of course, discredit our arguments. Even the most misguided person is occasionally right. There does not exist an idea so pure, noble and sublime that it cannot be perverted to some base end. Let us look at the arguments themselves, rather than those who use them.

But still, if our opponents raise the question of character, we should consider the question of their character too for a moment. Could we succumb to forgivable human weakness for a second, and consider how their attitudes arise out of their personalities? After all, if there should be some connection between personality and political attitudes, then it should apply to both sides in the debate, not just to us. And if, as I claim, our attitude is simply the attitude of reasonable common sense, then it is reasonable indeed to examine our opponents' personalities, to discover the origins of their perverse attitudes. I have lost count of both the number of times my own views have been attributed to some defect in my character or personality, and the number of times some deeply caring person has told me, in what is actually a deeply insulting statement, that I should look within myself to discover the reasons I think as I do. To remark, then, on the gullibility and inferiority complexes of some of our fellow citizens is only self-defence; and, as Wilde reminds us, 'on an occasion of this kind it becomes more than a moral duty to speak one's mind. It becomes a pleasure.' For a long time, the discovery of base motivations and self-interested reasons for what might seem to be generous, noble and disinterested actions has been a standard feature of iconoclastic intellectual life. Let us turn the tables. It is all too easy to suppose that the loudest complainers for the public are the most anxious for its welfare.

'Naturam expellas furca, tamen usque recurret,' Horace said. (You may cast nature out with a pitchfork, but she will always run back in.) We cannot alter our nature. If we suppress it in one way, it will come back again in another. And so it is with the inferiority complex that seems to have haunted us since the early days of European settlement in New Zealand. Innumerable observers have noted that many New Zealanders for a long time have suffered from a 'cultural cringe'; that we have always been conscious that we were not as civilised and as polished as the Europe that we had left behind. Gradually, we have cast off this 'cringe'; we have realised that, although there is still room for improvement, we have achieved a lot in the last century and a half; that in certain respects we may actually be better than Europe, while in other respects we are not better or worse, just different.

Yet the cultural cringe has not disappeared. Instead, a new generation of New Zealanders, while feeling no inferiority to Europe, now think of themselves as being inferior to Maoris. It is a remarkable circumstance that people who are not particularly impressed with the culture and learning, philosophy, religion, art, architecture, literature and music developed over two or three thousand years in Europe, should nevertheless feel awed and shy before the culture of a warlike and superstitious stone-age people. It requires a good deal of ignorance about the true nature of pre-European Maori life. But then, ignorance has never been in short supply. There is an unwholesome masochism about this adoration of the other. It involves a hatred of the self which can only be unhealthy.

The ignorant admiration of Maori life has the added advantage, for the admirers, that it offers a convenient excuse for their ignorance of everything to do with their own civilisation and culture. Why should they need to know these things, when they know that hakas, whares and stick games reflect some of the highest human achievement? I am continually depressed by meeting charming, lively, high-minded young people, who have been through our schools and even through some of our universities, but who do not know the first thing about our own culture's heritage of art, science, wisdom, skill and thought. They hardly ever read a book; their general knowledge of the most basic facts is lacking. But their Maori pronunciation is perfect and they know that Maori have been and continue to be deeply wronged.

We must not blame the existence of these beautiful savages solely on indoctrinating teachers. There are social and structural pressures on teachers to indoctrinate their students. In an age of television, instant gratification and pulp everything, it is hard enough to teach children anything. But the existence of a sizeable group of such ignorant, indoctrinated citizens, who know no better than to regard Maoridom as the highest source of wisdom, culture and community, is yet something else to worry about.

This inferiority complex is, perhaps paradoxically, accompanied by pleasant feelings of self-flattery and self-congratulation. The Treatyists, after all, are not deluded, (unlike so many others) by any belief in the superiority of Western civilisation. They see it as it is: they know it has always been completely bankrupt, both morally and intellectually. (If they paused to think, they might wonder how it is that it has survived so long, or been as successful as it has been.) They know, moreover, that anyone who disagrees with them is obviously an ignorant racist. What delicious feelings of moral and intellectual superiority they enjoy. How pleasurable it is to be able to despise ones opponents; how easy it is to label them as ignorant bigots instead of actually considering what they have to say.

Ignorance of one's own culture, and a general feeling of rootlessness, are necessary for this worship of the stone-age. Gullibility is important too, but would not of itself be enough. It is striking, as one considers the people one knows who have chosen to be concerned about racial injustice, to discover just how many of them are so ignorant of their own history and culture. One often notices also a significant number of recent immigrants among them. Perhaps these immigrants feel that the only way to be a 'proper' New Zealander is to be Maori; perhaps, cast adrift from their own settled ways in another country, they choose this obvious path to a ready-made community here.

One can perhaps blame the news media also, for their presentation of issues. The land on which the Moutua Gardens stand was freely sold by chiefs who knew what they were doing. Ken Mair, one of the Moutua Gardens protest leaders, acknowledged a legal sale, but refused to recognise it. Moutua Gardens and the old Pakiatore Marae were not the same area: the marae, on the riverbank, disappeared in a flood long ago. It is worrying, that, by and large, the news media did not mention these well-established facts. The news media, indeed, misrepresented one important point: they repeatedly stated that the Wanganui District Council was asking the High Court to decide on matters pertaining to ownership – thereby implying that the occupation might be legal. In fact, the Council was always asking that its ownership be affirmed. And the media downplayed the aggressive, intimidatory and violent aspects of the occupation in favour of set-piece public relations exercises, as when groups of women and children were ostentatiously welcomed on to the park.[15]

Our inferiority complex has reached the stage where a film about Chinese gold-miners in Central Otago can depict them as so innocent and naive as to be completely unaware of the idea of the surveying and division of land. The miners watched in amazement and almost incomprehension as these 'land-butchers' carved it up. In fact, the Chinese were ancient masters of surveying, and one could not run a peasant economy, let alone one with large cities, without drawing lines on maps. Yet so ready are we to accuse ourselves of

beastliness that we accept a fictitious Chinese noble savage as a pretext for our breast-beating.

Lurking behind both an inferiority complex and self-flattery is that old bugbear of our national life, puritanism. It was not something that Maoris ever suffered from, but was imported from England and Scotland, where ever since the Reformation it had appealed to a joyless, bitter section of the population. In this country, puritans may be referred to as 'wowsers', but the principle is still the same. Lord Macaulay, writing of the Puritans' brief and unpleasant rule of England after the execution of Charles I, said that they banned bear-baiting 'not because it gave pain to the bear but because it gave pleasure to the spectators'. This analysis remains as true as ever. Although reasons of health and safety and justice can always be found for this or that change, yet nevertheless, so often it seems that the reformers are, deep down, motivated by the awful lingering fear that someone, somewhere, might be happy.

Connected with this puritanism are the views advanced by many of the mainstream churches since the mid-1980s. Bruce Mason[16] describes the 1986 report of the Anglican Church's Bicultural Commission, which, while not defining 'partnership', was nevertheless 'convinced' that the Treaty implied it, and 'promised' bicultural development. No basis was offered for this assertion. Even the New Zealand Catholic Bishops have moved from the sound Christian principle that racism is sinful, to an unthinking acceptance that justice is largely on the Treatyists' side, and to the invalid and divisive call for 'constitutional supports for protecting the cultural, social and political rights of tangata whenua and for supporting the efforts of the Waitangi Tribunal as a court of inquiry to assess claims and define principles'.[17]

Christian principles are here being used to political and non-Christian ends. There is no reason in justice or Christianity why the state and the common welfare should be sacrificed to satisfy the imaginative guilt-complexes of a politically motivated and ill-informed few. *The WHOLE state to be given to Maori?*

La Rochefoucauld observed long ago that 'the old give good advice as compensation for no longer being able to set a bad example'. In the same way, many campaigners for worthy moral causes are those who, having abandoned ordinary pleasures themselves, find compensation in interfering with the pleasures of others. How many worthy campaigns in this country are essentially negative? The conservation movement is a fine exception, working for the protection of wonderful places and public access, and in the course of that, not just being 'against logging', but looking for alternatives to logging. But perhaps it is significant that one of the biggest social conscience movements is usually described in negative terms – the 'anti-racism' movement. We are all, I hope, opposed to racism – although what exactly it is can be a difficult question – but when we hear someone announce that he is 'against racism' it is not necessarily being glib to wonder: 'Is he *for* anything?' For that matter, were not some people who marched against rugby tours to or from South Africa motivated just as much by a dislike of rugby's place in our culture and society as by concern for black South Africans?

Moral highmindedness is of course good, yet it is tiring. When we hear another whining, concerned voice on Kim Hill's radio programme, discussing the dangers of trampolines, playgrounds, cannabis, alcohol, sport, and any item of behaviour, then the kindest of us can only wish that people paid as much attention to improving their own lives and making people happy, as they do to stopping other people from doing things.

Samuel Butler describes wowsers well:

A sect, whose chief devotion lies
In odd perverse antipathies;
In falling out with that or this,
And finding somewhat still amiss . . .
Compound for sins they are inclined to
By damning those they have no mind to:
Still so perverse and opposite
As if they worshipped God for spite . . .
All piety consists therein
In them, in other men all sin.[18]

Moral highmindedness is not only tiring, it can also be dangerous:

For virtue's self may too much zeal be had;
The worst of madmen is a saint run mad.

[handwritten margin note: ideologue must be different from morality]

For ordinary people, the rule of fanatics – into which category
puritans must fall – is unpleasant. Rule by human beings is to be
preferred.

Treatyists' belief in tolerance, too, is very limited. In the United
States, most civil liberties groups maintain that even the Ku Klux
Klan should have as much right to state its opinions as anyone else.
But after Pauline Hanson's success in the June 1998 Queensland state
elections, at least one prominent and caring New Zealand politician
suggested that it would be a good idea simply to not let such
people, and their parties, stand for election. So much for democracy
and the rule of law.

No Treatyists seem to be democrats. It will not surprise us, of
course, to reflect that our rulers for the last fifteen years have had
no time for democracy. They have consistently lied their way into
office and have made a virtue of promise-breaking, and they are only
too ready to use the easy methods of personal abuse, and dismiss
anyone who doubts their sublime wisdom as red-necked and reac-
tionary. It is perhaps a little more surprising in the case of those
labouring in the fields of social concern. On various occasions, in
private conversations, they have deplored the expression of my views
in the correspondence columns of the newspapers. One of my standard replies is to suggest that the socially concerned person should
also write to the newspapers, thereby engendering healthy debate.

double standards is THE point

But this, they reply, is pointless, for ordinary people simply would not understand the arguments. It is better for people to lobby and influence behind the scenes, and then impose their will on the nation.

These people believe, of course, in freedom of speech. But they say it must be 'informed' and 'responsible' speech. There are no rights to 'uninformed', 'prejudiced' and 'ignorant' speech. Yet how does one recognise this informed and responsible speech? Put simply, it is speech which agrees with their point of view and con-clusions. If it does not, it is clearly ignorant and can therefore be ig-nored, if not actually repressed.[19]

We live, too, in a godless age. The trouble with atheists, G. K. Chesterton observed, was not that they believed nothing, but that they would believe anything. Christianity has been replaced by the creeds of Marxism, Nazism and many bizarre new cults and sects, whether political or religious. We desire meaning; and in an increas-ingly anonymous and rootless age we desire a place to stand and a group to belong to. A good part of the support many offer the Treaty movement arises simply from Maoridom's usefulness in providing these psychological comforts.

Have our double standards disappeared? No: they merely apply in different areas. Instead of there being one rule for men and another for women, one for the rich and one for the poor, one for the rulers and one for the ruled, there is now one for Maori and one for everyone else. In our secular society, there would be many ob-jections if anyone ever attempted to offer prayers in English or Latin on any public occasion. That would be considered superstitous, and those involved would be accused of ramming religion down the throats of the unwilling. We can imagine very easily how vehemently it would be opposed. But when the same prayers are said in Maori, most will bow their heads as meekly as can be.

It is sad, indeed, to see so many good people labouring mightily to establish a system of special Maori privilege. Most of them are sincere in their folly; but even if a man die for a particular cause, that is no proof that the cause was right.

The pathetic eagerness of some Europeans to sign away their own hard-earned birthright is well illustrated by Charmaine Pountney, the well-known educational innovator, and Tanya Cumberland. Before buying rural land – not, it seems, in any legal sense, Maori land, just ordinary rural land – they thought, 'Hang on a minute: that means we would be wanting to buy Maori land'. They therefore consulted the local iwi, saying, 'We acknowledge this is your land. We would like to come and live here. Here are our hopes and aspirations. Can we come?' They intend to leave the land to the tribe after their deaths, and say their 'commitment' and 'support for sovereignty is about learning to be tenants and good neighbours' within this tribe's area.[20]

Nothing changes. Our schools, it is argued, were once 'bastions of conformity'. If so, they still are. With all their charters and mission statements mentioning the Treaty, they still foster conformity; the only difference is that unquestioned respect must now be paid to the Treaty, rather than anything else. Will concerned activist pro-Treaty school teachers really respect the views of pupils who disagree with the content of their indoctrination?

And how angry, too, some of these people are. It is not healthy for people to spend their lives in constant bitterness and rage – even if their complaints are well-founded, which they often are not. Some non-Maori supporters of radical Maori claims, in particular, seem to be very unpleasantly mixed up. Amid their negative emotions there often seem to be very few positive ones.

As their names reveal, Maori radicals usually have European ancestors as well as Maori ones. No-one can escape their ancestors: we are the product of them all . One cannot but wonder what perverse feelings have led these radicals to regard some ancestors as significant, and others as contemptible. One cannot but marvel that they seem to have acquired the worst characteristics of both races.

Supposedly high-minded would-be reformers are no more immune than anyone else to human weakness and temptation. They, too, can be swayed by the thought of riches, and they just as much as anyone else, would enjoy exercising absolute power. Their tone is clearly intolerant and autocratic. We must be on our guard. We must protect those principles, so long and so hard fought for, of the rule of law, and equality before the law.

We are being sold a pup over the Treaty, for there are two quite contradictory official views on Treaty claims. By one view – more popular with Ministers of Treaty Settlements – the Waitangi Tribunal process is concerned merely with righting the wrongs of the past. Once all those are righted, the whole business will be over; the

Tribunal can more or less retire, and we can advance harmoniously, if not as one people, then at least as two peoples with everything sorted out between us.

That is one view, which may incline us to tolerate the present fuss, since we can console ourselves that it will soon be over. But unless we do something about it, this is simply not going to happen. In part, this is because 'full and final' settlements do not mean just that: there have been, in various cases, full and final settlements before, and it is quite likely that in a generation from now, claims will resurface. The various references to the 'principles of the Treaty' in various Acts of parliament will ensure that Treaty issues will continue to be raised there. The Court of Appeal is keen to see Treaty principles 'evolve' over the generations. A Ngai Tahu spokesman has stated that of the claims by 'seventy major tribes' in New Zealand, only one has been finally settled. He did not estimate the number of minor tribes. Sixty-nine 'major' claims will clearly fester for many years. But over and above this, it is clear that claims for land, and for specific, alleged past injustices, are now only one part of what certain Maori are claiming before the Tribunal. Claims now, as we will see, complain of Maori poverty, crime and social deprivation and even cultural deprivation – issues far removed from any property rights contemplated in 1840. Even European use of Maori music is now

but resulting from changes in land communal to private

alleged to be a Treaty injustice, even though we might have thought that music was a path to harmony. Above all this loom the claims for political power. They may be the claims of a minority; but then, the Provisional IRA was never very big. Maori leaders have not been as active as they could have been in discouraging them, and the Crown's refusal to attach conditions to Treaty claims means that comfort, which stifles so many revolutions, will very probably not stifle this one.

The end of Treaty claims, then, is not in sight; but the end of a lot of European patience is fast approaching. *with what result?*

THREE

Justice and Treaty Issues

If one were to be continually enquiring, settlement would be indefinitely postponed.

process / closure

– Aristotle, *Ethics*, Book III

Justice is the crowning glory of the virtues: something which we must all favour – until our particular case comes along, anyway, when it may be that we do not like our just desserts. 'Injustice,' H.L. Mencken said, 'is relatively easy to bear; it's justice that rankles.'

Every law library has a good number of thick books on the subject of justice. So many authors have their own particular idea, expanded at excessive length and in exhaustive detail. And so few authors apply their general principles to actual situations, such as that which now confronts us. Indeed, it could be said that justice is so popular an idea precisely because it is so vague, so that everyone can use the concept as they please.

In the Institutes of Justinian, part of the Code of Roman Law compiled under that emperor, we read the famous definition, repeated from earlier sources, that 'Justice is the constant and perpetual wish to give to every man that which is his due.' But that is, of itself, little help, for it still leaves it to all comers to say what their dues are.

This is not the place for a lengthy and detailed discussion of justice as it was understood by Socrates and Plato, Aristotle and St Thomas Aquinas. Not only would such a discussion be tedious, and imperfectly done in my inexpert hands, but it would not necessarily come to any conclusions. One might not be able to say with certainty what these philosophers would have said about our situation. And even if we could accurately deduce their views, we are not necessarily obliged to agree with them. It is, in the last resort, for us to decide what is just and unjust in our time and place, not to be ruled by the hands of long-dead Greeks; or, for that matter, of long-dead Maoris and European settlers here. Nevertheless, we respect ancient philosophers because their observations and conclusions are so in accord with our own, and with the timeless truths of human nature and society. For these reasons alone their views must hold at least some weight.

At the risk of establishing a new philosophical school, let us consider some simple propositions about what justice must involve, before listing some commonsense and practical considerations too often ignored.

Justice is concerned with dealings between two or more parties. Justice must, at least on the face of it, involve respecting other people's property, and respecting agreements. 'Corrective justice', as Aristotle called it, deals with correcting and restoring intrusions which one person has made on the rights of another. But justice must also begin from the principle of equal treatment – equal treatment, at least, for all those people in the same class or category – and if we accept the principles of universal human rights, then it must involve a belief that, simply because of our common humanity, we all have certain basic and equal claims to participate in the earth and its fruits and in the running of our society. These are the principles of Aristotle's 'distributive justice'.

For society to function properly, some division of labour must be made. Some must rule the city, receive ambassadors, make laws and impose taxes; some must pray, some fight, some farm, some trade; some must labour with their minds and wits, others with their hands; some must build the walls and guard the gates, sweep the gutters and clean the sewers. None of these honest labours is cause for shame. All are necessary to the community, which can be harmed equally by the watchman who falls asleep at his post, the soldier who runs from the enemy, the politician who favours one faction over the legitimate claims of all, and the thinker who encourages decadence and self-interest instead of decency, virtue and the common good. Although equality is a fundamental principle, yet a division of labour must be made; and so, too, rewards and benefits need not be divided in absolutely equal shares, although as all contribute to the common good, so all are entitled to receive a proper share in that good.

If we are all brothers and sisters, all heirs to the earth and inevitably members of one common society, then justice must also be a social virtue, whose purpose is the common good. Just as it does not involve a mere mechanical and automatic equality, nor does it mean mere mechanical restoration – an eye for an eye and a tooth for a tooth. It must involve some restraint on the part of those injured, lest the blood feud last for ever. Even with the best will in the world, some wrongs cannot ever be righted; others, if they were, would cause other wrongs far more grievous. One man with a gun or a car, can in a few minutes do more harm that his later execution or perpetual imprisonment and the forfeiture of all his property could ever atone for. Again, someone whose life has been fine and blameless may, in a split-second of inadvertence, injure other people dreadfully. It is just, of course, that the injured should be compensated; but it could also be argued that it is not entirely just that, in so compensating, the entire life and career of the injurer, and his family, should also be destroyed. This is part of the reason why we still have the vestige of a system of accident compensation; that, and the belief that we all belong to a community that benefits from the fruitful labours of its members, and that accordingly owes duties, and not just charity, to those engaged in aspects of the great common enterprise of society.

We are, as Aristotle says, creatures of the *polis*, the social and political community. Solitude is a fit state only for gods and beasts. The state exists, not just to enable us to live, but to enable us to lead good and worthwhile lives, where we may be happy and good, and fulfil, to some degree, the potential within us all. This is not socialism, but the agreed philosophy of Western civilisation from the Greeks onwards, until the Business Roundtable and its friends decided that greed and self-interest should govern human dealings. It was people like them who announced, for the first time, that there was no such thing as society, only individuals: 'consumers and taxpayers', not citizens. Their appeal to our baser nature, their absurd belief that by being selfish we can somehow benefit all, has done much to diminish civilisation. But do not confuse their half-baked self-interested 'philosophy' for real wisdom.

To live in society, then, means that one must exhibit restraint. This is one's duty, in justice, to the community, because without restraint the community is harmed, to the great detriment of us all.

The law of 'an eye for an eye and a tooth for a tooth' is considered barbaric and cruel. Many of us would say that there are occasions when, say, the death penalty is the only proper penalty for murder; but this is not always the case.

This principle has important consequences. Some Maoris have claimed that 'justice' requires that an acre of land be returned for every acre wrongly taken. It has even been said, by several claimants, that simply to settle one of their claims 'justly' would bankrupt the country.[1] Since, obviously, the Crown would never make so generous an offer, statements like this ensure that, no matter how generous a settlement is now, an excuse will always remain, a generation hence, for renewing the complaint of injustice and extracting more from a gullible or weak government. But as a simple matter of definition, any treaty settlement that would bankrupt the country, or even significantly harm the prosperity of the whole community, and render the state incapable of aiding anyone – including, of course, other Maori claimants, as well as all the others who have some call on our charity and consideration – cannot be just. Other parties have legitimate interests. Justice involves mutual forbearance, not blind restitution.[2] But the furious rejection by claimants of the 1994 proposed 'fiscal envelope' of one thousand million dollars as far too little makes it clear that only the massive and unthinkable transfer of public funds and assets to claimants might satisfy them. Even already negotiated settlements may contain 'escalation clauses', so that, if the total sum of present settlements exceeds one thousand million, then the amounts of existing settlements will increase in order to remain at a certain pre-ordained percentage of the whole. This arrangement is itself a financial trap of appalling implications.

There is a popular legal maxim: *'Fiat justitia, ruat coelum.'* (Let justice be done though heaven falls.) The dedication to justice of those who say it is of course admirable; but those who say it are usually quite sure that heaven will not fall – or, at any rate, not on them. But as a matter of principle, this maxim is flawed, for any judgment that led to 'heaven falling' – social chaos and catastrophe – would hurt the common good, and is by definition not just.

I have spoken to influential persons who have wrung their hands in predictable fashion at the injustices daily visited on Maori. Some of these same caring people, later on in the conversation, have asserted very strongly that everyone should have to pay for his or her own health and hospital care, and that if anyone could not afford to pay, he or she should simply be left on the side of the road to die.

We may safely assume that the concern for Maoris expressed by these heartless persons was motivated largely by a mindless desire to follow fashion. This is comforting, for it offers some hope that when the present fashion passes, as fashions do, some sanity may reappear. But what faith can one have in claims that justice is on the Maori side if so many Treatyists display such heartlessness and contempt for social justice on many other issues? The same governments which, since 1984, have displayed such concern for 'justice' for Maori have presided over a society which, in so many other respects, is becoming increasingly unjust. Our old equality is disappearing, along with that comfortable decent middle class to which so many of us belonged, and which so many others hoped to enter. More and more our society is becoming one of a small group of rich businessmen, bureaucrats, consultants and the like, and a huge group of unemployed, precariously employed or low-paid workers. The health, education and other public services which we once more or less willingly contributed to out of our taxes for the greater good, are being deliberately destroyed. How can we have any confidence, then, that our rulers are on the right track for justice when it comes to Maori claims? On their track record, it is surely more likely that they are just as wrong, just as brutal and just as much favouring one or two special interest groups as they have been in everything else they do.

Do we accept that it is morally permissible for some to live in luxury while others lack even the necessities of life? Our new masters tell us that the unimpeded accumulation of riches is permissible, and somehow works for the common good. Most of us, however, hold by an older philosophy that, above a decent, or even generous, sufficiency for ourselves, our families and dependants, the rest of our property is subject to a 'social mortgage', and the community has some legitimate interest in it and even some claims over it.

Now many Treatyists – not the right-wing ones, but the socialistically inclined – would maintain this. They, even more than most of us, would condemn the sudden and unjust accumulation of wealth by a new class of vulgar snobs who, not content with being rich, want to rule us as well.

But, to repeat one of my principal themes, let us have no double standards here. If it is proper to tax European millionaires heavily for the common good, then it is proper to tax Maori ones. If it is unjust that a European family sit on vast lawfully acquired assets while thousands live in misery, then it is improper for a Maori tribe to sit on such assets. Was it proper for only two or three thousand or so Ngai Tahu to occupy most of the South Island to the exclusion of all others?[3] Was the breaking up of the large estates of last century's sheep kings proper? Presumably Treatyists would have to say it was not. If the state should not be in the business of handing public assets over to a handful of rich Europeans, why should comparatively small groups of Maoris receive them? If we do not want European capitalists, why are we so busy creating Maori ones? The evidence is abundant that some Maori enterprises, anyway – Ngai Tahu, if not some further north – will be every bit as hard-headed and hard-hearted as those run by white men can be.

No-one of sense would maintain that injustices were not done to Maoris during European colonisation and settlement. Maoris may consider themselves fortunate to have been colonised by the British, who, it could be pretty safely asserted, were largely humane and generous, compared with the French or Dutch, Germans or Belgians. Yet nevertheless, that good fortune does not of itself entitle us to ignore injustices that we committed. *What restitution will he suggest*

Perhaps in New Zealand the present Treaty mania might not be so strong if several earlier genuine complaints of injustice had not been treated so unsympathetically by governments. The Bastion Point and Raglan Golf Course cases were ones where genuine injustices had been done to Maori, injustices which could have been righted with very little trouble. The intransigence of the government of the time inevitably inflamed the sense of grievance, and assisted in developing an atmosphere where European institutions were distrusted and radical claims and actions favoured.

This book does not attempt to deny that injustices occured. They did not, however, occur all the time. Only the gullible – there are, alas, plenty of them – believe automatically every tale of injustice they are told. It is depressing to see how many self-flagellating Europeans automatically and unquestioningly accepted the baseless claim that Moutua Gardens, in Wanganui, were on Maori land – and the nonsensical stories recently told about Maori printing presses

a minor member of small James

being thrown into rivers, and thousands of Maori murdered with deliberately poisoned flour. The Waitangi Tribunal, in its interim report on the Taranaki claim, has spoken of Taranaki history as an 'on-going holocaust'. This we need not believe.

Injustice was not the usual result of dealings between Maori and European. And hindsight is irrelevant here. If, at the time, both Maori and European parties were happy with an arrangement, then the mere fact that generations later someone of Maori descent regrets the sale, or has fallen into misfortune, is immaterial. Justice does not allow the re-opening of closed cases. We must all take our chances with the future.

If Maoris were, as their advocates maintain and as few would deny, a clever, quick and intelligent race, then it is condescending in the extreme to suppose that they were constantly and usually duped in dealings with Europeans. Many wanted to sell land to new settlers, and resented Article II of the Treaty, which ordained that only the Crown could buy land from them.

Even when it is possible to recognise genuine injustices in the past, that of itself does not mean that it is clear what justice requires now by way of remedy. Some considerations relevant to those past injustices now follow.

Justice in particular

'*Pacta sunt servanda*', runs the Latin maxim: 'Agreements must be kept'. We must all agree that this is part of any principle of justice. But even this principle is not so simple. We pass over here the question of what exactly the agreement of the Treaty meant and said: that question we deal with in Chapter 4. But certain other points must be made.

For one thing, this principle that agreements must be kept is applied only very selectively. After all, for many years most New Zealanders had an agreement with the Crown whereby, in return for paying taxes all through their lives, the Crown would provide them with decent, readily available health and hospital care, education for their children, and a number of other services and facilities. Where is that now? The present Minister of Justice talks about 'the honour of the Crown': does he think of this great betrayal? Every day long-standing arrangements are torn up. Politicians may attempt to justify this on the usual tired old grounds that we live in a changing world, where new circumstances may mean that it is no longer appropriate . . . we have heard the spiel a thousand times. There may even be a grain of truth in it. But if it is true, then why does it not apply to the Treaty also? If, as is claimed, our circumstances are different from those of 1970 or 1930, they certainly are different from those of 1840.

One particular change must be mentioned here. Agreements like the Treaty, which, it is claimed, last forever, can last only as long as the parties to them continue to exist. Many agreements lapse when the parties to them disappear. A marriage is dissolved by death. The Treaty, too, had moral validity only while the original parties to it existed. And neither of those parties is what it was.

The Treaty was made between the Crown and Maori chieftains. The Crown is not what it was in 1840. Before the Treaty, after all, it was a foreign power. It had scarcely any subjects here. New Zealand had only a handful of European settlers – missionaries, whalers, sealers, and dealers in flax, grog and muskets.[4] The Crown acted by its prerogative: it was answerable to no-one in New Zealand. In 1840, indeed, Queen Victoria in the United Kingdom was little more than a constitutional monarch. Her powers were very limited. Her United Kingdom Ministers were even then the Crown. But the Crown now is, in practical and political terms, an entirely different thing. The Crown means the government of this country – the Governor-General (a mere cipher) and his ministers. They become Ministers because they enjoy the support of – and are in fact the leaders of – a majority in the House of Representatives – in parliament, in other words; and that parliament is elected by the people. We are all, including Maori, part of the 'the Crown'.

We can, and should, criticise parliament and politicians for many of their actions. Yet imperfect though our democracy may be, it is still better than – and it is quite different from – being ruled by the decrees of a monarch. It is impossible now to draw any clear definite line between Crown and people, rulers and ruled. Democracy is government of the people by the people for the people. We rule ourselves: parliament, after centuries of struggle, has captured the Crown, and the Crown does what it is told. The idea, which Maori claimants insist on, of a 'Crown' that is quite different from citizens ✓

is nonsensical. There simply is no longer any separate Crown; there are only New Zealanders; and any money and assets the 'Crown' uses in Treaty settlements come not from some secret hoard of gold, but from the taxes and public assets of us all.

The other party has also changed. In 1840 Maoris, despite some differences between tribes, were a distinct race and culture. This is no longer so. There has been intermarriage, and now many 'Maoris' have only a fraction of Maori blood. There have also been enormous social changes. It cannot be said that tribes represent Maoris, or encompass Maoridom. Many of Maori descent do not even know what tribe their Maori ancestors belonged to, and many others, although they may know, nevertheless have little actual contact with their tribes. They may live in other parts of the country. Even if they live in the territory occupied by their tribe in 1840 – the tribe's 'rohe' – the course and interests, and distractions, of their lives may mean that the tribe means little to them. Settlements to tribes will benefit only comparatively small numbers. In Ngai Tahu's traditional area, for example, 80 percent of those of Maori descent now living there are not of that tribe. Among Ngai Tahu themselves, a full third in the last census declared they considered themselves to belong to the European ethnic group. Only slightly more, 36 percent, considered they belonged to the Maori ethnic group, and 29 percent said they belonged to both.[5] Tribal settlements will create a 'Business Browntable', an elite of Maori capitalists who cannot be expected to have any more sense of obligation to their poorer Maori brethren than European capitalists have to theirs.

In the 1997 Tainui Trust Board annual report, Sir Robert Mahuta said that the government, not the tribe, had the duty to provide proper health care, welfare, housing, employment and all the basic needs of Maori people. Since the Treaty promises Maoris all the rights of British subjects, there is a case for this. But if the Crown must do all this, then what are Treaty settlements for? They are to establish Maoris – or Maori leaders, anyway – as a privileged class, not as an equal one. Tainui has already sold 410 houses, many rented by Tainui, which it received as part of the settlement. They were not offered to the tenants. One Tainui man said, 'The settlement might as well have been in blankets, axes and trinkets. I would have had more show of getting a blanket than a dollar.'

Various traditional tribal leaders stoutly maintain that Treaty settlements may be only with tribes, and that any claim which any Maori has to Pakeha largesse must be through a tribal connection. Sir Tipene O'Regan has described the suggestion that non-tribal Maoris might have some share in the benefits of the Treaty of Waitangi Fisheries Commission as 'sun-tanned welfarism'. Yet generosity to tribal Maoris means that many Maoris – and among them, many of the most needy – will receive nothing. Urban Maoris earlier this year went to the High Court to argue that their new urban organisations, cutting across old tribal divisions, are themselves a form of 'iwi' – although not, of course, iwis who signed the Treaty. But if we accept their very sensible claim that the old tribal identities are no longer relevant, there is no reason why we have to accept the invention of 'new' tribes instead. It would make more sense to say, consistently, that tribes are the past. Justice does not require the antiquarian revival of decaying institutions.

So decaying – or so fragmented, which amounts to much the same thing – is tribal 'authority' that even an official of the Office of Treaty Settlements can say, speaking of the necessity of dealing with Maoris with the requisite authority, that 'you have to be God, sometimes, to know who are the right people'. It is, in other words, impossible to know; and this perfectly reasonable requirement may 'have to be revisited' by the Crown in the case of the Taranaki claim. If the Crown has to 'revisit' – let us be plain, abandon – its requirements that Maori negotiators actually represent their side, finality is hardly likely.

Just as this book was going to print the news arrived that the Waitangi Tribunal has recognised 'a group outside the traditional tribal structure' as a 'Treaty partner'. It has given some form of recognition to Auckland's Waipareira Trust. The Tribunal maintains now, evidently, that the Treaty was not with tribes, but somehow with the Maori race. At the same time, contradictorily, its decision is to say that the Maori urban non-tribal group is an iwi (in this context effectively a tribe), at least for some purposes. The Tribunal goes on to suggest that any voluntary grouping of Maoris could be a legitimate Maori community, which (by Treaty principles) should be recognised by the government and should be eligible for government money. It gives such examples as Maori churches, welfare groups and cultural groups. The Tribunal says, then, that the state is under a duty automatically to recognise – and fund! – any voluntary group of Maoris. None, of course, of our thousands of voluntary groups and incorporated societies of non-Maori members can hope for such state funding. The Tribunal even suggests that gangs, such as Black Power, may be legitimate Maori communities. Up until now, the state – the community – has always claimed the right to choose which groups of citizens may and may not receive legal recognition. But now the Tribunal suggests that a state duty exists to somehow recognise – and fund – even Maori gangs. Non-association orders to gang members would presumably be breaking up a Maori community, and therefore against the Treaty. There seems no reason in principle why any other future Maori militia could not also claim recognition and support.

The justification given by the Tribunal for its decision is that it allows various worthy Maori groups to receive government funding. The Tribunal discovers that Treaty principles require further openings of the public purse. In fact, there seems no reason why the Crown cannot deal with non-tribal organisations now, and fund them to provide social and support services. The Crown, after all, has dealings with a myriad of private groups – church charitable services, voluntary societies dealing with one or another disease or affliction, employment trusts, Red Cross and Plunket – there is no reason why it cannot also contract now with a Maori trust. Perhaps the Tribunal's real purpose is to suggest to the courts, in a forthcoming dispute, that urban Maori should enjoy the bounty of the Waitangi Fisheries Commission. But in any case, the Tribunal's report is further evidence – if it were needed – that tribes are not what they were.

On various occasions now – in Taranaki, for example, and at Ngai Tahu's northern boundary – different Maori tribes cannot even agree among themselves as to whose land it was that was allegedly wrongly taken. If, after 150 years of peace, it is impossible to know which tribe is the 'rightful' occupier of that place, we will never know. The question of rightful occupation is clearly a metaphysical one; but that will not stop complaints of injustice from continuing.

There is injustice, also, in seeking to rely on a document one has not signed. Many tribes in the central North Island either chose not to sign or simply never had the opportunity. In all the South Island outside the Marlborough Sounds, and in Stewart Island, only seven signatures were obtained. The present Minister of Justice has stated that this does not matter. It is a strange sort of agreement whose morally binding force does not depend on whether one has actually agreed to it or not.

If European New Zealanders are to apologise and make reparation for their misdeeds, then should not Maoris also apologise for theirs – for their cannibal feasts of whalers and sealers, for a start? And if it is replied to this that those Maori actions were proper by their culture, and one culture cannot judge another – then how may Maoris condemn the actions of Europeans, which must also be judged only by the standards of their own culture?

Perhaps Mr Tau Henare, so concerned about the return of preserved heads of Maoris, could concern himself also with the return of the preserved heads of Europeans. The head of missionary Carl Volker is reputedly still hidden in a central North Island cave. The heads of various soldiers were smoked and vilified during the Hau Hau uprising. The last recorded victim was a farmhand, Timothy Sullivan, tomahawked near Cambridge in 1873, whose smoked head was carried around the Waikato. Given what we are told is the remarkable capacity of Maori oral history, there are surely people alive who know where these heads are. What a gesture of reconciliation their return would be. When is it going to happen?

For that matter, a Minister of the Crown concerned about the recovery of New Zealanders' body parts from overseas might do worse than start by bringing back the bodies of soldiers who died overseas fighting for this country, rather than the heads of those freely sold by members of their own race.

The dimunition of blood

The Maori chieftains who signed the Treaty were, like their tribesmen, full-blooded Maoris. Their descendants, who claim redress from the Crown for wrongs done to their ancestors, are not. Most have – or had, before their Maori 'reincarnations' – European Christian names and surnames, and many are little different in complexion appearance and lifestyle from most other New Zealanders. To what extent is it just that these people should be entitled to redress?

Most of us would say that it is perfectly just that any claims we have pass to our heirs and successors. Some, of course, would not:

socialists seem to favour death duties and inheritance taxes. (It is interesting to note that the same people who preach against social welfare benefits, on the ground that they sap initiative and encourage dependency, do not hold the same view about large inheritances, which are surely just as capable of doing the same thing.) Some of those supporting Maori claims would strongly oppose any suggestion that large landed estates and trust funds for a privileged few Europeans are a proper part of our society.

There is something to be said for hereditary right, although we would draw distinctions between various cases. If a fortune has simply sat in Chancery for the last century and a half awaiting a claimant, it is fair that it should go to someone who shows a good claim. But if, say, one branch of a family had dwelt in peace for that long on an estate, and was then expelled because of the discovery that a century and a half before there had been some error, and title should have passed to another branch, would we think the situation so clear cut? There would be some justice in the claim of the long-dispossessed branch – especially if they had lived in some disadvantage all that time – but it would not be clear cut. To throw out on to the street the innocent beneficiaries of that old mistake, who had relied on the situation they found themselves in, and shaped their lives accordingly: that too is not entirely just.

This analogy of separate branches of the same family does not, however, accurately describe the situation which faces us. That situation, to extend this analogy, is one where there has been intermarriage between the branches.

There is no longer a pure Maori race: nearly all Maoris are of mixed Maori and European descent. The law, in such statutes as the Electoral Act 1993 and the Maori Land Act 1993, defines a Maori as 'a person of the Maori race of New Zealand; and includes any descendant of such a person'. We hear statements that the number of Maoris is increasing. The number of people who so describe themselves may well be; but the figure is meaningless. All these people have European blood, and it would be just as accurate to say that the number of European New Zealanders with some Maori blood is increasing.

When any modern 'Maori', then, claims for an injustice done to his ancestors, he is in fact claiming for a wrong done to some of his ancestors – Maori ones – by others of his ancestors – European ones.

Is not this absurd? If his Maori ancestors suffered from the injustice, his European ancestors very possibly benefited. One disadvantage is wiped out by another benefit. *this is silly*

If injustices have been done, and if people today do actually suffer because of injustices done to their ancestors, then it is reasonable to make redress. But it is a question of fact in each case whether a person alive today has in fact been injured. The mere fact that (say) one of a claimant's sixteen great-great-grandparents suffered an injustice is no proof at all – indeed, hardly evidence at all – that this man or woman today has been injured. As a simple question of fact, it is surely unlikely that someone with only that slender strain of Maori blood has ever suffered.

The remedying of injustices should benefit only the victims of injustice. It is actually an injustice to the rest of the community to give special benefits to people who have not suffered injustices. It is, therefore, entirely reasonable to insist that anyone claiming under the Treaty should offer prima facie evidence, anyway, that they have suffered injustice; and part of such evidence must surely be a sufficient proportion of Maori blood to suggest that this person has suffered. In other words, anyone with less than, say, a quarter of Maori blood – certainly an eighth – should *ipso facto* be unable to claim any benefits under Treaty claims. Such a minimum proportion of ancestry is not thought unreasonable elsewhere in the world. The Alaska Native Claims Act 1971 defines 'native' as someone at least a quarter-caste Alaskan Indian.

Ngai Tahu has evidently enrolled as one of its beneficiaries someone who is, genetically, only one-256th part Ngai Tahu.

To say that someone of one-sixteenth or one-thirty-second Maori ancestry is, in any meaningful sense, Maori, is as absurd as the insistence, by Hitler and Himmler, on standards of racial purity – blond hair and blue eyes – which they themselves could never reach.

This absurdity is compounded by the fact that not a few Maoris now are descended from more than one tribe. Such Maoris will be able to claim three or four times as many benefits as others (perhaps even with more Maori blood) who have the misfortune to be descended from only one or two tribes.

When asked this question of degrees of blood and the identity of Maoris, certain Treatyists reply that this question 'is one for Maori to decide'. This is doubtless their desire; but it is an evasive and dishonest answer. It is, in fact, a refusal to answer, for there is no answer.

Treatyists claim also that Maoriness – the sense of being Maori – is not a matter of genetic make-up and degrees of blood, but rather of culture. Even if one has little Maori blood, one can still 'feel' oneself to be Maori. One can identify far more with the Maori strain in one's ancestry than with the genetically-predominant European or non-Maori strain.

Now it is certainly true that our cultural interests and preferences do not always coincide with our racial inheritance. A New Zealander of, say, largely English descent and little Scottish blood may well find that the Highlands, moors and misty isles, bagpipes and whisky appeal to him more than his own English traditions. Many good and worthy people spend much of their lives studying and learning about people of completely different races and cultures. (They usually do so, of course, without taking the extra step of claiming that they actually *belong* to that different culture. For someone without any Scottish blood to pose as a Scotsman – for someone without any Maori blood to pose as a Maori – would be bizarre.) But there is nothing wrong or particularly unusual about concentrating on only selected strands of one's ancestry. And we, tolerant people, would not presume to tell others what cultures they may or may not admire or adopt.

But the situation is different when one comes to Treaty claims, or any other claim that people have suffered injustice deserving of remedy, or in some other way deserve special treatment. Here, it is not enough to say, 'I am Maori if I think I am Maori.' Here, people are claiming that, as a matter of simple fact, they have suffered from unfair treatment; either indirectly (because their ancestors suffered, and they have inherited that disadvantage) or directly (as when they themselves are discriminated against). Most Treaty claims for compensation allege indirect suffering: people alive now claim to be disadvantaged because of the injustices done to their Maori ancestors. By all means let justice be done; but for justice to be done here, it must first be established, as a simple matter of fact, that these people in fact have been disadvantaged by the treatment of their ancestors. And it is unlikely that anyone who is only one-sixtyfourth or one-thirtysecond, one-sixteenth or very probably even one-eighth Maori has actually suffered disadvantage. Someone one-sixteenth

Maori may have had one Maori ancestor who was very hard done by; but he or she also had fifteen other great-great-grandparents who suffered no injustice at all, and who (if Treatyist rhetoric is to be believed) actually prospered unduly because of the injustice done to the sixteenth great-great-grandparent.

One's cultural identification may be a matter of personal preference; but whether one has actually suffered an injustice is a matter of fact, and it is entirely valid to consider ancestry and proportion of Maori blood here, to assist in making a decision as to whether injustice has actually been inherited. If one is merely a 'cultural' Maori, and not a 'racial' Maori, one simply has not, as a simple matter of fact, suffered any injustice. One is not entitled to fatten oneself off the taxpayer, and enrich oneself unjustly, by cultural camouflage. Call yourself a Maori if you please, but do not try to pretend that that automatically means that you have been oppressed or swindled.

Another point must be made here. If, as these Treatyists claim, Maoriness is a matter of culture, not race, then it would follow that the mere possession of a small proportion – or even a large proportion – of Maori blood, would not automatically make that person a 'Maori', and entitled to anything under the Treaty. By their own argument, some sort of 'cultural test' would be required. But any serious cultural test – we do not mean the mere ability to say a few words in Maori, or even sing a song: culture is deeper than that – would, of course, disqualify many at present sharing the spoils.

To those who claim that Maoriness is not degrees of blood, but simply whether, inside, you feel like a Maori, this reply can also be made: how would those people, with only a fraction of Maori blood, know what it feels like? If one's ancestry is, say, seven-eighths European, then so, surely, is one's brain, and very probably one's cultural background also. The only person who knows how a full-blooded Maori feels is a full-blooded Maori.

Moreover, it is highly questionable whether people of (say) one-sixteenth Maori blood can really know what it is like to be a full-blooded Maori – especially if they have such fair complexion and European features so as never to have known what it feels like to be discriminated against on the basis of colour.

The indigenous question

The whole idea of who is and is not 'indigenous' is a political question, not a simple scientific one answerable by referring to history or archaeology. An 'indigenous' person is (according to the Oxford dictionary) someone 'native to' or 'born or produced naturally in a land or region'. In one sense, then, all of us born here are indigenous: we are all native, are all in some sense 'people of the land'; in Maori, 'tangata whenua'. This is our home; we have no other. We may speak a language and have a culture that developed elsewhere in the world; but then, the first Maori settlers brought their language and culture from elsewhere also. If, on the other hand, 'indigenous' refers to people whose ancestors have lived in a place from time immemorial, then New Zealand has no indigenous inhabitants; for permanent human settlement on these island dates from only about eight centuries ago.

These are the only two things that the word 'indigenous' can mean – either, simply, born in a place, or, having been there forever. The word does not mean, and has never meant, 'having ancestors who arrived in that place before anyone else'.

It is fair enough, nevertheless, to refer to Australian Aborigines, whose ancestors arrived between forty and sixty thousand years ago, as 'indigenous', for so long a time is really beyond human comprehension. But New Zealand was the last of the world's large landmasses to be settled; Maoris arrived only about eight hundred years ago, and the few centuries between Maori and European settlement are not enough to give Maoris any claim to a superior title based on being 'indigenous'. *well, he must know*

The question of whether one is indigenous — of whether ones ancestry gives one some superior claim, to rule or to receive special treatment, is a question of politics and philosophy, not of fact. It is not a question which can be settled by science. Descendants of the first people – or the first surviving people – to settle a land – must base any claim to special treatment on principles of justice, not on something inherent in their ancestry.

An international body linking 'indigenous' peoples has produced maps showing where indigenous peoples live today. From them we learn with interest that the only indigenous people in Europe, for example, are the Lapps of Lapland. We can only conclude from this that this body defines the word quite differently from the dictionaries, and does not regard most Europeans as being indigenous to places they have lived in for thousands of years.

The same map claims that the only 'indigenous' people in Japan are the Ainu, now only a few tens of thousands in number. Ordinary Japanese are not 'indigenous' even though their ancestors settled Japan about five thousand years ago. Five thousand years, and not indigenous: yet Maori, whose ancestors arrived here only eight hundred years ago, are. The reasoning evidently is that no matter how long one's ancestors have lived in a place, one can never be indigenous if someone else's ancestors were there first. Time is irrelevant.

This is all nonsense. The Ainu in Japan are treated badly, and other peoples in other parts of the world may be also. The way to improve their lot, however, is not by inventing strange principles about special rights arising from ancestral settlement. An appeal to basic principles of non-discrimination and human rights would be a lot quicker and simpler, and make more sense. If one's concern is with the survival of some culture, one can protect that culture without having to claim indigenousness and special rights for the indigenous.

Judge Durie, of the Maori Land Court, is among those claiming that Ainu are indigenous to Japan, but other Japanese are not. He denies, however, that 'indigenousness' contains any implication that other people have no right to live in that place. That may be his opinion, but it is difficult to see the point of these claims if they are not intended to support some claim of superior status on the part of the 'indigenous'.

To take a homelier example: if an inhabitant of Canterbury were to claim, because some of his ancestors arrived on one of the first four ships, that he was entitled to some special place, consideration or privilege in the province, we would unanimously ridicule his snobbery and pretensions – and his failure to recognise reality. Why, when we change the ship into a canoe, does the argument become stronger?

Should Sir Edmund Hillary own Everest because he was there first? Should the United States own the moon? Given the course of history, it was inevitable that both Polynesians and Europeans would eventually both discover New Zealand. Discovery, then, can hardly be conclusive in any theory of sovereignty. The idea that first-comers have greater rights has some validity, but as an overall principle it is more appropriate to a queue for tickets than to political status. Otherwise sixth-generation New Zealanders (like me) would, by Treatyist logic, be entitled to greater political rights than the descendants of more recent immigrants. Can Treatyists really mean this?

The passage of time makes the question of justice more complicated. If a thief steals my property, then, other things being equal, justice certainly requires that he return it to me. What, though, if he has onsold my property to an innocent third party, and then disappeared? Two innocent parties now have a claim on the same thing; and, although we might still award the property to the original owner, we would do so with a little doubt and hesitation. If the original owner had been negligent in some way, and the later innocent purchaser careful, we might even be inclined to favour the later purchaser. And what if that property, over a century and a half, had had numerous owners, all of whom had worked on it, improved it, and invested in it their own sweat and tears and the skills, inventions, plants and animals they brought with them from overseas? To say that these assets, so improved, should be given back to the original owners is so simplistic as to be wrong.

When we consider justice, too, we must remember what benefits.

76

European settlement brought to Maori. They must be put in the balance. The earlier centuries of Maori settlement in New Zealand seem to have been ones of comparative peace, and abundance of resources. But by the time Europeans first sighted New Zealand, moas and many other birds had become extinct or very rare, seals and some fish populations were overexploited, and the human population, which had grown for some centuries on abundant resources, was facing what Dr Tim Flannery has called a 'resource crisis'[6] (see also Chapter 6). Tasman's men were the victims of un-provoked attack; Captain Cook, too, observed violent confrontation. Everywhere were signs of war and destruction. Cannibalism was practised as a matter of course. The evidence is clear, from Maori as well as from European sources, that warfare was endemic, the pre-occupation and obsession of the race, and that human bodies were a regular source of food. Cruelty practised on captives was just as barbarous as the punishments of Europe. The evidence strongly suggests that it was the destruction of environment and resources, and the ensuing threat of famine, which had turned this pre-human paradise into a war zone, and it is very possible that, had not Europeans arrived when they did, with pigs, potatoes and other foods, there might have been a catastrophic collapse of the Maori population. Maori life before European settlement was short, dark, savage, and full of fear.

From all of this European settlement delivered Maori. European settlers were welcomed in many places as a source of possible enrichment and as some guarantee of protection against raids by enemies. Let us remember, also, that many Maoris wanted to sell their land – and that Maoris, whatever their naivete in 1840, were not fools, and not naive for long. True, Europeans brought new dis-eases, but who can say if fewer Maori might have died of war, star-vation and their own diseases had Europeans not come?

Moreover, just as human exploration and colonisation of the globe was inevitable, so the appearance of the world's diseases in New Zealand was also historically inevitable. One cannot say that British explorers were guilty of a crime because they chanced to be the instruments of that appearance.

In 1845 the Akaroa police magistrate received a deputation from local natives asking him to purchase lands in the northern South Island and place settlers there. They said they would ask very little in payment, in consideration of the benefit of 'having a body of English emigrants stationed between them and their enemies in the Northern Island'.[7]

European plants and animals, labour and skill, inventions and knowledge, peace and order have made an overwhelming contribution to our country. Who has heard even the most radical Maori suggest that it would be desirable, even in theory, for Maoris to return totally to the way of life they endured before European settlement? Europeans certainly caused great environmental damage; but then so did Maoris (see Chapter 6). Our land now can support a vastly greater human population than it could in pre-European times, with long life expectancy and in comparative security. But to recognise the benefits of European civilisation is one spiritual challenge that Maori activists evidently find impossible to meet.

The European contribution has not only vastly enhanced the comfort and security of Maori life, but also the usefulness and value of land. If a tribe's land could, before European settlement, sustain indefinitely only a certain number of people, there is surely some force in the argument that justice would require them to be left only the area of land which, with European innovations, could support that same number of people – a vastly smaller area. I do not propose that as the general rule, but certainly it is unjust for Maoris to insist on the return of the same area of land as that taken. *doesn't he mean SOLD?*

It was the pioneering European ancestors who, with little more than their bare hands, turned the wilderness of 150 years ago into the prosperous, smiling land it is today. Our debt and our obligation is first and foremost to them. Colonisation rescued Maori from warfare and population decline. It placed the whole world and everything in it – the riches of its cultures as well as its comforts and *by our definition* necessities of life – at their disposal. These benefits have to weigh heavily in the scales of justice.

We have prospered, indeed, not just because of the hard work of the pioneers, but also because of the happy chance, which few even of the pioneers might have foreseen, that we were eventually able to sell our meat and dairy produce to a willing customer 12,000 miles away. We know of this market, and our past prosperity, only with hindsight. At the time of many land acquisitions it was unknown, and therefore it is unjust to declare with hindsight that the prices paid for land were absurdly low. Land alone is only one source of prosperity: plants and animals, capital, and , above all, skill and knowledge – for the most part brought from Europe – have made it what it is.

Our standard rhetoric is that we are a 'young country'. We have, of course, been a distinct and independent nation for much longer than many other members of the United Nations. In terms of our culture, too, we are not young. Maori brought a culture with them; Europeans brought several thousand years of their culture also.

We all look nostalgically back to the days of our childhood. But we cannot return there. The past is forever closed to us: 1840 will not return. Nor should we think like children. All races and cultures pass through a tribal phase. It is inevitable, but it is only a phase. It is not democratic, nor is it rational. It is, indeed, anti-social. Outside the tribal group are only outsiders – without rights. Tribes cling to grievances; the group defines itself by conflict with outsiders and enemies. Harmony with outsiders is difficult to establish; the motto of a tribe must be 'victory or death'. A tribe, like any other sectional interest, is committed to self-interest, not objective justice. Tribes look after their own; and, very often, it is only its leaders who make the rules. *→ so are nation state*

Here on these islands at the edge of the populated world we are still physically remote from the hearts of human activity. How much more were Maoris exiles before Europe arrived. They had a lot of catching up to do. Four to six thousand years ago the Egyptians and Indians, Persians and Chinese were more advanced than Maori were a mere 200 years ago. All of human history is expansion and encounter, struggle and saga, the development of consciousness and the development of civilisation.

In all our concern about what Maori thought in 1840, let us not forget what most Europeans thought then. Not even the missionaries intended to freeze in time the neolithic tribal culture they found here then, and few would have intended to guarantee that culture a permanent and high degree of power and influence. All people may be of equal value; but, although we should respect the good in all cultures, we cannot say that Maori and European contributions to civilisation are equal.

What does it take to make a culture into a civilization?

Revolutions and legality

About 150 years separate us from the signing of the Treaty. Almost exactly the same period of time – 152 years – separates the Treaty from one of the most momentous and significant events of recent British history: the so-called 'Glorious Revolution' of 1688. To consider that revolution provides a useful perspective on the Treaty of Waitangi.

In that year, the undoubted lawful king of England, Scotland and Ireland, James VII (of Scotland) and II (of England) was overthrown, and fled from his kingdoms to seek shelter in France. That king, son of Charles I and great-grandson of Mary, Queen of Scots, was Britain's last Catholic king. It was his attempt to introduce religious tolerance – not just for Catholics, but for non-conformists as well – which led to his overthrow. In his and his son's stead, his daughter Mary and her husband William of Orange were placed on the throne. After their deaths James's other daughter, Anne, was made queen; and after her death fifty-four Catholics with better claims to the throne were passed over in order to give the throne to the fifty-fifth in line, the first Protestant among them, George, Duke of Brunswick and Elector of Hanover, who became de facto king as George I.

The attempts of the unlucky Stuart princes – James Edward, the son of James VII and II, and James Edward's son Charles Edward, the Bonnie Prince – to recover the thrones of their ancestors belong more to Scottish, than New Zealand history, and need not be recounted here. Since the failure of the rising of 1745, led by the Bonnie Prince, Jacobitism (the name given to the Stuart cause) has been a hopeless cause. The line of the Stuarts has died out and their claim, increasingly shadowy, has passed to other European princes. Yet many still remember the pride and nobility of the struggle, and remember too that our present good queen, for all her illustrious ancestry and fine qualities, owes her throne to parliament, not to unbroken ancient right. *crown not without power from 1688*

Revolutions, by definition, are unlawful – by the law existing before the revolution. If the revolution succeeds, and the old legal order is overthrown, then a completely new legal order, (invalid by the old pre-revolutionary law) is created.

Treason doth never prosper. What's the reason?
Why, if it prosper, none dare call it treason.[8]

It has often been observed that if the American Revolution of 1776 had failed, George Washington and others would not be the revered fathers of their country, but would instead have been executed as traitors.

Queen Victoria, then, owed her throne to an unlawful revolution which, about 150 years before, had overthrown the old legal order. Yet, sooner or later, we must face facts. By 1840 any hope of restoring the ancient line had long disappeared. Even then, although the sentimental might be pleased to sing 'Will ye no come back again?' and 'Wha'll be king but Charlie?', Jacobitism would, with all charity and affection, have to be described as, at best, a charming but largely irrelevant eccentricity. *c . 1850*

Irrelevant, that is, in all senses but this: that the history of the Jacobite cause reminds us that the finest legal theory must sooner or later take account of brute facts. The lawful right of the Bonnie Prince to the throne of his ancestors was impeccable, and if the uprising of 1745 had succeeded, no-one could have denied his lawful right to reign after his father's death as Charles III. But to claim, in 1840, that England and Scotland's lawful monarch was not Victoria, but Francis of Modena (the then Stuart claimant) would be absurd. To claim in 1998 that our lawful monarch is not Elizabeth of Windsor, but Albert of Wittelsbach, the Prince of Bavaria (entitled to the throne by the old pre-1688 laws of succession) would be bizarre. A new regime has appeared, and sooner or later we must all accept it.

This is only common sense. We cannot live in a past that has gone forever. The history of every country in the world is full of wars and invasions, conquests, revolutions and usurpations, which, by the pre-existing law, would be illegal. We cannot ignore the Norman Conquest, or the Anglo-Saxon invasions of Roman Britain, or the Roman Conquest of Celtic Britain, simply because these things were constitutionally and legally improper. They happened. We must live with them. The ancestors of many European New Zealanders – Scots, Irish, poor English – suffered at the hands of the British ruling classes. We may not forget this, but we are not such fools as to let the memory rule our lives.

Some Treaty supporters, though, are the Jacobites of today. They suppose that since (they claim) Maoris never ceded sovereignty by the Treaty, that is the end of the matter. They consider irrelevant the fact that for well over a century we have been ruled by a settled and established legal system which behaves as if it had sovereignty. The fact that the Crown behaves as if it had sovereignty is surely some evidence that in fact it does have it: but no, this breath of common sense is dismissed at once. By international law the government of Elizabeth II is recognised as the lawful government of this country; yet some Treaty supporters, very keen to advance the (dubious) claim that the Treaty was valid by the international law of 1840, display no interest at all in the views of international law today as to who is sovereign.

By Maori custom itself, title always had to rest, ultimately, on physical possession and the actual exercise of rights of ownership. If, for three generations, cooking fires and camp fires were not lit, then title to that land lapsed.[9]

Maoris themselves, in 1840, made a treaty with Victoria. By doing so, they must be taken to have accepted that Victoria, and her house and regime, were lawful, and that the revolution of 1688 had validly established a new constitutional arrangement. Doubtless Maoris never actually considered such delicate niceties: they were sensible realists who recognised established power and order when they saw it. In logic and consistency, their descendants should do the same. *ugly*

The chief Maori method of obtaining title to land was not the occupation of unoccupied areas – for in theory all land in New Zealand was held by one tribe or another. Title was obtained mostly by conquest and held by strength of arms. Might was right. This was Maori land law: the rule of the strongest. Tribal title, obtained by conquest, was held only as long as a tribe was able to defend its right. Its 'right' hardly existed other than as a physical fact.

There has recently been a tendency among many pro-Treaty activists to ignore or even conceal this painful fact. The Ngai Tahu acquisition of most of the South Island, for example, has recently been described by a well-known tribeswoman as having occurred through 'intermarriage'. This is, to put it politely, untrue. It is beyond dispute that in the course of Ngai Tahu acquisition – as in the course of many another acquisition – many battles were fought, and many people killed and eaten. *always*

An old friend has often described how, as a young man, he strolled along a beach on the Chatham Islands, and how Maui Pomare, a descendant of the 1835 North Island Maori conquerors of the Chatham Islands Moriois, pointed out to him the landmarks between which the bodies of the slain Moriois were laid. For days, if not weeks, the bodies were eaten by the conquerors, until they became so rotten they could be eaten no more.[10] Maori life in pre-European times was not all aroha and stick games. Of course, women of child-bearing age were also taken by the conquerors. But even then, this would, in many cases, better be described as forced breeding – or rape – rather than 'intermarriage'.

A recent *North and South* article on Dunedin stated that 'for hundreds of years' before Europeans arrived Ngai Tahu had lived there. But they had done no such thing. Ngai Tahu themselves have chosen to celebrate, in the year 2000, 250 years of their presence and hegemony in the south. Banks Peninsula, among other places, still remembers not only Te Rauparaha's onslaught on the Ngai Tahu (after they had been so fatally weakened by the great Kai Huaka feud) but also the battles and devices by which the Ngai Tahu had earlier overcome their predecessors, the Ngati Mamoe. In other words, Ngai Tahu had established themselves in the south, by conquest, only about a century before the first four ships arrived in Lyttelton, and not very long before Captain Cook's visits. Tribes have appeared before the Tribunal whose ancestors had taken lands by conquest less than one generation before the Treaty; sometimes the conquest was only a year or two before 1840. Even assuming that European acquisition of these lands was improper, how unjust is it that so very recent a conqueror not be compensated fully?

This book does not claim that the Crown acquired sovereignty over New Zealand, or that Europeans gained title to Maori land by conquest. But certain Maoris do make that claim. They claim that Maoris never ceded sovereignty, whether by the Treaty or in any other way, and that the loss of land in wars and confiscations was, essentially, a conquest.

But in complaining of alleged European 'conquest' Maoris are being inconsistent. If Maori tribes may conquer and destroy each other, and thereby validly acquire sovereignty and title to land, why should not the same principle apply to the tribe of the white queen across the water? It would surely be surprising that the Maori

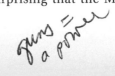

customary acceptance of conquest should only apply to conquest by other Maoris, and that successful conquest by other races was somehow invalid. Such a principle would be not only racist – and who is in favour of that? – but absurd. By definition, the conquered never like their conquerors.

If land in the South Island is being 'returned', not to Waitaha or Ngati Mamoe, but to Ngai Tahu, that is surely an admission by Ngai Tahu that the original owners' claim disappears with time.

These inter-tribal differences continue. Maoris fought with the Crown against their 'fellow Maori' during the Maori Wars (often referred to euphemistically today as the 'Land Wars'), and often played a crucial role in defeating, for example, Hone Heke and Te Rangihaeata. Ngai Tahu continue to deny that any remnants of the people they displaced, the Waitaha and Ngati Mamoe, continue to survive as a separate and distinct entity, even though people claiming to be Waitaha still exist. Ngai Tahu succeeded in 1996 in having themselves recognised by parliament as the Maori occupants of most of the South Island.[11] The Ngai Tahu Claims Settlement Bill now before parliament contained nothing at all for Waitaha except insofar as they form part of Ngai Tahu. Those Waitaha people – and there are some – who dispute that they form part of Ngai Tahu, do not receive anything. Rangimarie Te Maiharoa, the present head chief of the Waitaha, has complained that legal recognition of Ngai Tahu and them alone 'commits a gross injustice'. He has commended the government 'on its suggestion that Waitangi Tribunal powers be curbed'.[12]

Even an 'unjust' and improper purchase requires two parties, one a Maori vendor. When considering any moral guilt on the part of Europeans we must remember that some dubious land purchases, where the Maori vendors had little or no title to sell, were actually motivated by the desire of those Maoris to hurt their Maori enemies. For example, Teira, who offered to sell Governor Gore Browne the Waitara block at the beginning of the Taranaki wars, was moved to do so to hurt the chief Kingi.

Tony Simpson, the author of *Te Riri Pakeha*,[13] writes that 'sellers were often actuated by private tribal feuds. They sold the land of their enemies . . .' Simpson tells us that 'by 1848 the Maoris were doing well out of the colonisation of New Zealand', and describes how Governor Hobson had bought rights to Taranaki land from the

Waikato Maoris, who had conquered it before 1840 but never settled it. When settlers actually arrived, Ati Awa land in Taranaki appeared empty. 'But this apparently virgin expanse was a nest of claims and rights, a snare for the unwary.' Maori who claimed to be wronged by some Taranaki purchases were Maoris who had recently lost that land anyway to the Waikatos. Unjust land sales could be, to paraphrase Clausewitz, the continuation of tribal warfare by other means.

All duplicity, then, was not on the European side. Alan Everton remarks on Ngai Tahu's readiness to part with their lands, and believes that, although 'the Crown's early land-buying policy [was] based on the notion that the Maori were innocent primitives, ripe for exploitation by unscrupulous white men, in fact, if anything, it was Ngai Tahu who saw the white man coming'. Many sales of the same parts of Banks Peninsula were made, sometimes by chiefs whose rights to sell were debatable.[14]

This also must be said about Jacobitism. Given that our present regime and legal system owe their existence to the illegalities of 1688, it would be inconsistent for that regime to attempt to ignore plain facts, and attempt to recognise some long-abandoned and outdated principle, however valid it might once have been.

And, just as our present government was established by revolution and violence, so by that method we may again establish a new one in its place. There are enough Maori hotheads ready to talk of throwing bombs and re-establishing some Maori government or other by force. If our government displeases us, then, as the events of 1688 show, the power lies in us to replace it with one more acceptable to our attitudes.

As explained in Chapter 5, the Treaty is a blank cheque. It is, so wise judges tell us, 'an embryo, not a fully-developed set of ideas'. Its 'principles' are to be discovered only by judges and lawyers, after close, long and expensive examination. These principles, we are told, are 'developing', and so there may never be any final statement of what they are. It cannot be just that we be ruled by what is therefore, essentially, a secret law; by principles that we cannot know in advance but that we must unquestioningly receive. No-one can 'know' what these principles are. Some say they involve Maori sovereignty; others, separate and equal Maori and non-Maori parliaments. Others, obviously, say they mean something less. The

extraction of principles from that brief, terse document, the Treaty, is not like the extraction of a legal principle from an ordinary straightforward case. It is (as the diversity of views on what the 'principles' are shows) entirely a political decision, and it is no less political because judges do it. To accept the rule of the Treaty is to accept that we are to be ruled for ever by the metaphysical processes and political decisions of a handful of people.

Even if these interpretations of the Treaty were made by a more democratic body, it is still bizarre that the policies, laws and arrangements of an entire nation should be governed for ever by one page of words set down a century and a half ago. Thomas Paine, the author in 1791 of *The Rights of Man*, insisted that every generation was the master of its own law, and that while the revolution settlement after the overthrow of the Stuarts a century before was a good thing, it was hardly the last word on the English constitution.

The same principle must apply here. However fine the Treaty was, it may not by any principle of justice or natural law reach out its hand from the grave to rule us. We must certainly respect our history, and frame laws in harmony with our long slow constitutional development – although if we actually did that, of course, we probably would pay far less attention to the Treaty than we do, for it is a very recent mania. But in the last resort, our nation is to be ruled by us, not by the words that over a couple of evenings, a century and a half ago, were set down by half a dozen men in a ship's cabin.

We are, however, bound by the past to this extent: that if those before us, freely and without duress, considered a particular bargain or arrangement to be just, or if they considered some later settlement of an injustice to be just, and ending the matter once and for all, then the matter is settled. They were there at the time; they were better judges of the case than we are. Nor can we forever constantly relitigate the past.

Our criminal law, like that of England, has a rule against 'double jeopardy' – against being tried twice for substantially the same crime. Once acquitted or convicted, there is an end of the matter. This does not apply in the case of the Waitangi Tribunal: even after it has made a recommendation – and after that recommendation has been acted on – some disgruntled person can still lodge a new claim. We know, also, that previous 'full and final settlements', solemnly agreed to and happily accepted by previous generations of Maori, are dismissed as irrelevant and not binding upon their descendants. The stage is already being set for this to happen again. Already, some within Ngai Tahu have announced that the present settlement is unjust and are attempting to stop it. Doubtless in twenty or thirty years this will be cited as 'evidence' that the 1998 settlement was unjust, and not agreed to by many Ngai Tahu, but somehow 'forced' upon them.

No less a person than Charles Crofts, the then chairman of Te Runanga o Ngai Tahu, has said of the present settlement that 'justice is not attainable for the poverty, alienation and losses' endured since 1840. Compensation will be 'far short of what had been lost through broken promises'. Mr Crofts favours Ngai Tahu accepting this most recent settlement, but clearly he does not think it will hurt for Ngai Tahu to pose as a public-spirited martyr; and clearly he is, consciously or not, making it possible for fresh claimants a generation hence to claim that the 1998 settlement was also inadequate. Mr Crofts claims that Ngai Tahu's 'land losses' alone would cost the country about twenty billion dollars.[15] Indeed, the clause in the present Ngai Tahu Claims Settlement Bill forbidding further claims can be repealed just like any other statute; and the Bill itself contemplates that the Deed of Settlement (much of which is enacted by the Bill) can be amended in future.[16]

In a lengthy correspondence in the press several years ago, Te Okoro Runga firmly maintained that binding future generations is not 'the Maori way' and that it is not only improper but impossible so to bind one's descendants. Alamein Kopu would seem to share this belief in the transience of solemn agreements. So do others.[17] But to the extent that it is true, it has two consequences. One is that we can never hope for an end to Treaty claims. The other is this: If Maoris now cannot bind future generations, then the Maoris who signed the Treaty could not either. The Treaty was solely for their generations; no later Maoris may rely on it.

One cannot have it both ways: either Maoris can, validly and culturally, bind future generations, or they cannot. If they can, then the Treaty – whatever it means – abides, but only one settlement of any claim is ever possible. If they cannot, then the Treaty does not abide, and we may all quite properly ignore it completely, for it died when one party to it – the generation of Maoris alive in 1840 – died.

Moutua Gardens protesters wrote in the *Dominion* that 'one cannot sell forever the land, for that is to deprive future generations of their mother: parts may be gifted for others to nurture, but the iwi always retains the authority of ultimate custodial people. One cannot give one's mother permanently into the care of another. It is an idea that is spiritually incomprehensible and legally impossible.' As Simon Upton observes, 'things that are spiritually incomprehensible and legally impossible are, conveniently, impossible to debate with outsiders. Such is the essence of tribalism . . . profoundly corporatist, particularist and conservative . . . Talk of spiritual incomprehensibility and legal impossibility is a romantic and revolutionary withdrawal from the debate. Talk about the impossibility of private title to land and you risk a revolution.'[18]

In an interview on National Radio at the time of the Gardens occupation, both Dr Ranginui Walker and a Whanganui iwi representative conceded that the Gardens sale deed had been signed by 207 Maoris, that the land sale was properly registered, the land was subject to no Treaty claims and there had been no subsequent fraud or other illegitimate activity by the Crown.[19] The Maori occupancy was, they said, rather based on the claim that Maori had no concept of freeholding; that, as the *Dominion* article quoted above claims, they

could not imagine anything more than a lease, or something like it.

No claim, therefore, can finally be settled, because iwi are always there as the 'ultimate custodial people'. And, even more ominously, if Maoris are always the custodians, then no title to private land anywhere in the country is safe, regardless of how proper any original sale was. And Ranginui Walker and the iwi representative agreed that this was so.

Once we abandon legal title to land, however, then title must be the same as physical possession – in other words, there is no law but force. Whanganui Maoris would, then, have no right to complain if some other stronger tribe came down the river and swept them out to sea. They would have no right to call on the forces of law and order to intervene.

So are tribal warfare, and uncontrolled violence the blueprint for the future?

The latest full and final settlement[20]

A 500-clause bill supposedly settling the Ngai Tahu land claim was introduced into parliament recently. Politicians made wry comparisons with the Bill introduced the 'first time' the claim was settled, a mere three-clause minnow. They were referring to the Ngai Tahu Land Claim Settlement Act of 1944. That was actually the *third* rather than the first time the claim has been disposed of in a supposedly binding 'full and final settlement.' Barring some unexpected spine being discovered in the politicians, the 1998 Act will merely be the fourth and largest instalment yet paid out.

The 1944 Act was a masterpiece of clear legal drafting, especially in an era in which other Acts of the legislature used convoluted and superfluous language. This was an Act 'to effect a Final Settlement of the Ngai Tahu Claim', and provided for the payment of £300,000 in yearly instalments of £10,000 each. The settlement was negotiated by Sir Eruera Tirikatene, MP, the father of former Labour Cabinet Minister Whetu Tirikatene-Sullivan.

It is frequently claimed that earlier settlements were negotiated by those without a mandate, or that there was insufficient consultation with the affected iwi. Like much of the cant surrounding the Treaty grievance industry, this is simply not true. In 1971, when debating whether to extend the original payments to payments in perpetuity, Mrs Tirikatene-Sullivan angrily told the House that more than 80 meetings of beneficiaries were held in both islands over a period of three years. More importantly, she noted that in official delegations to the government since, the Ngai Tahu Trust Board, which administered the money, 'specifically endorsed their continuing acceptance' of the 1944 Settlement. Of the claim that the beneficiaries in 1944 had not been properly aware of the Act's provisions, Mrs Tirikatene-Sullivan noted that 'there were 109 movers and seconders of formal resolutions which accepted a compensation payment of 10,000 pounds a year for 30 years. This was the specific proposal they accepted.' Now dead of course, Sir Eruera himself cannot confirm her claims.

Going back further in history, there was a still earlier 'full and final settlement' in 1887 when further land was granted to the Ngai Tahu. This added to land granted to the tribe in 1868 in recompense for alleged chicanery regarding Kemp's purchase of twenty years before. By the end of the 1880s, tribal reserves totalled some 40,000 acres, more than sufficient for the needs of the 600 or so Ngai Tahu living in the area at the time. Contrary to claims accepted by the Tribunal, there had never been any promise by Kemp or any other government representative to set aside reserves of 10 percent of the land purchased. Given the Ngai Tahu population at the time, this would in any case have been absurd.

The 1944 Act was one of a trilogy of enactments which were naively supposed to settle all outstanding claims once and for all – an eerily familiar sentiment. Like the Ngai Tahu Act, each was clear and unambiguous. The relevant sections of the Waikato-Maniopoto Land Claims Settlement Act obliged the Crown to pay £6,000 per year in 'full and final settlement of certain claims which have heretofore been made or which may in the future be made regarding certain confiscations of land in the Waikato-Maniopoto district'.

The 1944 Taranaki Maori Claims Settlement Act was entitled 'An Act to effect a final settlement of certain claims relating to the confiscation of Native lands in the Taranaki and Wellington districts . . .' The payment of £5,000 per year 'in each and every year' was to be 'in settlement of all claims and demands which have heretofore been made or which may hereafter be made . . . in respect of or arising out of the confiscation of land within the Taranaki district . . .'

After fifty years, with rampant inflation for much of the last thirty, it is easy to assume (wrongly) that this and the other settlements were financially insufficient. Based on earnings statistics of the time, however, the annual payment was in fact worth about $4 million in today's money. To put it another way, until inflation took off in the 1970s, the government was giving Taranaki Maoris the value of two large dairy farms every year.

The claim is now made that the negotiators of these settlements did not truly represent the tribes. The Waikato claim was negotiated by none other than Princess Te Puea, a revered Tainui matriarch. The Taranaki settlement was negotiated by Sir Maui Pomare. Historian Michael King, in a work recommended by Tainui representatives, notes that the final offer of £6,000 per year for fifty years and £5,000 every year thereafter was more generous than that negotiated by the elders the night before. One of Te Puea's negotiators accepted with words translated as 'the matter is finalised satisfactorily'. The Waikato claim of course has just been the subject of a further 'full and final' settlement, and the Taranaki iwi are soon to begin negotiating with the government over the size of their latest instalment.

The lessons from all this are quite clear for all who will see. By the mid-twentieth century – if not earlier – *all* of the major claims now being renegotiated had been settled. The settlements were negotiated by respected kaumatua of the time, and the sums agreed were accepted as fair and reasonable by those negotiators. There can only be one 'full and final' settlement; once a second is negotiated, the precedent is set for the twenty-second.

There is a much more important and fundamental point than the money. It has been observed that the latest Ngai Tahu instalment represents only about two days of the annual Social Welfare budget. Clearly the country would not fall if such payments were made every ten years or so. The more important point of course is that if 'full and final' can now mean 'until the next time', where will that lead?

One of the most important principles of the law is certainty. Without it, parties cannot know the extent of their rights and obligations. If the government can shift the legal goalposts in this area why not change the criminal law to suit the particular crime or a particularly odious criminal?

The same fishhook-wearing liberals who are applauding the Ngai Tahu handout as moral and just would have a very different view if the government announced – after the fact – that the punishment for cutting down iconic trees on hills was now ten years' hard labour rather than three months' periodic detention.

If the earlier settlements were illegitimate why is that so? Is the current Settlement Bill simply the invoice for the latest instalment to be funded by the taxpayer? Is it in Maori interests to settle claims finally? What is the proposed response to the next lot? At the very least, the government needs to respond to those questions honestly.

One must add that $170 million is not, even now, the total of the Ngai Tahu settlement. Ngai Tahu has, in perpetuity, the right of first refusal on all Crown properties in its area. It has already made some very tidy sums by buying such properties and immediately on-selling them for a profit. Ngai Tahu boasts of the very rapid growth of its funds and assets; not surprisingly, given this advantage. Virtually all greenstone is now its property.

In deciding, also, what is just, we must not feel under any obligation to accept everything the Waitangi Tribunal tells us. As remarked elsewhere, the Tribunal makes its recommendations solely on the basis of what happened in the past; it does not, it cannot – and indeed it probably should not – consider the more important and pressing question of what justice actually requires now.

92

In the case of the 1996 Taranaki Report, the Tribunal published its thick 'interim' report even though, on many matters, 'the Crown was still to be heard.' This took place with the agreement of the Crown. It was published "to assist a settlement", even though the Tribunal's inquiry was incomplete.

It is this report that speaks of 'the holocaust of Taranaki history'.[21] Although the report records a sorry history of European dealings with Maoris over land and expropriation by force of arms, to suggest that the dealings between the races in New Zealand – the murder of Maori by European and European by Maori – are even remotely comparable to the horrors of German gas chambers, is the clearest confirmation that the Tribunal has lost its sense of proportion.

When hearing the Ngai Tahu claim, the Tribunal found as a fact that Codfish and the Crown Titi Islands, off Stewart Island, had been acquired by the Crown entirely properly and without any breach of Treaty principles. Yet it still (in excess of its jurisdiction) recommended 'returning' them to Maori hands. What would we think of a court which held that a plaintiff's claim is without foundation, but nevertheless the defendant should compensate him anyway? The Tribunal chose also to attribute Ngai Tahu's 'parlous' condition to the Crown's failure to honour Treaty principles, ignoring such other causes as economic depression affecting the whole country. Brian Priestley, who advised Ngai Tahu on public relations, has said that 'it would be hard to imagine any public body less well organised to get at the truth.' The Tribunal has claimed that the Resource Management Act is 'fatally flawed' because it does not put the Treaty ahead of everything else. Why should it? The Act has sustainable management as its purpose. It is a pleasant surprise to hear the Tribunal admit that some Maori practices are not sustainable, but then of course such practices would not be able to continue for ever anyway. Sustainability is hardly an objectionable principle; for the Tribunal to object to it reveals it as a group of politicians, not impartial arbiters.

Another reason not to believe the Tribunal automatically is because it has not always had all the facts presented to it. A good example is the Ngai Tahu claim. In its opening submissions to the Tribunal, the Crown adopted the stance of stating its historical researchers and other experts had been instructed to find out the truth about the matters in issue and neither to hinder nor blur the truth. They were told not to put forward the evidence in a manner that was partial to the Crown, nor act as advocates for the Crown.

However, when the Crown came to present its case – which it claimed would show that the conclusions of some of the claimant's historians whose enthusiasm had turned them into advocates would not be justified – its own historians failed to present all the evidence which could have been relevant. For example, in 1872, Canon James Stack, a good friend to Ngai Tahu, observed habits of indolence and dependence among the tribe. He was not the only contemporary witness to make that observation. Alexander McKay wrote in 1868, of a reserve at Otago Heads, that 'the poverty of the people is entirely attributable to their own indolence and apathy. They have plenty of land of good quality and might live in comparative comfort if they would only exert themselves.'[22] Instead, the tribe preferred to let its reserves to European farmers.

In 1882 Ngai Tahu's population was at most two thousand, and its reserves were 43,710 acres – more than twenty acres per head. French settlers at Akaroa in 1840 were allocated five acres per adult male. According to one researcher, Denis Hampton of Christchurch, there is little if any evidence that Ngai Tahu did other than fritter away the £14,000 – then a huge sum – which they received from their land sales.

The same researcher has commented that Crown witnesses in the Ngai Tahu case were sometimes ill prepared and others were employed at short notice or without appropriate background. He suggested the full and final settlement of 1944 was only lightly touched upon by the Crown's Counsel, and concluded that the Crown's case was at best half hearted.[23]

The rules of evidence applied by the Courts arose out of necessity. Some evidence is better than other evidence. The Waitangi Tribunal is free to receive whatever evidence it pleases: anecdote, reminiscence and hearsay are all acceptable. Such evidence has the dangers and defects of all oral history.

Words and ideas that are written are thereby pinned down, and although they may still change, they do not change so quickly. Without books and paper, words can change their meanings far more quickly and history itself can be revised far more readily. History is then, after all, stored in the memories of only a small handful of the learned. This knowledge is, of course, secret, the powerful possession of a privileged caste. It is a simple matter for those who possess it to adapt it – to insert an incident here, a marriage there, a wrong, an atrocity, an ancestor – in order to establish or avoid some claim. This is not to say that it is utterly without historic use; but it cannot be relied on as written documents can be.

Written documents, of course, must be accurate in the first place; but it is usually much easier to sort out written truth and fiction.

When Cicero was a boy, in the first century before Christ, every Roman schoolboy still learnt off by heart the Twelve Tables of the Law. These tables, the first code of Roman law, were first written down on publicly displayed tablets of bronze about 450 BC, and so by Cicero's time they were old-fashioned and superseded. Nevertheless they were vitally important: as important in Roman history as Magna Carta is in ours; for they mark the first time that the laws were written down and were no longer the private possession of the aristocracy who could use and re-shape them as they pleased. The Twelve Tables of the Law were a great step towards liberty; the acceptance of oral history, and allegation uncorroborated by evidence, is a great step away.

Professor Kenneth Cumberland wrote: 'Maori history, before missionaries invented a method of writing the language, was handed down in chants, stories and carvings. They grew more fanciful with each generation. Carvings became so intricate that even tribal elders were not sure what to make of them. But European scholars insisted on trying to find a literal interpretation, and Maoris obligingly embroidered stories to give their guesswork credibility.'[24]

Calculating Europeans and land confiscations cannot be entirely blamed for Maori economic woes. We have often heard descriptions of the fruitfulness of Maori commercial agriculture – in certain part of the North Island – before the land wars, with the implication that it was those wars and confiscations which destroyed them, as Europeans found Maori prosperity threatening. But this claim contains some basic logical and historical errors. Wars in the central North Island did not affect Maori populations in Northland, the southern North Island and the South Island; and Maori wheat-growing along the Waikato and Waipa rivers had already declined in the late 1850s because of the collapse of international wheat prices.[25] The attempts of some Europeans to encourage the development of Maori farms

Maori's fault?

were opposed by Maori traditionalists who feared it would lead to the subdivision of tribal estates. *Land was individualized*

The mere existence of money had certain inevitable effects. Before European settlement, wealth existed only in things likely to be available to all – meeting-houses, fine carvings, canoes, and food – food, which, of its nature, would not last more than a year or so. When money appeared, as payment for timber and flax, leases and sales of land, it need not necessarily be shared. Money paid to small groups of senior elders was often treated by them as their own property; it could be enjoyed without living on the land, and spent by some without the knowledge of others. There was therefore a strong Maori opinion that all names should be registered on land titles, and all owners should receive a share of rents.[26]

Somewhere, too, in all these calculations of benefit and disadvantage we must put into the scales at least a portion of the many millions of dollars that, over many years, have been poured into so many programmes and projects of special assistance for Maoris. They seem to have had little positive effect. Perhaps further gifts will have the same effect.

Justice and mercy

There is a difference between justice and mercy, between what punishment or treatment is due to us and that which, in pity and compassion, is actually meted out to us. The prodigal son, having squandered all his inheritance, was in justice entitled to no more; yet his father, in mercy, raised him up, kissed him and treated him with honour. It should be added, however, that although the father killed a fatted calf for him, he did not propose to re-divide his estate, or take anything away from the share of his other, dutiful son.

Yet in our own time these two qualities, justice and mercy, are confused. This confusion was referred to in Chapter 1 as what Robert Hughes has called 'the cult of the victim'. No-one could condemn mercy and compassion: they are noble and god-like virtues. But they are not justice, and, in the words of the old legal maxim, 'a man must be just before he is generous'. Our resources are not unlimited, and to be unduly generous with them to one person is automatically to short-change someone else. Moreover, mercy or generosity can easily become the easy way out. Instead of looking carefully into the facts; instead of making enemies by stating a few plain home truths, it can be all too easy to say to someone, 'We'll let you off.' By being excessive in mercy the whole social system is harmed.

Sir Kenneth Clarke observed[27] that 'we are so much accustomed to the humanitarian outlook that we forget how little it counted in earlier ages of civilisation. Ask any decent person in England or America what he thinks matters most in human conduct: five to one his answer will be "kindness". It is not a word which would have crossed the lips of many of the earlier heroes of civilisation. If you had asked St Francis what mattered in life, he would, we know, have answered, "chastity, poverty and obedience"; if you had asked Dante or Michelangelo they might have answered "disdain of baseness and injustice"; if you had asked Goethe he would have said, "to live in the whole and the beautiful". But kindness, never. Our ancestors did not use the word, and they did not greatly value the quality . . .'

In ordinary life, politeness means that we do not always say what we mean, because we do not wish to offend. Sometimes we do not call laziness, stupidity, ugliness and ignorance by their proper names, because that would hurt the lazy, stupid, ugly and ignorant. In this way an entire moral climate can be altered or even destroyed. A confusion can arise whereby people expect kindness as their due, and anything less than kindness – such as, for example, being held liable and answerable for one's own actions – is claimed to be injustice. The idea of responsibility becomes injustice, and no-one is regarded as being responsible for anything. The world owes us a living; and when Maori prodigals return to their parent Crown and taxpayer, having squandered their substance, they consider themselves very hard done by, even bitterly duped, if they do not receive what is actually unjustified generosity.

FOUR

Sovereignty

In friendship false, implacable in hate,
Resolved to ruin, or to rule the state.

– Dryden, *Absalom & Achitophel*

We know what sovereignty is. As the dictionaries tell us, it is 'supremacy in respect of power, domination or rank; supreme dominion, authority or rule'. We all know, too, as a simple matter of fact, that for a very long time the Crown has been recognised, by both New Zealand and international law, as possessing that sovereignty.

We do not need to go into the arguments about the precise moment when British sovereignty was acquired: whether it was on the day when the Treaty was first signed, or after some later days of signing, or after some later act of the Crown. It has recently been argued by Professor Jock Brookfield, of the University of Auckland, that the sovereignty of the Crown came not from the Treaty, but from some later 'revolution' and simple physical assertion of dominion. Although this may sound radical, it is in essence little different from the older view that the Crown acquired sovereignty by its own prerogative acts following the Treaty. The standard view for many years has been that sovereignty passed to the Crown not by the Treaty – which was merely a necessary preliminary political proceeding – but by royal proclamation of 21 May 1840, which mentioned the Treaty, and Maori agreement, in respect of the North Island, but which claimed the South Island (perhaps inhabited by only two or three thousand people) by right of discovery. New Zealand, on then becoming a possession of the British Crown, automatically became part of the colony of New South Wales and only some months later became a separate colony.

For our purposes, we need note only two things. One is the

Crown's holding of sovereignty now, and for a long time past. The other is that, even if one accepts that the Crown did not acquire sovereignty by the Treaty, yet nevertheless the words of the Treaty are capable of granting it to the Crown.

In the English version of the Treaty, the chiefs ceded to the Crown 'all the rights and powers of sovereignty' which they possessed.[1] In return, Her Majesty guaranteed the chiefs 'full, exclusive and undisturbed possession of their lands, and estates, forests, fisheries and other properties . . .' As a matter of logic, of course, she could only make this guarantee if she now had sovereignty over the land.

Various activists, however, claim that there is a difference between the English and Maori versions of the Treaty. They claim, essentially, that the Maori version of the Treaty did not cede sovereignty at all, and that, by the *contra proferentem* rule, the Maori version must prevail.[2] As argued in Chapter 5, if there was in fact that complete difference of belief as to what the Treaty meant, there was no meeting of minds, and therefore no agreement at all from the beginning. And, as various Treatyists themselves claim, it is not clear who was the disadvantaged party in 1840 (it could well have been the Crown) so the *contra proferentem* rule could therefore be taken to mean that the English version should prevail.

But leaving these point aside, the activists' argument is this: the Maori version grants the Crown 'kawanatanga'. This word come from 'kawana', the Maori pronunciation of the English word 'governor'. It therefore means governorship. This governorship is, it is alleged, limited, and less than sovereignty, which therefore remained with the Maoris. If the Treaty meant the Crown to have sovereignty, it would have used some such word as 'mana'.

Moreover, they say, the chieftains by the Treaty retained 'te tino rangatiratanga', which means 'full chieftainship', which, they say, is essentially sovereignty. Sovereignty therefore remained with the Maoris, and, they say, remains so to this day. The Treaty, therefore, gave the Crown only some right of governance over European settlers, or some other lesser right. Maoris such as Sir Tipene O'Regan, who recognise the sovereignty of the Crown, however it arose, are accused of being 'Uncle Toms'.

For various reasons, both legal and practical, this argument simply will not hold water. Some arise simply out of the words of the Treaty.

Translations of the Maori version of the Treaty do not assist those supporting 'Maori sovereignty'. The 1869 translation ordered by the Legislative Council[3] has the Chiefs 'giv[ing] up entirely to the Queen of England for ever the government of their lands', while they retained 'the full chieftainship of their lands, their settlements and all their other property'. Professor Hugh Kawharu's translation, used in the Court of Appeal's 1987 decision (*New Zealand Maori Council* v. *Attorney-General*), and accepted by both Crown and the Maori Council as a good translation, has the chiefs 'giv[ing] absolutely to the Queen of England for ever the complete government over their land,' and the Queen in return agreed 'to protect the chiefs, the sub-tribes and all the people of New Zealand in the unqualified exercise of their chieftainship over their lands, villages and all their treasures.'[4]

Even the Waitangi Tribunal[5] accepted 'that the essentials of sovereignty were not lost on Maoris in the debate at Waitangi . . . From the treaty as a whole, it is obvious that it does not purport to describe a continuing relationship between sovereign states. Its purpose and effect was the reverse: to provide for the relinquishment by Maori of their sovereign status and to guarantee their protection upon becoming subjects of the Crown. In any event, on reading the Maori text in the light of contemporary statements, we are satisfied that sovereignty was ceded.' The Tribunal went on to suggest that 'tino rangatiratanga' was merely 'tribal self-management . . . similar to what we understand by local government.' But it is difficult, of course, to see how that could outlast the existence of the tribes themselves as living entities. It is also impossible to see how any such tribal self-management could outlast the sale of tribal land. Indeed, even the Dunedin Ngai Tahu Maori Law Centre has conceded that rangatiratanga over land is extinguished if that land is validly and properly sold and purchased.

Although rangatira is a Maori word, rangatiratanga – the concept of chieftainness or chieftainship – is said to be, like kawanatanga, a word coined by the missionaries, and little more certain in its meaning. Moreover, although the Treaty did not grant 'mana' to the Crown, nor did it guarantee that 'mana' to the chiefs – which it surely should have if, as alleged, 'mana' is the pre-eminent word for that sovereignty which the chiefs supposedly retained.

Again, the third Article of the Treaty makes Maoris British subjects, and that is quite inconsistent with any continued Maori sovereignty. How could the Queen give any guarantees of protection to Maori unless she first had authority over them?

By 1840 various Maori chieftains had travelled overseas, to Australia or even to England. Many more obviously had heard, in general terms, about the position of the Crown in those countries. They knew what British authority involved; they were not fools.[6]

In order to understand the Treaty, one must read it as a whole. This is, after all, what the signatory chiefs did in 1840. One gets the impression from some Treatyists that chiefs in the 1840s assented only to Article II, but this is hardly so. The Treaty has a preamble and three articles. Anything it might, or might not, say about chieftainship in Article II has to be read in the light of Article I, which, even in the Maori version, has the chiefs give the Queen 'complete government', and Article III, whereby the Queen gives Maoris 'the rights and duties of citizenship'.[7]

To say that Maoris and 'the Crown' – or, Maoris and non-Maoris – are 'partners' at once denies the sovereignty of the Crown, and the status of Maoris as subjects who, by the Treaty's third Article, are supposed to enjoy the Crown's protection. It also creates inequality between New Zealanders as individual citizens. If Maoris and non-Maoris are two equal groups, then the rights and influence of each Maori are greater than those of members of the majority group.

To say that one's personal influence and power depends on one's racial ancestry is racism. How can this simple truth be ignored?

Indeed, in 1840 the most significant part of Article II was perhaps the declaration – abandoned long ago without complaint – that the Crown alone could buy land from Maoris, thereby preventing sales to dubious foreigners by those without authority to sell. It is difficult to find in it any promises of separate legal systems.

Separate legal systems for different racial groups have been tried before. The barbarians who settled in the ruins of the Western Roman Empire were often governed by laws different from those of the Roman citizens among whom they lived. But these laws were always awkward, and could only ever apply when law was simple and when it was quite clear to which group someone belonged.

It is not as if there exists now some living body of Maori law which needs only to be recognised. It would have to be re-created from nothing. It would inevitably be something completely new, and those who made it would have an immense amount of power to affect all our lives. It would be a constant source of great irritation, and of course an inexhaustible goldmine for lawyers.

Doubtless no Maori chief who signed the Treaty could foresee the shape of constitutional government in the 1990s. Nor can we predict what our constitution will be like in another 160 years. Amid the various versions of the Treaty – in Maori and English, in what was said in speeches and at meetings – it is impossible to reach any sort of conclusion about what Maoris believed or agreed to, and it is pointless to try. But we can say that Maori saw the treaty meetings as, in the words of James Belich, 'significant ceremonies marking some kind of new deal'.[8] It is clear also that, as he further points out, 'British law and the machinery of state often received a surprisingly enthusiastic reception among Maori from 1840 right into the 1860s', and there was also 'Maori enthusiasm for settler neighbours and willingness to sell land for them to settle on'. These were all acts of consent to a European state and society.

It may seem that this discussion is pointless and academic: the fact is that the Crown has sovereignty now, regardless of how it was acquired. Tribes and chieftains, as vital authority-wielding entities, have disappeared. What relevance can these arguments have?

The relevance is that various Treatyists are claiming that the Treaty means that Maori still 'rightfully' have sovereignty now. No matter how generous we are with land and money, they will not be satisfied, because they want power as well.

To some extent, the Treatyists who are claiming sovereignty are a different group from those claiming land and money. Many – not all – of those claiming simple riches would probably be quite happy to live under the sovereignty of the Queen. Many – not all – of those seeking political power are unlikely to benefit a lot from rich settlements. But let us note that, whether or not all Maoris receive cash and land from us, those are not the last things which many of them will be demanding.

It is impossible to define exactly what those people demanding 'Maori sovereignty' actually mean by the term. If one refers to the book *Maori Sovereignty, The Maori Perspective*,[9] one finds an immense jumble of different individual views.

One notes in this book, incidentally, a misguided attitude to European culture held by many of the contributors . They seem to regard it as purely mercenary and acquisitive, and generally without any redeeming characteristics. Several contributors remark that European society in New Zealand 'is only 150 years old' – as if European settlers had no history before they came here – but that Maori society is much older. Ranginui Walker claims that Maori 'are rooted in the land. Pakeha are not. They are refugees from the slums of Britain . . . We have been here for more than a thousand years.' This reveals a surprisingly snobbish and unproletarian tinge to his thinking – a tinge which might almost suggest some belief in the racial inferiority of those 'from the slums'.

One finds also, incidentally, some surprising omissions from the list of contributors. Mike Smith, of One Tree Hill notoriety, appears, but people such as Moana Jackson, Annette Sykes, Titewhai Harawira, Tama Iti and Ken Mair are conspicuously absent.

Moana Jackson's activism and theorising are well known. He maintains that by the Treaty 'Maori allowed for a house of Pakeha culture to be built alongside their house'. It is not enough, therefore, to have 'bicultural' room for Maori in the Pakeha house. The Treaty guarantees both peoples the right to house their cultures adequately, and Maori people therefore need an entirely separate independent house.[10] The Maori race – whatever that is, these days – must be, it seems, entirely independent of Pakeha. In advocating dual sovereignty, Jackson has commented that 'at the very least there are more than twenty different sovereignties in the land area of Europe and they seem to operate without too much bitterness or debate.'[11] Yet how much blood has been shed even this century in European wars? How many men and women, young and old, soldiers and civilians have been killed? Does Mr Jackson actually know of this or does he not care? At other times he has gone beyond this 'separate but equal' view, saying that 'the Treaty says that people are permitted to live in peace in this country under the mentor of Maori rule.'[12] His English is not perfect, but we understand his message.

Tama Iti believes that sovereignty is 'repossession of all Tuhoe lands, total control of Tuhoe resources by Tuhoe and determination of the future of Tuhoe by Tuhoe'.[13] Te Ururoa Flavell, of the group Tino Rangatiratanga, maintains that 'basically, Aotearoa should be in Maori hands'. He adds, 'I don't think anybody [at this hui] is about personal violence but that's not to say it's going to happen or it's not going to happen – all strategies are being looked at to achieve a goal.' The group is also keeping an eye on Maori 'collaborators' who were signing away Maori rights and resources – such as in the Sealords fisheries deal. 'At the end of the day, Aotearoa must return to Maori hands, and they'll be held accountable.'[14]

Niko Tangaroa, after entering Australia on a New Zealand pass-port, tried to insist on returning to this country using a 'Maori passport.' He insists the issue is recognising 'Maoris as a nation'. Eva

Rickard had plans to declare the Raglan Golf Course an independent state, and a Maori lawyer, Mr T. Anaru, claimed this would be 'entirely valid within a constitutional framework . . . consistent with tikanga Maori'. Ken Mair has stated that he does not consider himself a New Zealander, and that any decision of the courts on Moutua Gardens (or, presumably, anything else) is 'an irrelevance'.

Perhaps, however, among these bizarre claims, we can obtain reassurance from the actions of two of the protesters who occupied the Takahue School in Northland. They were demanding tino rangatiratanga, but two of their number obtained Social Welfare grants to replace clothing destroyed when some of the protesters burnt the school down.

Perhaps the editors of *Maori Sovereignty* thought these people had little of interest to say; perhaps the editors thought rather that their views would alarm and alert us in an undesirable manner. Who can say? It is also difficult to say how much of what anyone claiming Maori sovereignty says is big talk and bluff, and how much is myth and misunderstanding. But even among the views expressed by more solid, less bizarrely-thinking Maori leaders, there is much to be concerned about.

Mike Smith claims that the 'Kawana', or governor, was merely a 'chief for the Pakeha'. Maoris 'have the main contract to look after this place and we subcontracted out some functions, some limited authority to the kawanatanga to look after their own people and ensure that they lived peacefully within . . . our society. We have the authority, the predominant or primary say in what happens here . . . Increasingly Maori are saying, ". . . If you [Pakeha] can't live up to your responsibilities, then we are going to have to make you subject to our jurisdiction, in terms of sorting you out."'[15]

Wira Gardiner, former chief executive of the Ministry of Maori Development, Te Puni Kokiri, rejects 'the common criticism that tribalism is divisive and is holding Maori back . . . what we are seeing in Bosnia is a desire by Bosnians to return to ethnic roots. The Bosnians, Croats, Serbs and Muslims were forcibly placed together this century. The breakup of Yugoslavia shows that tribalism is not dead. Of course it is going to cause trouble. But just because it creates problems doesn't mean that it's wrong.' The unspeakable atrocities and bloodshed of Yugoslavia are, it seems, just problems, about which the former head of a New Zealand government department is not unduly concerned. In his chest, it seems, there beats the heart of a warrior and statesman, not afraid to contemplate the breaking of a few eggs in the new tribal Yugoslavia of Aotearoa. We have been warned.

Sandra Lee considers Treaty negotiations as a 'nation to nation' issue, like the negotiations on the GATT treaty. Parliament has no business interfering in the matter.[16]

Maarire Goodall believes that 'many actions taken in the name of the Crown . . . given a false veneer of legality by parliament, have been quite unconstitutional and illegal. In due time the courts will recognise these mistakes . . . Parliament eventually will recognise a mixed sovereignty originating from both Maori and the Crown.' Parliament should not be able to legislate against the Treaty – although he offers no suggestions as to how this principle is to be enforced or applied in practice.[17]

For Hekia Parata, 'there is no Maoridom without the tribes,' and 'sovereignty is about restoring iwi decision-making'.[18] She does agree, though, that things have changed, and tino rangatiratanga 'does not have to be territorial sovereignty; it can be cultural or political sovereignty'. The recognition of change is sensible, although it would be even more sensible to acknowledge that change means that any 'rangatiratanga' is a dead letter. The idea that 'rangatiratanga' can mean all sorts of other things beside what it meant in 1840 is again a guarantee that Treaty claims will never end.

Ranginui Walker talks of 'models' for the realisation of Maori sovereignty. He thinks that government of this country will become 'untenable' unless we have, say, an upper House in parliament with an equal number of tangata whenua and 'tangata tiriti' (treaty people – i.e. non-Maoris). Maoris would have to be able to prevent legislation. Otherwise, they might 'engage in civil disobedience all over the country. [The government] couldn't police it. They couldn't control it. Especially with modern technology – explosives, arson and things like that.'[19] We must clearly ponder Professor Walker's warning very carefully.

Other Maoris in the same book say very sensible things. Ella Henry is not at all keen on imitating Bosnia and Rwanda. Kara Puketapu does not think the old system of chiefly authority is possible today. Sir Peter Tapsell, keen for the advancement of Maoris, regrets the return to tribalism and would like Maoris to be self-disciplined and well educated. He believes that Maoris might have been better off if past governments had taken a more hard-line attitude, saying 'you're only going to have money to do something useful.' John Tamihere, although he believes that Maoris should have no choice but to be put on the Maori electoral roll, and wants the Treaty written into a new constitution, nevertheless urges Maoris 'not to trade on purist mythology from the 1840s . . . Maori cannot turn the clock back.' Tamihere blames the present Maori leadership for allowing the government to turn them into 'hand-out merchants', and for the dependency of large numbers of Maoris on benefits. 'Such problems will not necessarily be solved by going to the Waitangi Tribunal in grievance mode. That settlement money is likely to be wasted like so many tribal resources.' It will do nothing for those without close tribal links. Sovereignty for him, he says, is 'regaining my mana, my dignity and respect for myself so that [poverty and degradation] do not happen'.

The Waitangi Tribunal, it should be noted, sometimes expresses different views on sovereignty from those mentioned before. In its report on the Taranaki claim – the report written without hearing the Crown's side 'on many matters' – it declares that, with respect to Taranaki Maori claims, the main claim, more significant even than that of land deprivation, is that of 'disempowerment' – by which it means the 'denigration and destruction of Maori autonomy or self-government'. It bombastically declares that 'if the drive for autonomy is no longer there then Maori have either ceased to exist as a people or have ceased to be free'.

The Tribunal considers that Maoris 'should be respected as founding peoples . . . and not merely as another cultural minority'. As long as the Tribunal considers that the Treaty requires 'self-government' for Maoris – but not, of course, self-funding – there can be no hope that Tribunal claims will ever end until the country is physically divided into white areas and Maori homelands. I cannot be called a legal twister of words, proving black to be white and white black; I am an amateur by comparison with those who consider apartheid to be objectionable and racist in South Africa, but who find it the highest expression of justice and non-racism here.

There is no agreement among Maoris, then, as to what 'sovereignty' means – quite apart from the claim that the Treaty never granted it. The mere fact that there is no agreement is proof – if proof were needed – that things have changed since 1840. There is a school of thought, also, within Maoridom that tribalism, and generous Treaty handouts, are not the answer. There is no reason why it is racist to agree with that sensible opinion.

But we should note what other voices are saying. We should not be blackmailed by dark mention of war-torn states elsewhere in the world, but we should be conscious that influential elements in Maoridom are attempting this blackmail. We must not give in to it; but we cannot ignore it. We can only deal with it clearly and firmly.

We cannot condemn desires for autonomy and independence out of hand. We all value independence and freedom, for states and for individuals. To love one's people, however one defines them, and to desire their happiness, are admirable attitudes. Various of these Maori spokespeople condemn, as we all should, the continuing sale of our country to overseas interests, and our increasing loss of the ability to influence our own future.

But the remedy in the Maori sovereignty pill is worse than the disease. Much as we might like to, we cannot cut ourselves off from the world. A retreat into the narrow insular inward-looking world of tribalism is no solution, even if one could actually turn tribes back into living entities. Tribalism will not stop foreign control and the inhuman workings of international market forces. The world will still be out there, and one cannot escape into the past. One will only add bitter racial strife to all our other problems, and those two groups who have perhaps the most to gain from standing together – poor young Maori men and poor young white men – will waste their energies fighting each other, instead of standing and working together to struggle against the injustices daily afflicting more and more in our increasingly troubled times.

FIVE

The Law

I cannot think that it was a brilliant day in our legal annals
when . . . the dead hand fell with a resounding slap upon the
living body.

– Sir Frederick Maitland, *Essays*

There is little law about the Treaty. What follows is of course a summary, but not a particularly brutal one. What Treatyists present as law is often nothing but political claim in legal dress. Long courses of study on the subject must, to fill in their time, either go into mind-numbing detail on minor points, or else devote as much time to background, speculation, metaphysics and politics as to law.

The leading case, as we shall see, is the 1987 decision in *New Zealand Maori Council* v. *Attorney-General*. Already, a mythology is developing about it. People who should know better have been heard to make the unintelligent claim that it establishes the Treaty as our supreme law. People who know very little about the matter may believe the same thing, or believe that Maori are now equal partners with the Crown in some or all matters, or make some similar error. The mythology bears little resemblance to what was actually decided. Perhaps a century hence people will look back and say that this case did establish these things, just as people look back to Magna Carta, unaware of what it actually said. But I doubt it.

It is a great pity that the law is involved in these essentially political questions at all. Lawyers, trained to ferocity and disputation, do not help to settle anything. Lawyers do not approach history as historians do. They are not interested in accuracy. They use history only as a quarry from which they can obtain ammunition for their sides. The result, in the seventeenth century, of turning English lawyers loose on the question of constitutional rights, was civil war.

The law is quite simple and easy to understand. Non-lawyers should not feel intimidated.

International law

The Treaty is a nullity in international law. This was so held in *Wi Parata* v. *Bishop of Wellington*,[1] and there is no reason to suppose that that case was not an accurate statement of international law as it was understood and practised last century. The reasoning underlying the judgment is that treaties can be made only between states, and Maoris, not formed into an organised state, lacked the 'political pen' necessary to conclude a valid treaty.

It may be objected that international law shows a certain bias if it regards certain agreements as binding and not others. That may be so. The simple fact is that the world's international law is European in origin, and, developing at the same time as European nation-states, concerned itself with the behaviour of those states. The mere fact that an agreement is void in international law may be irrelevant to the question of whether or not that agreement should be kept. But it is a good reason why people should not say that it is legally valid.

There is a modern revisionist school of thought which argues that the Treaty is valid in international law. Its supporters say that the nineteenth-century view expressed in *Wi Parata* was uncharacteristically narrow. They say that various scholars of international law last century believed such treaties could be valid. They point out that on various occasions treaties such as this were actually made with peoples lacking the 'political pen', and that Captain Hobson (who was also made consul) based his proclamation of sovereignty over the North Island on the Treaty. The Treaty is also said to be consistent with the law and practice concerning aboriginal title.

These are all correct points, although by simple logic they do not all lead automatically to the desired conclusion. All of us, individuals or governments, occasionally make agreements and say things that are politically wise but not legally binding; and if the Treaty is consistent with aboriginal title, that could be taken as an argument that it was intended by the Crown to be no more than a political confirmation of that title. Nevertheless, there are the arguments. No-one can say if they are 'right' or 'wrong'. In the case of such arguments, one simply has to wait a century or two to see which side eventually becomes 'accepted'. In the meantime, the arguments do not yet seem to have acquired great scholarly support.

Even *if* the Treaty were originally valid in international law, yet, even in international law, treaties do not last forever. They are made void by actions inconsistent with them. The Russo-German Pact of 1939, to take an obvious example, was effectively ended simply by Hitler's invasion of Russia. It would be absurd if Russia or Germany were now suddenly to suggest that it was still valid and applicable. It may be a question of fact as to whether a particular event is so inconsistent with a treaty as to nullify it, or is merely a lesser breach. But it is surely arguable that last century's wars between certain North Island tribes and the Crown would, as far as they were concerned, have extinguished any binding aspect of the Treaty. Such wars also diminish any morally binding effect the Treaty might have.

Even *if* the Treaty were originally valid in international law; even if it were made between two sovereign powers; yet the Treaty was one by which one of the parties extinguished itself as a sovereign power. Maori agreed to be no longer independent, but to become subjects of the Crown. Having thus yielded up their old status, they could not later claim against the Crown as if they still enjoyed that status. They simply are – as they have already agreed – subjects. This argument is even stronger, of course, if the Maori parties to the Treaty, i.e. particular tribes, no longer have much actual practical existence and influence today.

In the same way, individuals have no claim in international law against the Crown, even if the Treaty were valid. The Treaty was not with individuals; and even if it were, they are all dead. International law, by and large, does not concern itself with the dealings of individuals but of states.

As mentioned in Chapter 4, some Maori activists deny that the Crown has ever acquired sovereignty in New Zealand, because by the Maori version of the Treaty (they argue) the chiefs retained that sovereignty. There is a rule of international law – the *contra proferentem*[2] rule – which states that in such cases, the interpretation which should be chosen is that which favours the weaker party.

But this appeal to the *contra proferentem* rule and international law is bound to fail. For the rule, not unreasonably, applies only in the case of valid treaties; it would be absurd to use it to interpret something which legally is a nullity – and by international law the Treaty does not exist. International law also clearly recognises the Crown as now possessing sovereignty over New Zealand.

The Treatyist argument that Maori never intended to give up sovereignty suffers from another flaw. The *contra proferentem* rule applies only to genuine and undoubted agreements, where there are nevertheless differences of opinion over some details. But if the Maori and English versions of the Treaty mean two entirely different things – if Maori at the time believed they were retaining sovereignty, and the English believed *they* were obtaining it, then there was simply, on this fundamental matter, no agreement at all. There was no *consensus ad idem*: no meeting of minds. As a simple matter of fact, and regardless of questions of international validity, there simply never was an agreement in the first place. (The Waitangi Tribunal itself is familiar with this principle. In its Taranaki Report, for example, it is quite ready to allege that certain contracts for the purchase of land were 'nullities for lack of common understandings'.)

Even if one were to apply the *contra proferentem* rule, that is no guarantee that one would choose the Maori version of the Treaty. Maori were a majority at the time of signing: it was only in 1859 that New Zealand's European population first outnumbered them; and even then, three-quarters of those Europeans were in Auckland,

Wellington, and the South Island. 'In main Maoridom, 50,000 Maori interacted with 25,000 Pakeha. Here, Maori had the power to impose their definition of consent, or at least to force Pakeha to negotiate with it . . .'[3] Therefore, in 1840, it could well be argued – and is, by many Treatyists – that the Crown, for all that it drafted and translated the Treaty, was the weaker party. It is arguable, at least, therefore, that by the *contra proferentem* rule the Treaty's English version should prevail.

In any case, the Treaty is so vague and general that it cannot simply be incorporated into our law without further ado. It would of necessity need specific laws to put it into effect.

In the absence of the Treaty's legal status in international and New Zealand law, talk of its being our founding constitutional document is so much hot air. It may be politically and racially admirable; in the present political climate one certainly has to gesture in its direction; but it is not part of our constitution, let alone the basic part.

Judicial activism

In the following description of New Zealand law it will become plain that the legal status of the Treaty is far less than some of its supporters would like. It must be explained, however, that even the present legal status is only as much as it is because of the improper political adventuring of certain judges.

Judges are only human, and are, in their own way, as much prey to fashion and popular attitudes as anyone else. This may come as surprising and unpleasant news to laypeople who suppose them to be impervious to mortal weakness; but perhaps we have all seen sufficient judicial frailty and folly – some, indeed, even of a criminal nature – not to be too surprised. Accordingly, then, we find judges being so foolish as to meddle in politics. Shortly before the 1996 general election, indeed, one judge made what was essentially a political speech attacking government policy. Some of us may perhaps have agreed with the judge's words; and judges, like everyone else, inevitably have political views – but, just as justice must be seen to be done, so judges must be seen to be beyond politics. No judge should have said publicly what she said[4] – and indeed, if one could offer nothing better than the collection of worthy tired platitudes she delivered, one would probably not have bothered. Incredibly, the Chief Justice, instead of maintaining a dignified silence, or even reprimanding her, was so unmindful of a judge's proper role as to attempt to defend her.

This interest in politics has been appearing for some time. Whether or not we approved of the proposed 1985 All Black tour of South Africa, the decision to go or not go was a political one, which was better left to the Rugby Football Union, the government and the legitimate lobbying of the anti-apartheid movement. For a judge to decide that the general references to the good of rugby in the RFU's constitution meant that the All Blacks could not go was a clear case of political meddling, and the disrepute into which that decision brought the judiciary was as inevitable as it was deserved.[5]

There have been other political decisions since. We might even agree with the politics of them; but they should not have been made.

Ours, too, is the age of the manager. Management, it seems, is the only skill that matters. No longer, it seems, are there issues where people have different points of view and irreconcilable differences. There are only failures to communicate, and poor management. This idea has infected judges and lawyers. They, too, like to see them-selves as involved in management. There is no longer, in this world-view, any distinct area called 'law' which judges should limit themselves to. All is management – so why should a judge accept the traditional boundaries of his occupation?

Some readers will know that I usually have very little time for the Business Roundtable. Yet I must agree with their condemnation of judicial activism and misunderstanding of the proper judicial role.[6] Roger Kerr describes various decisions of the Court of Appeal, in par-ticular, which reveal it 'in a frolic', or where the Court 'consciously snubbed Parliament's intentions'. In *Treaty Tribes Coalition* v. *Urban Maori Authorities*[7] – the dispute over urban Maoris' share of the fish-eries settlement – the Privy Council accepted a complaint that 'the Court of Appeal did not answer the question posed on appeal. The parties did not know what question the Court in fact posed for it-self. Neither issue was raised, nor discussed, and the parties had not notice of what the Court of Appeal had in mind . . . what the Court did was to pre-empt the function of the Commission on the point.' The Privy Council in the *Goldcorp* case[8] said, of one of the Court of Appeal's favourite devices (often mentioned in Treaty cases) that 'to describe someone as a fiduciary, without more, is meaningless'. The Business Roundtable, it must be added, is not alone in voicing these criticisms: others less devoted to the free market say the same thing, though perhaps more shyly.

Professor Stephen Todd[9] finds the evidence 'compelling' that parliament, when it made the Bill of Rights Act 1990, did not intend to create new legal remedies for courts to grant. *Hansard* – to which courts may now refer, when it suits them – makes this quite clear. Yet the Court of Appeal has not hesitated to set itself above parliament in this matter.

Some years ago, family court judges held meetings with members of the Ministry of Women's Affairs in order to help them 'to understand the effect of their decisions on women's lives'. The meetings were held in private and at the request of the judges. Would we tolerate private meetings between judges and any other government department such as Police, Social Welfare, Inland Revenue? It is a basic axiom of procedure that anything said to a judge should be said in a court, in public, where it can be subject to challenge and cross-examination. But here the court was allowing itself to be lobbied by one particular interest group. Yet if one interest group may lobby judges, why should not all? But if any interest group – men, for example – tried to lobby judges, they would soon be told that they were behaving improperly.

The simple answer is that no interest group should ever lobby judges, in private, or even in public. Judges are not policy-makers or legislators. They should – with humanity and good sense – stick to their accepted role and apply the law as it is.

Judicial independence is a precious and important thing. Like all other freedoms, however, it can exist only while it is exercised with responsibility. Now, Roger Kerr says, 'judicial independence is apparently regarded by some as a licence for judges to remake the law the way they personally see fit . . . Justice Thomas was appointed to the Court of Appeal after writing a lengthy personal manifesto putting forward the view that the doctrine of precedent should be severely diluted and judges given more free rein to decide cases according to "principles" discerned by each judge.'

There already are reassuring signs that the present president, anyway, of the Court of Appeal, has more respect for our supreme law-making body and the will of the people as it expresses itself in national and local elections. But it is a sad day when the composition of the Bench and the personal characteristics of judges become so crucially important. Particular laws may be bad, or sometimes have undesirable consequences. But it is for parliament to change them. If courts defy parliament, if they substantially re-fashion law, then there will be an end to the constitution.

Judges, it seems, are as liable as anyone else to the great modern disease of wanting something for nothing, and power without responsibility. They seem to want the power and thrill of making political decisions while refusing (for high-minded constitutional reasons) to accept the burdens we impose on politicians. We cannot vote judges in or out; it is quite improper even to lobby them. To treat them with a fraction of the vigour we accord to MPs would result in immediate proceedings for contempt of court. They enjoy these privileges because, traditionally, they have not behaved as politicians. Yet some of them are now casting off the proper limits of their powers as they cast off their wigs. And so a Northland judge, faced with the clear facts of native-pigeon poaching can, it seems, act contrary to the wishes of parliament and discharge the accused, saying that he did not consider him a criminal.[10]

This engagement of judges in politics often goes by the name of 'judicial activism'. It would be more accurate to call it judicial politicking. We do not live in the Middle Ages, when a parliament might meet for just several weeks once every few years, and where there might be some excuse for judges to deal with matters which parliaments left untouched. Parliament is always here, and for all its imperfections, which none of us would deny, it is more in touch with the needs and desires of New Zealand life than are judges.

A recent legal conference in New Zealand had as its theme 'the quest for simplicity'. This is also a code for politicisation. We live in a complex society, where legal arrangements are often inevitably complex and intricate. To reduce everything to 'ultimate simplicities' is an excuse for ignoring the law and rewriting it, using a judge's own political opinions.

We have had something of a mood of judge-worship ever since Mr Muldoon's time, when we all feared for the constitution, and thought judges might save it for us. The mood has lasted too long, and judicial activism may itself now threaten the constitution.

The 'separation of powers' cuts both ways. We usually think of it as existing to protect judges from interference by wicked ministers of the crown. But it also exists to keep judges to their proper duties, and their oath of office, to administer justice *according to law*. If judges wish to be politicians, the only honourable option is resignation from the Bench. Courts, designed to hear disputes between two parties, are simply inappropriate places to settle what are essentially political arguments. If the arguments are not best forgotten, then parliament is the best place in which to settle them.

Even the pro-Treaty writer Paul McHugh has written[11] that 'No-one pretends that the language of "partnership" and "fiduciary obligation" was exchanged . . . at Waitangi in 1840. The Courts have stressed their construction of what amounts to a contemporary mythology of the Treaty.' The Ministry for the Environment has observed that statutory references to the 'principles . . . have provided room for the Courts to rewrite and moderate the actual terms . . . Partnership has no little or no intrinsic meaning and so can be made to mean whatever it is wished to mean. It is an empty box to be filled by whoever wields power on the day. The concept cannot be found in the words of the Treaty.'[12]

We may quote here even Sir Geoffrey Palmer's observations that the Treaty document is 'essentially political' and that 'some of the scholarship surrounding [it] is highly suspect, fuelled as it is by political motivation rather than detached analysis'.[13] Prominent among these activist judges is Sir Robin Cooke, the former president of the Court of Appeal. In his many years on the bench Sir Robin constantly emphasised the need for fresh approaches and understandings, appropriate to a young independent country, and has often disapproved of being bound by the traditional approaches of English law. Sir Robin's acceptance of a life peerage in the House of Lords – surely a foreign and outdated institution – was therefore greeted with surprise by many. Sir Robin has expressed his keenness to participate in legislative debates in the House of Lords. His keenness to legislate will surprise no-one here.

Even Sir Geoffrey Palmer has complained that Sir Robin has set himself up as a 'super umpire' above parliament. The court's attitude in the 1987 Maori Council case was, in one writer's words, 'the Court taking upon itself responsibility to supervise government policy at a high level'.[14] So much for the separation of powers, and indeed democracy. Sir Robin has spoken of following the 'middle path'. It is not for judges to follow any path other than the law. If the law leads them to either side of the middle, so be it. The middle path is for politicians.

Over the years, Sir Robin has suggested that it would be impossible for parliament to make laws on some matters (e.g. legalising torture – admittedly a perhaps extreme example, but then, 'torture' could possibly be widened to include, say, corporal punishment) and has often hinted at some unexplained power in the courts to supervise legislation.

This power would arise from the theory that sovereignty lies not in parliament but in 'the constitution, which consists of the framework of principles, such as democracy and respect for human rights, which are fundamental and cannot be denied, even by Act of Parliament.' This summary is that of Lord Irvine of Laing, the British Labour Party's Shadow Lord Chancellor in 1995. But Lord Irvine said[15] that such views are: '(i) contrary to the established laws and constitution of the United Kingdom and have been since 1688, (ii) an expression of "extra-judicial romanticism" in believing that judicial decision could hold back what would, in substance be a revolution (i.e. if Parliament passed legislation assaulting the basic tenets of democracy), and (iii) "smack of judicial supremacism".'

Judges cannot claim some right to review Acts of Parliament on the grounds that they subvert democracy, because the very questioning of parliament is itself a subversion of democracy. We may not like everything that parliament does; but there is no guarantee that a judge can better express the popular will, and it is all too easy for even the finest of us to see the 'true' will of the people in what is no more than our own opinion.

Some judges are politicians. Other judges display an excessive level of tolerance. Judge Hobbs, who tried the Takahue protesters, said that he had 'been spoken to . . . in a manner that any judge would find thoroughly offensive, but had said nothing and done nothing'. His lenient sentences (in fact, most of the sixteen were simply convicted and discharged) were criticised by the local marae trust chairman, who said they sent the wrong message to the protesters and others like them. The judge said that 'there was no question of jail, and no periodic detention centre in the area. The defendants had made their refusal to recognise the court abundantly clear, and [he] doubted they would consent to community service

. . . Imposing fines would probably be pointless.' What sort of message is this sending to those who would go beyond the law?

In another case, involving trespassing at Kaitaia Airport, it has been alleged that the judge was booed and jeered at, a Maori police officer was assaulted, and defendants were able to leave the court at will and made political statements from the gallery.[16] The judge denied that the hearing was ever reduced to a shambles or a spectacle, but did agree that there were 'one or two' instances where less than normal courtesy was offered. The local Bar, incidentally, refused to provide a duty solicitor on the ground that his safety could not be assured.

Judge Bollard, who convicted Mike Smith for attacking One Tree Hill's tree, allowed prayers and waiata by Smith's supporters, and also allowed two and a half hours of submissions about Smith's character and cultural background. At the end of this, Judge Bollard sentenced Smith to six months' periodic detention. The maximum penalties were two years' jail or a $200,000 fine. Maori elders, among them Mr Graham Rankin (a descendant of Hone Heke) were among those who condemned this laxity, and who were sure that if the positions were reversed a non-Maori would not have got off so easily. (Smith replied that Mr Rankin's opinions were 'colonised', and his understanding shallow.)

Even a Maori MP, Mr Dover Samuels, has complained that European judges are scared to come down too hard on Maori fishermen who abuse customary fishing rights, and that they are guilty of 'cultural naivety'. He was speaking after Judge Everitt acquitted a Maori commercial fisherman who took more than a tonne of scallops over his quota on the last day of the scallop season. The fisherman claimed the scallops were not for sale, but for two huis.

It must be added that these strictures do not apply to all judges. Many – most, perhaps – go about their duties in a responsible manner. It is just a pity that not all do.

New Zealand has had, since 1986, a Law Commission. Its functions are to 'review in a systematic way' the law, and 'to make recommendations for the reform and development of the law'. It is given an ideological slant from the beginning, also, for in making its recommendations, it must 'take into account te ao Maori (the Maori dimension) and shall also give consideration to the multi-cultural character of New Zealand Society'.[17] The Commission needs no second bidding. It does not limit itself to mere technical matters. It has a clear political agenda on many matters, and its recommendations would be more appropriate to an elected political body than to a small clique of appointed progressive intellectuals. Shonagh Kenderdine, now a judge of the Environment Court, reports[18] that 'the Law Commission argues for law reform to restore and affirm Maori fishing rights' and that it 'argues that the courts, legislature and executive should see the Treaty as the source of public policy'.[19] Whether or not one approves of these principles, it is simply not appropriate for an unelected body to push this political agenda into law.

It is not unknown, either, for judges to be appointed from law commissioners. One must, with the very greatest of respect, wonder if the attitude of a law reformer – even a non-political one – is appropriate to the office of a judge whose duty it is to declare the law as it is, not as it should be.

Parliaments and politicians, however, must share the blame. As we shall see, judges have engaged in disgraceful political adventures; but they have been able to do so only because ministers have inserted clauses into legislation referring to Treaty principles. Let this be clear: no judge has said that the Treaty is, simply in itself, part of our law. Judges have made it clear that they refer to the principles of the Treaty only if, or when, parliament tells them to. For politicians to suggest that they are simply the humble slaves or prisoners of judicial statements about the Treaty, statements which they have no responsibility for, is quite untrue.

New Zealand law

Even if the Treaty were valid in international law, it has for centuries been an elementary principle of the English legal system that treaties cannot alter the rights of subjects. Treaties do not affect our local law. If a treaty is to have the force of law, then it must be adopted into our law by parliament. This has not been done.[20]

The Treaty is therefore in itself a nullity in New Zealand law. This has been constantly repeated by recent Court of Appeal judgments. If it has any place in the law, that is only because it is referred to here and there by some statute or other, and its legal efficacy is only to the extent that that statute requires. In other words, it is the statute that is the law, not the Treaty. A statute can refer to the Treaty in the same way that it can refer to any other document.

In several cases, certainly, the courts have considered the Treaty in itself, and unconnected with particular statutory references. In *Baldick* v. *Jackson*,[21] concerning the ownership of a harpooned whale, the Chief Justice, Sir Robert Stout, considered that one reason why the royal right to whales known to English law did not apply to New Zealand was the Treaty guarantee of fisheries to Maori. It seems clear, however, that these whales were in fact never caught by Maori. Sir Robert also recognised European rights to whale here. It must be added, also, that it is clear that the ancient royal right to gold and silver has always existed in this country, despite any promises about 'taonga'; so perhaps we cannot say that the Treaty did renounce the royal prerogative. Perhaps the other reasons for Sir Robert Stout's judgment were the real ones.

In *Huakina Development Trust* v. *Waikato Valley Authority*,[22] Mr Justice Chilwell held that the very general words of a statute allowing public objections were wide enough to cover Maori spiritual and cultural values. Those values were not to be conclusive, of course, but could be considered along with all others. His Honour said that the Treaty, although not part of our law, was part of the social background and situation in which law is made, and was 'part of the context in which legislation is to be interpreted'.

Various statutes do refer to the Treaty. One is the Treaty of Waitangi Act 1975. Despite its perhaps slightly misleading name, that Act only established the Waitangi Tribunal, and gave it the power (now slightly altered) to make recommendations only. The Tribunal will be described more fully later.

Various other statutes refer to the Treaty. Several of them concern the environment in one way or another, and they are dealt with in Chapter 6. The general approach of all these statutes is to require that, in the administration of an Act, some degree or other of respect has to be paid to the principles of the Treaty.

Note: 'the *principles* of the Treaty'. These are quite different from the *terms*. The terms of the Treaty are simple. By the first Article, the chiefs ceded sovereignty to the Crown. By the second, the Crown confirmed the chiefs and tribes in their possessions. The chiefs also, by the second Article, yielded to the Crown the exclusive right of purchase of whatever lands they wished to sell. While some declare the Treaty unalterable for ever, this particular provision disappeared long ago, and no-one seems to have disputed the validity of its disappearance. By the third Article the Maori received all the rights and privileges of British subjects. The terms of the Maori version state something similar – the main disputed differences are discussed in Chapter 4.

The terms are clear. They are so short and simple as to be of practically no relevance at all, in a state where the Crown has sovereignty, the property of all is guaranteed, and people of all ancestries enjoy the rights of free-born subjects of the Crown. For any statute – or any future written constitution – to refer merely to the Treaty or its terms would mean very little.

Statutes, however, do not refer to the terms of the Treaty. The few statutes that do refer to the Treaty speak instead of the rather more elusive and mysterious 'principles', whose implications no-one can hope to understand without the help of highly paid lawyers.

The leading case on the principles of the Treaty is *New Zealand Maori Council* v. *Attorney-General*.[23] It arose out of the breaking up of the old Department of Lands and Survey, Forest Service and other government departments, and the division of the lands they had administered among the new Department of Conservation and a number of state-owned enterprises. The State-Owned Enterprises Act 1986 established these enterprises. Their principle objective was to operate as successful businesses. Crown assets, including land, could be transferred to them by the Crown. Section 27 provided that if land was transferred which was already subject to a Treaty claim, then when the Act came into force the enterprise could not transfer the land to another; and, pursuant to a Waitangi Tribunal recommendation, the Crown could later recover the land. But nowhere in Section 27 or anywhere else in the Act was there any provision dealing with claims lodged *after* the Act came into force.

It was only when the Bill was proceeding through parliament that the Labour government had inserted into it a new clause, which eventually became section 9. This section said: 'Nothing in this Act shall permit the Crown to act in a manner that is inconsistent with the principles of the Treaty.'

There can be little doubt that this clause was actually intended to be little more than a pious and reasonably meaningless piece of lip-service. When the Maori Council brought its case, relying on section 9, there was actually great consternation and surprise among the wise legislators and constitutional experts in the Beehive, and emergency meetings of ministers were held to consider it. The Solicitor-General also argued before the Court that if this section applied to all land transfers to state-owned enterprises, that would frustrate the Act's purpose: the enterprises would be able to operate only 'in a withered and crippled way', and that could not have been Parliament's intention. Sections 9 and 27 had both been inserted following the Waitangi Tribunal's suggestion, but it is clear that parliament thought section 27 was enough in itself, and section 9 little more than window-dressing. Sir Robin Cooke accepted in his judgment that Parliament 'thought the Act would have the effect now contended for by the Crown'.

Section 9 became law, along with the rest of the Act. The Crown then prepared to transfer large amounts of Crown assets to these enterprises. The Maori Council then sought a judicial review of the proposed transfers, claiming that many of these lands, although not subject to a claim in 1987, might be the subject of claims in future. In addition, it said that even if land proposed for transfer in 1987 never became the subject of a claim in future, yet its alienation from the Crown would reduce the 'land-bank' which the Crown could use in settling claims, in substitution for land successfully claimed but now unavailable. It claimed, therefore, that these land transfers would breach section 9 .

The Solicitor-General argued, as seen above, that parliament must have intended that these transfers should take place, because otherwise the Act's, and parliament's, purpose would be frustrated. Land was not the only Crown asset to be transferred, but it was certainly the main one. He argued also that section 27 (dealing with claims already lodged) was a complete and self-contained code covering claims, and that it implied that the more general words in section 9 did not apply to land claims, where there was this more specific provision.

Nevertheless, the Court of Appeal held that section 9 did apply to transfers of land, and made a declaration that land transfers would be unlawful unless some system was established to consider compliance with Treaty principles. The transfer of Crown land was one of the Act's 'central subjects', although there was certainly 'a range of assets other than Crown land'.

This decision by the Court was not inevitable. If the Court had decided in the Crown's favour, then no lawyer could have called that decision wrong. Cautious, perhaps; conservative, unimaginative, or perhaps sensible; but not wrong. Nor can one actually say that the decision the court came to was wrong. Either decision was a valid interpretation of the statute. It is in cases such as this that judges have choices, and make law as they interpret it.

One can however fairly describe the Court's decision as 'adventurous' and 'political'. Even in 1987, the Treaty was a contentious topic. Our wise legal tradition says that judges should not meddle in politics. Any sensible court would have chosen the cautious path, and made it plain that any radical moves were for legislators, not judges. The Court's decision that the Maori Council should win was a political decision, not required by the statute.

What were the principles? The entire judgment runs to 79 pages in the *New Zealand Law Reports*, and much of that concerns them. A very brief summary is given below. With his usual generosity, Sir Robin observed that the Act's interpretation 'should not be approached with the austerity of tabulated legalism. A broad, unquibbling and practical interpretation is demanded . . .' After later describing the terms of the Treaty, he said that 'the Treaty has to be seen as an embryo rather than a fully developed and integrated set of ideas.'

The choice of the word 'embryo' is significant, for this approach – that in 1840 the Treaty was just a seed full of potential – allows the Court to develop it into whatever social and political views it pleases. Certainly it was Parliament that, by enacting section 9, obliged the judges to consider the question of principles. But the Court was not obliged to be so expansive in its development of the 'embryo'.

You will forgive me if I do not painstakingly list which judge said exactly what. The Treaty was a 'solemn compact'. The Crown obtained sovereignty by it in return for promising protection to Maoris. Its principles require its parties to act towards each other reasonably and with the utmost good faith. It is a partnership between races. The Crown would behave honourably. A duly elected government must be free to follow its chosen policy, and to make laws for the whole community. The Crown has a duty to active protection of Maoris in the use of the their lands and waters to the fullest extent possible. The Crown should grant redress where the Tribunal recommends it. Maoris have a duty of loyalty to the Queen, full acceptance of her government, and reasonable co-operation. There may be a duty on the Crown to consult Maoris.

Few of us would find fault with most of the items on the list. That is part of the trouble: the list is so vague that it means everything and nothing. It could be used to justify any conclusion anyone wanted to come to. From the list, the Court in this case chose those items which led to declaring that the Crown's actions were unlawful. It could just as easily have chosen other parts dealing with the Crown's right to sovereignty and to govern, and decided the other way. A list of platitudes is not a helpful guide to anyone. No-one will ever know, in any particular case, what Treaty principles require until a matter has, at great expense, been submitted to a judge, who will be justified by the list above in making almost any decision he pleases.

It is plain, too, that the 'embryo' has not yet fully developed. There is an old legal maxim that the end of litigation is in the interest of the state and the community. Decisions such as this one are invitations to litigation.

The Court of Appeal's *Tainui* decision[24] declares that 'the principles of the Treaty have to be applied to give fair results in today's world'. Grab hold of the Treaty, then, and any judge is entitled to re-write law as he or she pleases for 'today's world'. In the *Muriwhenua* case[25] Sir Robin declares that 'the position resulting from 150 years of history cannot be done away with overnight. The Treaty obligations are ongoing. They will evolve from generation to generation as conditions change.' Sir Robin and his followers clearly do not believe, or even hope, that Treaty claims will all disappear by the year 2000. The task of interpreting Treaty obligations 'from generation to generation' will preoccupy courts and academics for many years, as they continue to be generous with the property of second-class citizens. The principles of the Treaty are, essentially, nothing more than what judges today – or tomorrow – would like the Treaty to say.

The general attitude of the common law for centuries has been that each generation should be the master of its own law. The 'rule against perpetuities' and the various methods of ending the dreaded fee tail[26] were intended to make it impossible for those long-dead to rule their former lands from the grave. Sir Frederick Maitland condemned a court's application of the law's dead hand to the living body of an entirely new situation. But recent Treaty decisions evidently herald a change of policy.

The Court spoke of the Crown's duty to behave honourably to Maori, to behave reasonably and in good faith, and to protect them and their possessions. This is surely the duty of the Crown towards *all* its subjects. By saying that the Treaty imposes this duty on Maori, the court implies some sort of 'special relationship' between Maori and the Crown – and implies also that non-Maori subjects are not entitled to the same degree of fair dealing by the Crown. (Sir Geoffrey Palmer has said the same thing, claiming that 'Maori people have a special constitutional status'.) Yet all these propositions are intolerable. A special relationship between the Crown and one class of citizens makes all other citizens second class. So much for equality. So much, for that matter, for the Treaty's promise in Article III that Maori were thereafter British subjects like everyone else.

Sir Geoffrey has also written with approval[27] that Judge Durie (of the Maori Land Court and the Waitangi Tribunal) has summed up best the essence of the Treaty – 'the gift of the right to make laws and the promise to do so so as to accord the Maori interest *an appropriate priority*'. Sir Geoffrey has also applauded the contribution of the Tribunal to the 'Maori constitutional revolution', whatever that means.

We must say some things, however, in the judgment's favour. It still made it plain that the Treaty was in itself a nullity. The court could apply it as part of the law only because, and to the extent that, a statute authorised it.

Although the 'principles' of the Treaty are vague and capable of being abused, they could have been worse. The Waitangi Tribunal has its own list, which of course has no legal status. The Maori Council, too, proposed its own list to the court in this case. That list included the principles that Crown and Maori would be of equal status, and that the Crown had a duty to return land for land.

Moreover, the decision has often been misquoted by people with their own axes to grind. In particular, the myth is constantly repeated that this judgment declared that Crown and Maori are 'partners'. This is simply not the case. Bruce Mason, in his analysis of the decision,[28] has pointed out that the word 'partners' is used more or less interchangeably with the word 'parties'. Various judges spoke of a relationship, not of partnership, but 'akin to' partnership.

Sir Robin Cooke in a later article[29] spoke of 'the *analogy* of partnership'; and both there and in the *Tainui* case[30] he reminds us that even in real partnerships, partners can be unequal – some senior, some junior, some more powerful than others – and that the concept of partnership does not mean 'that every asset or resource in which Maori have some justifiable claim should be divided equally'. But this message has not yet got through. Perhaps it may never.

Regrettably, the Ngai Tahu Claims Settlement Bill before parliament at the time of writing refers to Ngai Tahu at least once as the Crown's 'Treaty partner'.[31] But then, what does parliament know? The legislators also believe the 1944 Settlement Act was enacted 'without prior consultation'. The preamble of The Maori Land Act 1993 also refers to the 'Treaty partners'. These references are unjustified even by the Court of Appeal's decision. Parliament is making a rod for our backs.

Any idea of a partnership between the Crown and Maoris puts non-Maori New Zealanders into an inferior position. Even if the Treaty were a 'partnership between races', as Sir Robin Cooke says at one point, there can be no equality between citizens. If a larger and smaller group are equal, obviously the rights of each member of the smaller group are greater than those of members of the larger.

'Partnership' is in any case a meaningless term. It can be used to justify anything. Bruce Mason, quoting Alex Frame,[32] suggests that if any term is to be used that has meaning and practicality, the idea of 'co-operation' makes more sense. Most people know what it is, and can recognise its presence or absence without too much trouble.

As for the remedy in the 1987 case, the Court allowed the Crown time to negotiate with Maoris to reach some mutually acceptable solution. The solution eventually agreed to, with much amendment of statutes, was essentially this: that these lands could be transferred to the state-owned enterprises, but they would always be liable to be taken back. A memorial on the Certificate of Title would give notice of this possibility. If the Waitangi Tribunal were later to so recommend, then the District Land Registrar would be obliged to transfer the land to the person named in the recommendation. This is the one situation where the Tribunal can, in effect, make a binding order, and require private property to be given to Maoris. As mentioned below, the very existence of this threat might well have significantly influenced governments already.

The Court of Appeal is not the only body to have proposed a list of Treaty principles. As we have seen, the Maori Council proposed its own list to the court, and commentators have extracted a list from decisions of the Waitangi Tribunal. The 1988 Royal Commission on Social Policy found three fundamentals – partnership, equality of peoples and protection of Maori interests. The Justice Department has proposed five 'Principles for Crown Action of the Treaty':

1. Government: The Government has the right to govern and make laws.
2. Self-management: Iwi have the right to organise as iwi, and under the law, to control their resources as their own.
3. Equality: All New Zealanders are equal before the law.
4. Reasonable co-operation: The government and iwi are obliged to accord each other reasonable co-operation on major issues of common concern.
5. Redress: The government is responsible for providing effective processes for the resolution of grievances in the expectation that reconciliation can occur.

None of these other lists, however, has the legal standing which the Court's list has. The courts have said, however, that the Tribunal's views, in particular, may be of assistance in deciding what the principles actually are.

In two cases concerning Maori broadcasting[33] the Court of Appeal – in particular, Sir Robin – has been inclined to hint that the Treaty might have some status in itself as common law. Sir Robin, alone among the judges, opined that 'at the present day the Crown, as a Treaty partner, could not act in conformity with the Treaty or its principles without taking into account any relevant recommendations by the Tribunal'. Even though the Radiocommunications Act 1989 made no mention of the Treaty, three of the five judges (the present president of the Court of Appeal and the present Governor-General dissenting) thought that for the Crown to proceed with its proposed sales without awaiting a further report from the Tribunal would be a failure to take relevant considerations into account.

In the second of these cases, Sir Robin did suggest in passing that 'Treaty principles of partnership and taonga, past neglect . . . and international obligations can be argued to [require] the Crown to [protect Maori language and culture] by broadcasting.' But no-one explicitly agreed with him.

The Privy Council, however, when considering the question on appeal,[34] based its decision firmly on the obligations of statute – the State-Owned Enterprises Act. The possibility that there might be a status for the Treaty independent of statute was not mentioned as even a remote possibility. The Privy Council also thought that any obligation of the Crown was not absolute and unqualified, as 'that would be inconsistent with the Crown's other responsibilities'.

In the 1987 case there was no 'duty' of the Crown to consult Maori. Sir Robin Cooke thought it was 'unworkable' to lay down a duty in an unqualified sense. Other judges agreed that good faith does not necessarily require consultation. By 1989, however,[35] Sir Robin believed that it is 'really clear beyond argument' that there is a duty to consult on 'truly major issues'.

In *Te Runanga o te Ika Whenua Inc. Society* v. *Attorney-General*[36] the Court of Appeal did mercifully hold that 'however liberally Maori customary title and treaty rights might be construed, they were never intended as including the right to generate electricity by harnessing water power'. Sir Robin Cooke did not miss the opportunity to add some unnecessary passing remarks. He opined that an extinguishment of aboriginal title by less than fair dealing would likely be a breach of the fiduciary duty 'widely and increasingly recognised as falling on the colonising power'. All the New Zealand cases he offers as authority are his own. Sir Robin evidently hopes that if he repeats something often enough it will become law.

Mason-Riseborough v. *Matamata-Piako District Council*[37] was a decision of the Environment Court. It refers to the *Whale-Watching* case as an authority – Sir Robin Cooke's remarks in that case about how it should not be a precedent are ignored. It admires Sir Robin's view of the Treaty that 'what matters is the spirit' and maintains the Treaty is 'a living and continuing document which calls to be interpreted and applied not simply as at 1840 but in a contemporary setting'. Such waffle would justify a judge in doing absolutely anything.

There has been a change in Treatyist attitudes of recent years. Once their cry was for 'justice'; law was irrelevant. The white man's law was a tool used to separate Maoris from their land. Now there has been something of a change in their thinking. Treatyists have become pragmatists and positivists; now they want their 'legal' rights; and law, all of a sudden, is not so bad. Leaving aside the fact that the law may still not be all they hope for, this appeal to the law is dangerous and hypocritical, for Treatyists are the first to complain about the law when it is against them, and – as they themselves have said so often – the law proves nothing about justice.

The Nurses Act contains no reference to the Treaty or cultural safety. Treatyist activists have found in the Nurses Regulations some very general and innocuous words about 'the administration of safe and competent nursing care', and have forced their absurd interpretation, that this refers to 'cultural safety', onto feeble educators without any legal justification.

It may well be unwise even to tie ourselves down with a detailed written constitution, for it would transform many essentially political questions into legal ones, and hand much power over to unelected and unaccountable judges. But how much more unwise it is to be tied down by a document as vague as this, and surrounded by myth, propaganda and controversy. We must resist the determined effort being made by a small group of activists to foist the Treaty onto us as law. As Guy Chapman has written,[38] 'It is not often in political life that such a determined conventicle is seen at work. In the universities there have been mass conversions, and it would be a brave court that would do other than genuflect.'

Clarity and certainty must always be the foundations of law. 'Treaty jurisprudence' offers us neither. The Treaty was a modest little document, with a limited and political purpose. It was not drawn up by lawyers. It promised no-one any fundamental rights. It is not a constitution or an environmental charter. If we want these things, we should make them ourselves, not try to find them in the Treaty. Attempts to make the Treaty law will divide the country racially, will obscure and muddy the law, and take power from the people to give to the judges.

The Waitangi Tribunal

The Waitangi Tribunal was established by the Treaty of Waitangi Act 1975. Originally it had the jurisdiction only to consider laws, policies and acts of the Crown which were made, agreed on or done after 1975, and which were 'inconsistent with the principles of the Treaty'. At this time many of its decisions did not concern loss of land, and some did the public a great service in their concerns over environmental degradation. Of the eight major reports issued by 1989, only two were concerned with land, one with the Maori language, one with sea fisheries; and four with broad environmental questions, mostly pollution and the contamination of the sea where food was gathered.

In 1985, however, the Tribunal's jurisdiction was changed by a caring government. It was given the power to consider any alleged wrong or inconsistency with Treaty principles since 1840. Obviously, since then the Tribunal has spent a lot of time examining historical injustices. But it has jurisdiction to examine *any* law or act or policy of the Crown, which at any time since 1840, up until the present, is 'inconsistent with Treaty principles'.

The Tribunal has, with one exception, never had the power to do more than make recommendations, and even then only if it finds that a claim is well-founded – that is to say, if there has been a breach of 'Treaty principles'. The one exception, where it can make a binding recommendation – an order, in other words – concerns state-owned enterprise land transferred to the enterprise by the Crown.

This power of the Tribunal to order state-owned enterprise land to be given to Maori claimants has just been exercised for the first time, and it may have been of great importance for a long time. It has always existed as a threat. In at least one case the Tribunal has threatened publicly to exercise it; we do not know in how many other cases the threat has been made privately or hinted at. It may be that the absurd generosity of some recent settlements has been prompted by the fear that otherwise the Tribunal's power will be exercised. Even the present Minister of Treaty Settlements has evidently contemplated repealing this part of the law. One cannot help but think that the Labour government which enacted it – after first mindlessly throwing section 9 into the State-Owned Enterprises Act – was among the biggest afflictions this country has ever had to bear. The transformation of Sir Geoffrey Palmer to wise old constitutional expert must remain forever a mystery.

Winston Peters has warned that a mandatory order returning state assets for the settlement would be 'disastrous' and, if spread over other settlements, 'could bankrupt the country'.[39] Even the easy-going Doug Graham has warned about the harm such a mandatory order would create, because it would boost other settlements, in proportion, to many more hundreds of millions of dollars.

Sir Robin Cooke suggested in the 1987 *Maori Council* case that if the Crown did not act and follow the Tribunal's recommendations, that would of itself be another breach of the Treaty. To suggest that is, of course, to suggest that in fact the Tribunal's recommendations *do* of themselves have *some* binding force, which is, of course, not the case. Sir Robin Cook is, not for the first or last time, attempting to rewrite a statute. In any case, he seems to have regretted this generous statement later, for in the *Muriwhenua* case,[40] he was very careful to say that the Tribunal's recommendations 'are not binding on the Crown of their own force. They may have the effect of contributing to the working out of the content of customary or Treaty rights, but if and when such rights are recognised by the law it is not because of the principles relating to the finality of litigation'. In other words, the Tribunal does not actually have any power finally to decide anything or make binding judgments.

The Tribunal has, then, never had any power to make orders over private land (other than that which might, since 1987, have been purchased from a state-owned enterprise). But that is not to say that its recommendations could not affect private land. The moment the Tribunal made some recommendation, or even observation, concerning private land, the owner of that land, and any potential buyers, were entitled to expect trouble ahead. Land occupations were possible. At the very least the land would drop a great deal in value. It was too glib for politicians to say – as many did – simply that the Tribunal could do nothing to affect private land.

It was for this reason that a 1993 amendment to the Act inserted a new section, section 6(4A), which says that, subject to the state-owned enterprise exception, 'the Tribunal shall not recommend . . . the return to Maori ownership of any private land or the acquisition by the Crown of any private land'.

This is very well as far as it goes. But it does not, of course, stop the Tribunal from finding that (in its opinion) the land was originally, long ago taken unjustly; and that may be enough to prompt the threats of trouble and a drop in land value which are the subject of concern.

The membership of the Tribunal has been increased on several occasions. The chairperson is the Chief Judge of the Maori Land Court. There may be up to sixteen other members, to be appointed by the Governor-General 'on the recommendation of the Minister of

Maori Affairs after consultation with the Minister of Justice'. In considering the suitability of persons for appointment, the Minister must have regard not only to ability and so on, but also 'must have regard to the partnership between the two parties under the Treaty'. No more than seven Tribunal members act to hear any claim. There can, therefore, be two 'divisions' of the Tribunal sitting at one.

It is unclear who has the right to appear before the Tribunal. Clause 7 of the Second Schedule seems to imply that only claimants, and the Crown, may. The Tribunal – which may 'regulate its procedure as it sees fit' – has adopted the practice, at least on occasions, of allowing groups representing significant matters of national interest – conservation societies or farmers' representatives, for example – to appear before it, but this seems to be entirely discretionary. Occasionally, private landowners have had their legal expenses paid by the Tribunal, although usually, it seems, expenses are not covered.

The Tribunal may, essentially, receive what evidence it pleases. It may act on 'any testimony, sworn or unsworn, and . . . any statement document information or matter which, in [its] opinion . . . may assist it . . .' whether it would otherwise be legally admissible as evidence or not. Anecdotal evidence and hearsay are acceptable. So is secret evidence. The Crown, moreover, in the Ngai Tahu claim, considered that cross-examination was 'for the purpose of elucidating factual matters rather than the testing of evidence'. This is also the Tribunal's own attitude. How then can oral evidence be tested? How can one sift truth from a mishmash of gossip and hearsay? How can one be sure that some researcher or consultant in any particular case was not in error, or had not been swayed, in his evidence, by his own attitudes or expectations?

There is something magical about the Maori race. Not all members of the Tribunal need to be Maori; but if, at a sitting of the Tribunal, some members of the panel are not present, the hearing can still go on, as long as the chairman and at least two others are present, *and* 'one of the members present is Maori'.

There is no appeal from the Tribunal. There are appeals against decisions of the courts, for it is accepted that judges are only human, that they can err, and that the freedom and property of the subject are so important that decisions affecting them should, if necessary, be tested by an appellate body. Since the Tribunal's recommendations can have such momentous consequences and its evidence-gathering procedures are so dubious, the argument for a right of appeal from its decisions is so much stronger. But none exists.

Sir Geoffrey Palmer has claimed recently that the setting up of the Waitangi Tribunal has been an enduring contribution to the constitutional position of the Maori people. He thinks, evidently – in his kindly paternalistic way – that there *is* a 'Maori people', that they all wish to remain separate, and that it is a good thing that they have a 'constitutional position'.

As one might expect from a body whose members are appointed 'having regard to the principle of partnership', the emptying of Parihaka (not a glorious incident, but one that caused no-one's death[41]) was described in the Tribunal's Taranaki Report as 'one of the most heinous [acts] of any government in any country in the last century'. Yet how does this compare with the Russian pogroms, the Peterloo massacre, and the Highland Clearances (which were still continuing well into last century)? And what of the Turkish massacres in Greece, and the Great Famine in Ireland, where one or two million people died? Do any of the Tribunal members know the first thing about history? As mentioned in Chapter 3, the Tribunal has also spoken of Taranaki history as an 'ongoing holocaust', evidently to be compared with Nazi Germany.[42]

Even a member of the Office of Treaty Settlements, in speaking to a conservation group, stated that those Maori who make claims to the Waitangi Tribunal, rather than deal directly with the Crown, do so because they believe they will get a better deal; they see the Tribunal as more susceptible to suggestion.

Several years ago a senior Waitangi Tribunal staff member spoke publicly in favour of claimants in a case where the Tribunal refused to have an open hearing process. Chapter 6 describes the Tribunal's consideration of the claim for Codfish and the Crown Titi Islands, where the Tribunal recommended Crown action even though there had been no breach of Treaty principles.

The Waitangi Tribunal is not equipped – or, indeed, authorised – to answer complicated and delicate questions of justice. The Tribunal – in dealing with the case of some *past* alleged injustice – merely considers that historical question. If a wrongdoing was actually committed, that certainly raises a claim for *some* redress of *some* sort. But the nature and extent of the redress is another question. The

Tribunal does not consider the interests of non-Maori New Zealanders – or indeed of Maori New Zealanders of other tribes. It does not consider the various arguments raised in this book about, for example, the diminution of blood, and whether claimants now have, as a simple matter of fact, ever been disadvantaged. It does not consider the benefits of European colonisation, or the claims of the non-human world. It does not, in short, consider a great deal.

Brief mention must be made of two other matters: aboriginal title, and fisheries.

Aboriginal title

The word 'aboriginal' here has nothing to do with the Australian aborigines, although the word is the same. The principle of aboriginal title (or 'customary title') is a common law principle, derived ultimately from Spanish writers on Spain's rights to the Americas. It means that even after British sovereignty was acquired in New Zealand, and the Crown became feudal lord of this country, the Maori inhabitants' right to use and occupy their lands and water continued until extinguished, in one way or another, by the colonial power. Obviously, a purchase of land could extinguish it, as could a statute of confiscation. Very recently one or two commentators have suggested that to be valid, an extinguishment of title must be fair – and so a statute on confiscation would not do. But this seems to be nothing more than a new political theory rather than law, and it is not for the courts to question acts of parliament.

The principle of aboriginal title is quite independent of the Treaty, although the Treaty is often said to be consistent with it. It is a rule of common law, recognised in the same case of *Wi Parata* v. *Bishop of Wellington* that Treatyists profess to despise, and in many other cases since. It was recognised, obviously, by the Crown in making purchases of lands after 1840, which purchases would have the effect of extinguishing that title. On occasions, Treatyists admit that such sales by Maori are valid endings of the 'te tino rangatiratanga' promised under the Treaty, although this is not a conclusion they like to reach.

Recent decisions of the High Court of Australia – the *Mabo* and *Wik* cases, the subject of such controversy – held that the rule applies in Australia also. Before *Mabo*, the view had always been that this had not been the case, and that Australia, upon European discovery, was *terra nullius* – no-one's land. The *Wik* case held that when a pastoral lease (similar in some ways to high-country pastoral leases in this country) existed, aboriginal title could still exist, although in the case of a conflict the lease prevailed.

For most of this century, statutes have forbidden the bringing of any action against the Crown to uphold or enforce Maori customary title to land. This means, in effect, that a class of the Queen's subjects has been debarred from bringing actions in the royal courts of justice to protect their private property rights – an unfortunate state of affairs. Since, however, aboriginal title cannot prevail against a statute, and since any remaining Crown land in the country is governed by statute, it is unclear if this prohibition prevents many valid claims from coming to court.

This prohibition was continued by section 406B of Te Ture Whenua Act 1993 – the Maori Land Act – which says that the general rules about the limitation of actions apply to Maori customary land. (In other words, the time period for bringing those actions expired a long time ago.) However, Paul McHugh has made an interesting and worrying suggestion,[43] when he points out that the same statute now gives the Maori Land Court a *general* jurisdiction to determine whether *any* specified land is held by any person in a fiduciary capacity (i.e. to Maori), and, where it is, to *make an appropriate vesting order*. Although the Waitangi Tribunal may no longer make recommendations concerning private land, yet, he also says, actions concerning non-territorial aboriginal title (discussed below) may continue to lie over land owned by the Crown, state-owned enterprises or even private individuals. Mr McHugh points out that the preamble to this Act speaks of the 'special relationship' between Maori and the Crown, and the principles of the preamble are, by section 2, to apply in the Act's interpretation.

The Maori Land Court has recently held that a legal road – unformed, certainly, but that is legally irrelevant – which runs between blocks of Maori land can be held by the local district council 'in a fiduciary capacity'. The court therefore ordered the land to be vested in the Maori plaintiffs.[44]

The High Court has evidently rejected this particular claim on appeal, but has confirmed the principle that the Maori Land Court can order local authorities to give land to Maori. The Department of Conservation, rather than support the struggle for public access, chose to side with the adjoining Maori landowners and discourage public access. Claims evidently include ones over foreshore and seabed, roads and forest lands, if this 'fiduciary relationship' exists. A Maori Land Court judge in 1997 considered that Maori title to the seabed could still exist.

As well as this aboriginal title to land, there is another form of such title – the 'non-territorial aboriginal title'. This does not refer to ownership of the land itself, but rather is a claim that Maoris still have rights to enter that land for certain purposes, such as the gathering of food. This form of title can also be extinguished by any sale to the Crown which, either expressly or impliedly, included forests, plants, animals and fisheries.

It can also, of course, be extinguished by a statute which, for example, protects certain land or certain species of plants and animal on that land.

In *Te Weehi* v. *Regional Fisheries Officer*,[45] Te Weehi claimed to be exercising a traditional Maori fishing right, the existence of which was preserved by Section 88(2) of the Fisheries Act 1983. Mr Justice Williamson recognised this right as being not only guaranteed by statute but also based on non-territorial aboriginal title.

Te Weehi's case, and the opinion of the Waitangi Tribunal in the *Muriwhenua Report* that traditional fisheries guaranteed under the Treaty had a commercial aspect to them, were the underlying reasons for the fisheries settlement – the 'Sealord Settlement' – embodied in the Treaty of Waitangi (Fisheries Claims) Settlement Act 1992.

Fisheries

The general provisions of the settlement are well known. The Crown paid $150 million towards the acquisition by the new Treaty of Waitangi Fisheries Commission of a 50 percent interest in Sealord Products Ltd., a major fishing company, and promised 20 percent of any new fishing quota to the Treaty of Waitangi Fisheries Commission. The Commission would be 'empowered to allocate' its assets and income. This allocation has, of course, been the source of much disagreement between coastal and inland tribes, and between tribes and non-tribal urban Maoris.

The Sealord deal was signed in 1992. Since then, there has been immense argument as to how the assets and benefits of that deal should be distributed. Maoris from coastal tribes have argued that they should receive most if not all of the benefits. After all, they say, the fisheries in ancient times belonged to them, not to inland tribes; and, with perfect reasonableness, they point out that when other tribes receive some benefit – cash, for example, or land – they keep it for themselves, and do not share it with all Maoridom, so why should coastal tribes be obliged to share their fishing benefits? Fisheries benefits, the coastal tribes say, should not be distributed *per capita* among all those of Maori descent, but to those tribes, and *only* those tribes, who held coastline, and then in proportion to the amount of coastline they once controlled, not in proportion to their present populations.

Urban Maoris maintain that any settlements with tribes do little or nothing to alleviate the lot of those Maoris most urgently and genuinely in need. They say that plans to distribute on a tribal basis do not meet the Deed of Settlement, by which all Maoris were to benefit from the assets. Auckland urban Maoris have claimed that the 80 percent of Maoris who live in urban centres would be deprived of their rights. To this, tribal Maoris reply that many of these urban Maoris can discover their ancestry and rely on it, if they want to (this may or may not be so – and in any case is hardly any help if the ancestors are not of a coastal tribe.) Tribal Maoris ask why other assets, given to other tribes, are not also claimed by urban Maoris as the property of all. Sir Tipene O'Regan has described urban claims that all Maoris should participate in Sealord benefits as 'suntanned welfarism'.[46] The matter continues to be fought out in the courts. The Court of Appeal has said that urban Maoris should be included in any settlement, but Charles Crofts, of Ngai Tahu, described this as setting 'a dangerous precedent in social engineering', and applauded the Privy Council's overturning of the decision. The matter has gone back to the High Court, which, just as this book was going to print, has evidently decided that distribution must be on some sort of tribal basis.

We need not decide the rights and wrongs of the issue here and now. Let us observe that it will be interesting if some Maoris, who believe themselves to have been wronged by Europeans, will soon also believe that they have suffered a similar wrongdoing from their own race.

In return for the Crown's payments and promises, all current and future Maori claims in respect of commercial fishing, however arising, whether in respect of sea, coastal or inland fisheries, are 'hereby finally settled', and no inquiry can be made into them, by the Waitangi Tribunal, the Courts or anyone else. Much of the objection by some Maori radicals to the settlement is to this provision; it is alleged that Maori negotiators short-changed their people.

The agreement and statute covered only commercial fishing. The settlement recognised that pre-existing Maori claims to non-commercial fishing continue, and to that end regulations are to be made 'recognising and providing for customary food-gathering . . . to the extent that such food gathering is neither commercial . . . nor for pecuniary gain or trade'. These areas are the 'mahinga mataitai' areas, where Maori alone will have rights to gather food, and others will have access by invitation only. At the time of writing, the first regulations are scheduled to appear in late 1998.

Completely separate from the settlement is the Maori Fisheries Act 1989, which allows 'taiapure' to be created. Any person may propose the creation of a 'taiapure – local fishery', and there will be public notification of the proposal and the right of objection at a hearing. If established, it will be managed by a committee nominated by persons 'representative of the local Maori community', but any rules made concerning the fishery must not discriminate against anyone on the grounds of 'colour, race or ethnic or national origins'. Maoris have already proposed taiapure as a tactic to prevent the establishment of marine reserves in particular areas.

Section 26ZH of the Conservation Act (as amended) declares that 'Nothing in this part of the Act shall affect any Maori fishing right'. That part of the Act deals with freshwater fisheries. This is the section relied on in the recent claim in Wanganui that Maori could lawfully fish for trout and salmon without a licence. The claim has been dismissed by the High Court.

It is depressing to observe, though, that even District Court judges are not immune from the desire to play politics. We have already seen a Northland judge discharge Maoris charged with pigeon poaching because, in his opinion, that kind of behaviour should not be against the law. So much for parliament. Nothing in the law obliged Judge Becroft to declare that Maoris could fish for trout and salmon without a license. There was an argument put forward by the defendant to that effect, but there were also good arguments put forward by the Crown. The judge chose the adventurous political path. The judgment was a political statement as much as a legal one. The High Court has now reversed the judgment. Maoris have announced that they will postpone their mass protest of fishing without a licence until after the Court of Appeal has heard their appeal.

The Treaty of Waitangi Fisheries Commission has assets now worth $554 million.[47] Because of disputes within Maoridom, no dividends have yet been paid out. The main dispute at present is between iwi and urban Maori, but that doubtless will not be the only one. It will be a long time before a general consensus is reached about how dividends are distributed, and it may never come.

These inevitable and insoluble arguments are not, however, the only reasons why dividends are not being paid out; the commission is also keen to invest and strengthen its assets before it begins to pay dividends. This is wise, of course, but can become an end in itself.

Often, local Maori do not benefit from leases of the Maori fishing quotas. Maori authorities may choose to lease their quota to outsiders rather than to their own people According to *North and South*, (March 1998), 'during the 1996-97 lease rounds, iwi on-leased 52 percent of wetfish and paua quota and 11 percent of crayfish quota. Just 1 percent of the wetfish and paua quota was actually used by iwi or Maori fishermen, although another 36 percent was used by an iwi, iwi company or iwi joint venture . . .' There may, in some cases, be good practical reasons for this. But in other cases the desire seems motivated more by a simple desire to maximise profit.

The simple fact is that here is a final settlement of a Treaty claim which cost the Crown, one way or another, about $250 million, and which is already being ignored by some very visible and determined elements within Maoridom. They do not even wait a generation before complaining that the settlement was inadequate and imposed upon them. Yet they would also complain if the Crown actually waited for that impossible day when all Maori would agree. $250 million is a very decent sum – and it has since more than doubled – but it is not enough. What amount will be?

Moreover, the actions of the rogue Maori fishermen in the far north who fish without quota are at base a denial of the sovereignty of the Crown. John Utu-taonga, a witness at the trial of John Hikuwai (and described by the accommodating Judge Everitt, who acquitted Hikuwai, as 'the most impressive witness'), has declared that he does not recognise New Zealand law, and that he regularly sold or traded his customary catch. Utu-taonga purports to issue fishing permits for members of the self-styled 'Confederation of Chiefs of the United Tribes', which does not recognise 'Pakeha' law at all.

There is no doubt that our already strained and struggling fisheries will suffer from this new assault on them. Many Maoris, including many local Northland Maoris, disapprove strongly of this piracy, have no patience with the idea of Maori customary exemptions, and want European law applied to such pirates.

It is not good for the fishery, for respect for the law and for race relations when there is one law for one race and one for another, when Maori fishermen go unchecked and when Europeans are checked rigorously.

It must be added that if Northland Maoris were not as poor and wretched as they often are, many of these issues might not have arisen. This poverty is caused, in part, by the fishing quota system; but that quota system was made necessary by the over-fishing that occurred during the last thirty or forty years.

Having said that, how are we to solve the problem of Maori poverty? If the 1992 settlement produces only a drop in the bucket, then the sum of, say, $1000 million – four times that settlement – would produce only four drops. No Treaty settlement is a solution. There may not be a solution at all; but draining the rest of the country and inciting bad race relations is clearly the wrong solution.

SIX

The Natural World

We are imperfect and unhappy creatures, and, whatever age we live in, we find reason to complain. We often give force to our complaints by contrasting the present imperfect state of things with some other age, of the past or the future, where things were or will be better. In almost every age and society there has been a nostalgia for some better, and usually older, time. The Greeks and Romans sang of a golden age; Englishmen have yearned for the days of King Arthur or Alfred, the laws of Edward the Confessor or of Magna Carta. Today we may long for the honest labour and freedom of the pioneers, and some radical Maoris, of course, openly state that a simple return to a forever-departed tribal past is Maoridom's only hope of salvation.

From the eighteenth century onwards, however, it has been a distinct fashion in the West to seek our ideals not in our own past, but in other cultures. European explorers were then beginning to encounter fine healthy Polynesian and North American peoples, and these soon became idealised as Rousseau's 'noble savages', living in John Locke's 'state of nature': beautiful and free of prejudice, hypocrisy and the curses of civilisation.

This attitude is still with us. It manifests itself in sometimes surprising ways. In the 1960s and 70s, for example, it was fashionable, among less thoughtful environmentalists, to blame all environmental ills on Christianity, which (it was claimed) placed man over nature, and made nature itself mere inert matter for human use. There was no divinity in Nature, and man was free to exploit it as he pleased. Christianity was the problem, and a change to another religion would, by implication, save the environment.

This anti-Christian argument, of course, ignored many things. It ignored the Christian belief that God created nature, rejoiced in it and 'saw that it was good'. It ignored the many Biblical commands to be good stewards of creation. It ignored the fact that, in the ancient world, it was not the Jews, but other cultures, who were the scientists and the ones who altered nature. It ignored the fact that for many centuries, Christian Europeans lived in a rough harmony with their environment, and that that harmony was broken not by Orthodox or Catholics – who, between them, form most of Christendom – but only by the handful of Protestants living in America and the edges of Europe. The argument suffers, in fact, from the misguided belief that Protestantism and Christianity are identical. If we are to blame any event in history for environmentally unsound practices, it should perhaps be the Reformation rather than the Incarnation.

But in fact the plain evidence is that all ages and cultures have been responsible for environmental degradation. It is not the prerogative of Christians or Europeans. Plato lamented the felling of Greece's forests, and the loss of soil from hillsides which thereafter would grow nothing more than thyme for the bees. The deserts of China have been growing for millenia, and the Yellow River is so called because of the immense loads of silt which it has carried down to the Yellow Sea. There are strong indications that environmental destruction was responsible for the end of such American Indian cultures as the Maya and those of the southwestern United States. In the Pacific Ocean there are many bare and empty islands where humans lived until their destruction of their bird populations and forest – a source of timber for houses, fuel, weapons and canoes – drove them, also, to flight or extinction. Archaeological evidence suggests that the Polynesian settlement of Hawaii, about AD 500, led to the extinction of at least fifty species of bird alone, and Captain Cook observed the early signs of serious soil erosion there.

It would be surprising if the history of human interaction with nature in New Zealand were any different from this sad catalogue of destruction, and the evidence is clear that it is not. We are all aware of the environmental destruction and extinctions which Europeans brought to this country. Yet we may not realise that the coming of the Maori caused a far greater wave of extinctions and destruction. Until eight hundred years ago, Dr Tim Flannery says,[1] 'New Zealand had the most extraordinary, indeed unbelievable, assemblage of birds. Nothing like it was found anywhere else on earth.' As well as about a dozen species of moa, the first Maori settlers would also have seen the giant swan and pelican, the flightless goose and coot, the fearsome giant eagle (larger than any bird of prey now alive), the mysterious adzebill, and many others. Estimates of numbers of species vary, but it is generally estimated that Maori were responsible for the extinction of between twenty-eight and thirty-five species of birds, and the destruction of about one-third of New Zealand's pre-human forest cover.[2]

Europeans, by contrast, have seen the extinctions of only seven to nine species of birds – still, of course, seven to nine too many – and the destruction of about the same amount of forest.[3]

Even some of those European extinctions perhaps should not be blamed entirely on Europeans. The huia, Dr Flannery says, was in pre-human times common throughout most of New Zealand. It was Maori hunting that restricted its range to just a small part of the North Island, and its eventual extinction, made more likely by this reduction in range, was caused not just by European collectors but also by Maori hunters. Dr Flannery quotes a prominent late nineteenth-century ornithologist who recorded eleven Maori hunters killing 646 huia in a single month.

**Auckland University researcher describes Maori rat
as a living treasure**

There can be no doubt but that it was Maoris who were respon-sible for these pre-European extinctions. It is clear that the bird species spoken of above were all present in abundance when the first Maoris stepped ashore. Natural causes cannot be found. In Jared Diamond's words, 'It would have been an incredible coincidence if every individual of dozens of species that had occupied New Zea-land for million of years chose the precise geological moment of human arrival as the occasion to drop dead in synchrony.' It is surely clear beyond reasonable doubt that the destruction of habitat, hunt-ing and egg-gathering, combined with the effects of the Polynesian rat were responsible. Atholl Anderson concludes, in *Prodigious Birds*, that 'it can hardly be in doubt' that human colonisation caused moa extinction.[4]

Nor can there be any doubt but that moa-hunting was not only unsustainable, but also immensely wasteful. Barney Brewster, in his book *Te Moa*,[5] and Dr Flannery both describe the conclusions of archaeologists that many more birds were often killed than could be eaten and that a lot of meat therefore often went to waste, with only the choicest cuts being taken.

Not surprisingly, the destruction of the Maoris' environmental resource base had serious and unfortunate effects on Maori society. In the times of the first colonists, the so-called 'Moa-hunter period' of Maori culture, resources were abundant, there was little for peo-ple to fight over, and little or no evidence of war. When the moa and other large birds became extinct, Maoris were forced to rely on other, less accessible resources. If early European sealers found seals only around Fiordland and other very remote places, it is because they had been exterminated elsewhere. Middens show a decline in the size of shellfish. Dr Flannery quotes archaeologists who believe that Maori fishing for snapper was at unsustainable levels. It was as a consequence of this resource crisis that Maoris began to turn to pa-building, and to war. Pas were built to defend kumara crops and people themselves from hungry human predators.

'By the seventeenth century . . . the land of milk and honey once possessed by their ancestors was, as the Maori would say, *'Ka ngaro, i te ngaro, a te moa'* – Lost as the moa is lost. By the time Europeans first sighted New Zealand, the resource crisis was in full swing.'[6] War, cruelty and cannibalism followed. It is hardly surprising that Maoris were expert in warfare by the time of the Land Wars. It is quite possible, Dr Flannery concludes, that were it not for the appearance of Europeans and their new foods, there would have been a catastrophic collapse of the Maori population.

This ancient history may seem surprising in a book that intends to deal with the present, not the past. But it is highly relevant to the present; far more relevant than those fruitless arguments over the precise nuances of every word written in the Treaty.

I do not relate this sad history in order to claim that Maoris are more environmentally destructive than Europeans. Doubtless if Europeans had arrived here first their environmental record would have been similar. It is petty and pointless, this arguing over whose ancestors were worse. The point of mentioning it here is simply to explain that Maoris are *not better* at environmental sustainability and wisdom than Europeans. We should blame neither the Maori nor European pioneers for the damage they caused. If we blame one lot, we must in fairness blame the other also. Both were pioneers in a strange land. In both cases, it took a long period of trial and error – and destruction – before the limitations of the land, and the remaining resources, were eventually learnt.

If, at the time of European settlement, Maoris had laws of tapu and rahui governing their taking of food from the wild, they had them only because they were forced to adopt them by circumstances – in particular, the circumstances arising out of their own earlier destructiveness. At present we are again fashioning environmental laws, which we can all look upon as the successors to those later Maori ones.

It is important to say all of this, for among some Maoris and sentimental but ignorant non-Maori Treatyists there remains this belief in the noble savage; the belief that somehow Maoris are *inherently* better at conservation and environmental responsibility; and therefore, that we can give our conservation lands away to Maoris, or grant them special rights over land or native species, and have no worries that the natural world might suffer. There have been countless emetic racist effusions on the environmental superiority of the brown man. Even Geoff Park, in *Nga Uruora*,[7] does not allow his passing light references to early Maori destruction to interfere with his rhapsodies of Maori wisdom and denunciations of pioneering ways; and in marked contrast, he sneers at the great Linnaeus as a mere 'warehouse clerk'. Science and classification are evidently wicked things – although evidently class distinction is not.

Among the most inane effusions must be Douglas Graham's belief that 'to most of us a river is something to use. We fish in it, swim in it, launch our boats into it and may enjoy just looking at it flow by. But we don't revere it as Maori do.'[8] Not only, then, is Mr Graham himself out of touch with the natural world, but he affronts the many non-Maori New Zealanders, subjects of the Crown, who revere and love their land and landscapes just as much as Maoris do. But instead of representing them in negotiations with Treaty claimants, he has become the apologist for those claimants, and a party to their delusions of greater environmental sensitivity. Whether this is because of Mr Graham's gullibility or claimants' powers of persuasion must, at present, be a matter of speculation.

A Ngai Tahu spokesman, worried doubtless by the destruction of the myth, has recently thought it necessary to announce that Maoris were not responsible for the extinction of the moa; although he then turned around and conceded that they 'may have been a factor'.

The evidence of the present day should make it clear that Maoris can be as environmentally unsound as anyone. The native pigeon is so heavily poached in Northland forests that, by present trends, it will become extinct in the area within ten or twenty years.[9] Some Ngai Tahu support the creation of an enormous new dormitory sub-urb outside Christchurch, very close to the site of the historic Kaia-pohia pa, on what is now mostly good farmland. In several places Maoris have opposed plans for marine reserves, often wanting instead a 'taiapure' area, whose committee would be nominated by local Maoris. Investigations into national park additions, such as that of Rangataua Forest to Tongariro, or even the creation of new parks such as Northland's proposed Kauri National Park, have been halted by Treaty claims.

Sir Tipene O'Regan has claimed that fur seals are a nuisance to commercial fisheries and caused problems on the Muttonbird Is-lands, and should be 'harvested' because they are no longer endan-gered. On these islands, off Stewart Island, muttonbirders have killed protected birds and bats. They have illegally released goats, cats and wekas on various islands. It is almost certain that mutton-birders inadvertently allowed rats to reach Big South Cape Island and cause the extinction of two more bird species. Ngai Tahu have opposed shifting endangered species from one of the Crown Titi Islands to

BREAKFAST AT TIPENE'S

another. They have at times greatly restricted DOC's presence and research. A Treaty Fisheries Commission analyst has urged that Maoris should be able to trade in whalemeat, and a Ngai Tahu spokesman has said that his tribe 'might support [whale] culls for food' if numbers were sufficient.

In southeast Otago and Southland, forests owned by Maoris under the Landless Natives Act 1906 are exempt from the laws on sustainable logging of native forests, which bind all other private forest owners. These forests are still occasionally the victims of vigorous and unsustainable logging. For many years elements within the Waitutu Incorporation were planning the logging of Waitutu forest. In the late 1980s Maoris felling forest around Mt Titiraupenga in the southern Waikato did not even stop at their own land boundaries, but logged at least 150 rimu and matai in Pureora Conservation Park. The response of a Maori Land Court judge was to urge the Crown to give the land to the loggers.[10]

For some years before its latest Treaty settlement Ngai Tahu was suggesting that a tourist monorail be built in the Greenstone Valley, whose peace and remoteness it would at once destroy. The new 'customary' fishing rights practised by many Maoris clearly often involve overfishing. Evidence suggests, also, that Maoris complaining of

DOC's drops of 1080 poison to kill possum are often motivated just as much by the desire to preserve the lives of the pigs they hunt, and the pigdogs used in that hunting, as by any deeper spiritual feeling.

Indeed, if the widespread attitude of Maoris to the natural world was one of deep respect and love, we might expect to find rather more Maoris in the conservation movement. Yet the conservation movement, which has served us all so well in fighting for public lands, national parks and wild New Zealand, has among its members an enormous preponderance of European New Zealanders, and even recent immigrants.

Some Maoris seem determined to take a very hard-headed, businesslike approach to their future. Sir Tipene O'Regan has said that Ngai Tahu were 'just too damned pragmatic', in contrast to the attitude of non-Maori conservationists. This approach may be very sensible. But it is completely incompatible with any claim to have greater spiritual, cultural or environmental sensitivity, and is a clear statement that we can expect those Maoris to be no less prone to commercialisation and exploitation of nature than anyone else.

It may be said that this environmental destructiveness is forced on Maoris by circumstances. But that could be said of anyone. Anyone can be environmentally sensitive when nothing forces them to behave in any other way.

So then: even *if*, by the time of European settlement, all Maori practices were environmentally sustainable,[11] the situation today is very different from then. Even among Maoris, tribal authority is a real living force to only a very few. It is absurd to suggest, as some do, that we should hand our environmental problems over to Maoris and make them our environmental governors; that we can give them our wild lands with perfect confidence as to their management. Sound cure rests on correct diagnosis. To misdiagnose our environmental problems as simply 'failure to respect Maori ways' is not going to lead to a cure. We must all look within our own cultures for the cure, not pass the problems to someone else. And to suggest, as a respected Canterbury academic has done, that the Treaty is some sort of blueprint for a sound environmental future, is fatuous nonsense.

The environment and the law

As noted above, the Treaty has no legal standing of itself, and forms part of our law only insofar as some statute expressly requires that it be considered. A disproportionate number of these statutes are concerned with environmental matters. Accordingly, the Resource Management Act 1991 lists as one of five 'matters of national importance': 'the relationship of Maori and their culture and traditions with their ancestral lands, water, sites, waahi tapu and other taonga'. Section 7 requires the consideration of 'kaitiakitanga', which is the 'exercise of guardianship by the tangata whenua of an area according to tikanga Maori . . .' The Act requires that iwi be consulted on various matters. I do not object much to these references, although it would be less racist if European links with historic and ancestral places were also a matter of national importance, and I note that as a matter of strict law there are more requirements to consult with Maoris than with non-Maori New Zealanders.

The Resource Management Act also mentions the Treaty, although, refreshingly and courageously, it simply says that those administering the Act must 'take into account' Treaty principles; and it is clear, from the context, that Treaty principles, once considered, can nevertheless in the end be ignored. The Act's primary aim is sustainable management; and, as mentioned elsewhere, the Waitangi Tribunal has claimed that the Act is 'fundamentally flawed'[12] because it does not give the Treaty primacy. The Tribunal offers no reason, however, why a sustainable environment for all New Zealanders is less desirable than Treaty rights for some.

It must be stated, however, that Maoris – along with others – are sometimes using the Act as a source of enrichment. It is absurd when a Maori consultancy charges a fee for determining whether the site of a proposed development is sacred or not, when local body and Historic Places Trust records already exist. The present Minister of Conservation is among those who have expressed concern that iwis are using the Act for pecuniary advantage instead of ensuring good environmental standards.[13]

The Crown Minerals Act 1991 also requires its administrators to 'have regard to' Treaty principles, and the long title of the Environment Act 1986 refers very briefly and cryptically to those principles.

Rather different, however, is section 4 of the Conservation Act

1987, which established and now governs the Department of Conservation (DoC). Section 4 states that: 'This Act shall so be interpreted and administered as to give effect to the principles of the Treaty of Waitangi.'

As explained below, this section has been so shamefully misused and misinterpreted, not only by enthusiasts within DoC, but also by the courts, that its repeal would be a very good idea.

The most fundamental part of the Conservation Act is section 6, which makes it absolutely clear that the Act's, and DoC's, chief purpose is conservation, and anything else must be subsidiary to this.

This is supported by section 4 itself, which simply speaks of 'interpreting and administering' the Act. Clearly, the words and aims of the Act are fundamental; it is only in interpretation, and in pursuing that fundamental aim of conservation, that there is any scope for Treaty principles. To the extent to which Treaty principles do not further conservation, then there can be no scope for applying them.

In practice, section 4 is a constraint on conservation. Normally, if something concerning Maoris was good for conservation it would, presumably, be done anyway. In effect, then, Section 4 will only be used to justify matters that would compromise conservation, and to impede the Crown's right to govern. This improper use of it may well be based on misunderstanding of its real effect; but the misunderstanding seems widespread and incurable. It is time that section 4 was done away with.

There have already been suggestions that it imposes some duty on DoC to give Maori names to reserves and to give Maoris preference in employment. It is claimed that the Director-General should consider allowing the taking of native plants and animals, even though the general aim of the Wildlife Act surely makes it clear that such taking must be for the species' own good – as is the case, for example, in most scientific research. At the time of the Chatham Islands' sesquicentennial celebration, local Maoris referred to section 4 when seeking permission to gather albatross, a 'traditional food', for a banquet. (In the end, permission was granted to gather chicks which had fallen from their nests and which would have died anyway. But because of bad weather, none were actually gathered. This avoided a potentially embarrassing incident, for the then Governor-General, Dame Cath Tizard, to her great credit, had already let it be known that if albatross were served she was not going to eat it.)

It has been suggested that DoC may have some duty under section 4 to give Maoris rights to deer on conservation land, and this suggestion is also implied by the *Whale-Watching* case mentioned below. Such rights would not, of course, involve any duty to control deer rigorously and reduce their numbers to acceptable levels.

DoC has claimed it is under a section 4 duty to allow two launch operators, one Maori and one non-Maori, to ferry visitors to Kapiti, and that in other matters also there should be an equal Maori and non-Maori split.

DoC's October 1993 'Greenprint' publication stated that 'what is needed is a partnership [between DoC and iwis] that achieves the Crown's conservation responsibilities, while also recognising the real grievances and ongoing interest of iwi as Treaty partners . . . This partnership must involve equal participation in . . . an appropriate level of shared management.'

The New Zealand Conservation Authority's papers on 'cultural harvest', mentioned below, base themselves on the principle that DoC's duty is to do whatever Maoris – or at least one particular Maori lobby group – want. Even the less outrageous second paper claimed that 'In all its work the Authority is required under section 4 to give effect to [Treaty] principles.' The paper also refers to the Waitangi Tribunal's views on Treaty principles as if they were as influential as the views of the courts, and, like so many other documents, refers to the 'Treaty partners' and partnership; a relationship which, as we already know (as seen in Chapter 5) does not exist.

The 1996 Abel Tasman National Park Draft Management Plan proposed, as an objective, 'scientific taking *and traditional gathering* in a manner consistent with park values and the recreational setting'. Kaka and wood pigeon were specifically mentioned. It did not apparently occur to the plan's authors that 'park values' would require no gathering at all. 'Gathering of native plant or animal materials' would be 'permitted only for Maori traditional purposes'. Only non-Maori, it seems, would be bound by the preservation purpose of the National Parks Act. National Parks, to judge by this draft, are in danger of becoming places where Maori could go to kill protected species.

DoC's regional conservancies are obliged by the Conservation Act to produce plans called 'Conservation Management Strategies' – hereafter referred to as CMS's. Many of these have gone overboard in their Treaty enthusiasms. The Northland CMS seems to believe that Maori actually have a statutory responsibility for conservation. But nowhere in section 4 or in the Court of Appeal's 'treaty principles' is there any suggestion that DoC may abdicate its duty to manage its land and resources. To consult Maoris – along with everyone else – is acceptable, but no more. The Northland CMS even proposes a committee of 'tangata whenua' who will 'assist' DoC 'in understanding the scope' of section 4. This could well be an unauthorised dictating to the proper decision-maker. The East Coast CMS speaks constantly of 'partnership' with DoC and Maoris 'working together', and it even seems, in some matters, to propose giving power of veto to iwi. The Auckland draft CMS gave as its first principle 'bicultural management of natural and historic resources . . . by giving effect to the principles of the Treaty'. Nature conservation and preservation come second and third. The preservation and protection objectives of the Reserves Act, the Conservation Act and the Wildlife Act are hardly mentioned: it is mostly concerned with kaupapas, mission statements, strategic approaches and management charters. The first objective for almost all of the twenty-five key land management areas is 'to restore tangata whenua links with the [island or land] and its taonga through the exercise of mana whenua, jointly with departmental authority'. The document defines 'mana whenua' as 'customary rights or authority.' Does this mean that DoC intends to relinquish Crown sovereignty?

It is certainly healthy to encourage Maoris – and, of course, non- Maoris – to get to know nature and our wild lands better. But non-Maoris do not feature much in this document at all, and the concern for Maoris goes far beyond what the law, let alone the wider public, ever contemplated.

There is another way, also, in which the scope of section 4 is far more limited than some in the Department believe. The Town and Country Planning Act 1977 contained a reference rather similar to the Resource Management Act's reference to Maori 'ancestral lands'. The Court of Appeal has affirmed that that expression includes lands not owned now by Maoris, but traditionally important to them;[15] but Mr Justice McMullin, in that judgment, observed that 'if there has been a voluntary disposition in the past by Maori to Europeans, the considerations made relevant by [that reference] may be considerably diminished in their impact'.

This is entirely reasonable. If one has freely sold lands, then that is some indication that those lands were perhaps not desperately important and dear to one; and if one has freely sold them, then why should one continue forever to have rights over them? The same principle must surely apply here. Even the Dunedin Ngai Tahu Maori Law Centre agrees that chieftainship can be extinguished by land sales.[16]

In other words, if lands are validly sold – or, surely, if claims have since been validly and finally settled – then the Court of Appeal's Treaty principles – the Crown's duty to act reasonably and in good faith, active protection of Maori interests, and redress of grievances – simply do not apply. The principles of the Treaty are directed to protecting Maori interests; but if there are no Maori interests to protect, then obviously the principles do not apply. This must be the case whether the matter under consideration is conservation or anything else. Maoris do not have any greater rights over those parts of the conservation estate. So, when the Ngai Tahu claim is again settled, the only special rights which Ngai Tahu will have over the conservation estate should not arise from section 4, but simply from the words of the latest settlement.

Section 4 cannot mean, then, that Maoris must be involved at all (let alone as an equal party) in each and every conservation decision. They are to be involved – over and above ordinary involvement by any interested members of the public – only if Maori interests are involved. If there are no such interests, the Treaty and its principles must be irrelevant. So if Maoris have freely sold land to the Crown, they no longer have any interest or role in the management of that land over and above any other member of the public. The same principle must surely apply for all plants and animals on that land. If land – and everything on it – is sold, no Treaty principle says that Maoris can, in effect, renege on that sale. The scope of section 4 must actually be considerably less than many in DoC believe.

In 1995, in the case of *Ngai Tahu Trust Board* v. *Director-General of Conservation*[17] the Court of Appeal, under Sir Robin Cooke, considered section 4. One feels that the Court of Appeal was ashamed of this decision, for it attempted, in its judgment, to suggest that its value as a precedent would be 'very limited' – in effect, a desire that the decision would be ignored. It remains to be seen if this request will have any effect. Various Treatyists have enthusiastically quoted the decision and attempted to use it as a precedent on several occasions, and, as mentioned in Chapter 5, at least one Environment Court judge has readily used it. The decision is legally and logically shoddy, and is one of the most blatant pieces of political meddling ever to have been made by the court in the disguise of case law. DoC has already used it to justify giving one of its two Kapiti launch permits to a Maori operator.[18]

The case concerned the proposed granting by the Director-General of a further permit for whale-watching at Kaikoura. Ngai Tahu claimed that they were entitled to special consideration. The Director-General claimed that they had already received it. The Marine Mammals Protection Act (which governed whale-watching permits) did not specifically mention the Treaty, but there was nothing in the law to stop the Treaty being considered when the decision was made.

Section 4 of the Conservation Act says that only *that Act* is to be interpreted and administered so as to give effect to Treaty principles. *That* Act – not other Acts, such as the Marine Mammals Protection Act, the Wildlife Act, the Reserves Act, the National Parks Act and the many other Acts administered by DoC. Parliament could very easily have made section 4 apply to them also, but it did not. Indeed, several of those other Acts even contain a section similar to section 4, which is surely a strong indication that Parliament believed that section 4 itself did *not* apply to them. Yet the Court chose to ignore this point, and in effect rewrote all these other statutes by holding that section 4 applied to them also. The Court seemed determined to choose the politically adventurous path, despite good legal signposts pointing in the other direction.

It is not even clear that other sections of the Conservation Act apply to these statutes – but the Court of Appeal believes that the Treaty section does. Quite possibly, then, Maoris must in future be given a 'reasonable degree of preference' (the Court's phrase) in job appointments under these statutes. Maoris might be entitled to preference in the allocation of opportunities to hunt and control deer and other pests: since DoC administers the statute dealing with this, and hunting deer is 'similar' or 'analogous to' hunting native birds, just as the Court thought that whale-watching was 'similar' or 'analogous to' whaling (which, the Court admits, Ngai Tahu very probably did not practise).

The Court raised the possibility that any Ngai Tahu control over whales was connected with its title to land, and therefore was extinguished when that title was. How did it deal with that possibility? After raising it, it said 'Putting aside that possibility, however . . .' And it never mentioned the question again.

The Court agreed that whale-watching is 'a very recent enterprise . . . distinct from anything envisaged in or any rights exercised before the Treaty'. It agreed that even if indigenous rights could develop (e.g. from whaling to whale-watching) the newly developed right would not necessarily be exclusive. The Court admits it was not clear that Ngai Tahu ever hunted even small whales, and that they certainly did not hunt the sperm whales that are now being watched. It agreed that the tribe controlled European whaling only to the extent that it owned the land where whaling stations were based. The Court thought that it was significant that the whale-watching was organised on a tribal basis, although it is difficult to see how a right can be created out of nothing just by tribespeople acting together. The Court noted that whale-watching was pioneered by two other people who obtained the first permit in the name of their own company and were later bought out by Ngai Tahu, but later in the judgment the Court considered it significant that 'Ngai Tahu were the pioneers of whale-watching'.

Arguments like these would be unacceptable from a first-year law student. The Court tried to link the claim to the Treaty by saying that whale-watching 'is so linked to taonga and fisheries that a reasonable Treaty partner would recognise that Treaty principles are relevant. Such issues are not to be approached narrowly.' Once more, in other words, the Court is very generous with other people's rights and interests. Its generosity of spirit is a smokescreen for an absence of basic law and logic.

In fairness, the judgment is not totally bizarre. It does reaffirm that the Treaty recognises the right of the 'Queen in Parliament' to make laws protecting and conserving natural resources. 'The rights and interests of everyone . . . Maori and Pakeha . . . alike, must be subject to that over-riding authority.' It does make plain that conservation considerations are over-riding and paramount, as regards whale-watching. It repeats that the Crown-Maori relationship is only 'akin to' a partnership. And it affirms that the Treaty has no independent legal life of its own, but depends on particular statutes to incorporate it into the law. But how much use are these principles if court decisions, having only a loose connection with law and reality, still grant Maoris substantially what they seek?

I actually have no great objection to Ngai Tahu having all the whale-watching permits. I am concerned, as we all should be, about monopolies. (The Court of Appeal was not: although concerned about many social issues, it seems that anti-competitive attitudes have to play second fiddle to assisting Maoris). I think it would be better for Ngai Tahu to be involved in whale-watching than in taking over conservation land. It is a pity that Ngai Tahu did not obtain whale-watching rights as part of their Treaty settlement, but only in addition. But I do object to the violence done by the Court to the law in the process. Judges cannot declare what the law is, and then expect other judges to ignore what they have said. The decision may, in the long run, do conservation and the country a lot of harm. The decision is certainly one which should have been made only by real politicians, not would-be ones completely unanswerable to the public.

Claims over conservation land

In an age of financial stringency, a government is always going to seek cost-effective ways to settle Treaty claims; and in an age when the privatisation of everything is a guiding principle, how great the temptation is to settle claims at little expense by privatising to Maoris public lands that at present are held for conservation. Many in Treasury and elsewhere in government have, for ideological reasons, opposed the Department of Conservation ever since it was established; that is why it has always been so poorly funded. In the last year the Business Roundtable has publicly called for the privatisation of much of the conservation estate. Doubtless they would prefer the new owners to be rich foreign corporations; but Maoris would do at a pinch.

Surprisingly, even some people who should know better support such proposals. The leaders of the Green Party have no problem with Maoris holding most of the conservation estate, and have told me that I am 'racist' for opposing it. The argument which they – and some Maoris, and the Crown – put forward is that it is not the

details of land ownership that matter, but rather how that land is managed. If, they say, it is managed, as now, for conservation purposes, why object to a merely formal change of legal owner?

The obvious answer to this is simply that different owners manage in different ways. Change the owner and manager, and you inevitably change the management. This is why we have public property, because any private landowner will (perfectly reasonably) put his own interests before those of the public. Management by private parties for public purposes is doomed to failure. Maoris may complain that the conservation movement does not trust them. The reply must be that no private interests, Maori or European, can be trusted – or even expected – to seek the common good.

The Crown's proposal, described below, that Maori claimants could be given 'a significant management role' in relation to conservation land will therefore inevitably conflict with the principle, also proposed by the Crown, that a change in management 'will not be approved if it results in a loss of protection to natural and historic values'. Managing conservation land now costs money. If Maori assumed that management they would, not unreasonably, desire to recover their costs, and all the other costs of ownership. That could only be done by changing management.

The Crown's 1994 proposals

The Crown's policies were once found in the 1994 *Crown Proposals for the Settlement of Claims* – the infamous 'fiscal envelope' proposals. The Crown stated that conservation land was 'not readily available' for settling claims. There were, however, the following exceptions:

(a) Some special sites of great significance, such as burial and pa sites.
(b) Sites of 'special importance' such as certain lake beds, river beds and mountains, and land required for access to greenstone.
(c) 'Discreet parcels of land where the overall management of conservation values will be maintained or enhanced as a result of their use in settlement.'

The Crown proposed that class (a) sites could have ownership vested in Maoris, with or without conditions on the title. For (b) and (c), land could be vested in Maoris under the Reserves Act or other legislation, 'with the capacity for returning title to the Crown if conditions are not complied with,' or else there could be a 'transfer of a significant management role' to Maoris.

Probably few of us would quarrel with vesting in Maoris an acre here or there, the site of an important pa or burial ground, should Maoris desire them. But the other two exceptions may possibly allow very significant losses to the conservation estate. In financially tight times, conservation land is always a cheap and tempting option. The Waitangi Tribunal is still allowed to recommend that conservation land be used in settlements. Nor was any part of the conservation estate exempt, by the Crown's proposals, from possible use in settlements. The use even of national parks was not ruled out. And parts even of national parks have been used in the Ngai Tahu settlement: 12,000 hectares around Mt Cook is a sacred 'topuni' area.

Moreover, it is not clear what status these policies now have. The 'fiscal envelope' itself has – perhaps – got the chop. The latest Tainui settlement raised hopes that conservation lands were still unavailable. But the proposed Ngai Tahu settlement gives that tribe generous rights over conservation lands. Politicians can change their minds and their policies. Future politicians might prefer a more generous use of conservation land. Indeed, even the government which made these proposals may have contemplated not actually being bound by them. A 1991 Cabinet paper on the Ngai Tahu claim proposed using the Crown Titi Islands, Codfish Island and Arahura Valley lands in settlement because this could be done 'at little cost to the Crown'. In 1992 Mr Bolger informed Federated Mountain Clubs that 'the government will be looking to optimise benefits to Maori under the existing statutes . . .', and in a letter to Sir Hepi Te Heuheu in 1995 – after the Crown proposals were published – Mr Bolger told him that 'the government can be flexible in some areas of the settlement policy, for example on conservation estate issues'.

The dangers of co-management

Even if Maori management were only 'co-management' with DOC, that would be most unsatisfactory. Co-management would mean that land is no longer public land, as before, but managed at least in part for Maori. It would mean a greatly increased administrative workload for the department – many more boards, committees and trusts would have to be established, services provided and meetings attended. The public would still be significantly excluded from management. Any accountability of the private party to the public will of course be highly unlikely. The Crown's ability to act will be severely limited. If DOC were actually to stand up for conservation against its co-managers, there would be unpleasant fights. Political correctness in the Department would make it likely that DOC would often merely accept *de facto* total management by Maoris – as it already has, for example, over the Crown Titi Islands. It is certainly difficult to imagine that DOC would ever revoke any co-management privileges. Political pressure or a threatened resort to the Tribunal would ensure that. Already the sorry saga of Mt Hikurangi has shown how unwilling or incapable the government is of enforcing the simplest and most basic conditions. What willpower did the Crown show at Moutua Gardens, or in the Urewera occupation?

It is, in fact, completely unclear how any effective action could be taken against inadequate co-managers. Although the Crown is the senior partner in the Treaty's relationship 'analogous to partnership', a timid and underfunded DOC is unlikely to behave as anything but the junior partner.

If co-management were so benign there would be no objection to it extending to those who hold some sort of concession or other interest on conservation lands – skifields, tourist flights and the like. But, significantly, the Crown has ruled this out. So a national park could be co-managed, but not the commercial skifield on it. Private property will not be exposed to co-management's high risks, only the public estate.

In the present climate of ambitious Maori aspirations it is inevitable that any special rights which any Maoris obtain over the conservation estate will be regarded by them not as a final settlement, but as just a foot in the door. They will not docilely accept DOC's advice. Having some interest in the land, they will seek more. They will invoke *tino rangatiratanga* to seek to turn it into a freehold. So would any European. In reference to Mt Hikurangi, a Maori Land Court judge has already remarked that if the Crown's intention were to give an interest, that interest could be readily extended to full ownership and control. A tribal representative at the same hearing denied the Crown's right to impose any conditions at all.

This preparedness of the Crown to sacrifice the conservation estate has not gone unnoticed. Tuwharetoa have taken DOC to the Waitangi Tribunal to bring pressure on the Crown to give the tribe control, and other tribes have also begun agitation. DOC leans over backwards to consult iwis.

Maoris, like all other New Zealanders, have full access to conservation land now. Indeed, they already enjoy privileges over it, including some 'harvesting' rights. For example, totara and other trees may, in certain circumstances, be taken for canoes and traditional buildings. Plants may be taken for cultural purposes. Muttonbirds are taken in some areas, and horses may be used in Urewera National Park. There are feather recovery programmes from dead native birds. There are Maori representatives as of right on the Conservation Authority and several conservation boards.

More than sixty claims have already been lodged over much of the conservation estate. Hardly any part of the country is exempt. We may be confident that investigation of some of them, anyway, will reveal no injustice. Even the Waitangi Tribunal dismissed Ngai Tahu's 'hole-in-the-middle' claim, and found that in the 1848 Kemp purchase, Ngai Tahu had indeed sold the Southern Alps and all the mountainous areas between eastern and western coasts. The claim that, in the 1853 Murihiku purchase, Ngai Tahu had not sold the land west of the Waiau River – Fiordland – was also dismissed. If Ngai Tahu is now to receive the Routeburn, Caples and Greenstone stations as part of its settlement, that is not because that land was wrongly taken, but as substitution for other lands which the Crown cannot or will not provide. Mt Cook – and many other places whose sacredness Ngai Tahu claims – were sold and purchased properly.

Since the re-organisation of government departments in the 1980s, the conservation estate is the only remaining holder of large areas of Crown land. But the use of conservation land as a cheap substitute for other land no longer available is unthinkable. Even *if* justice requires that land be given to claimants, it is unthinkable that dedicated conservation lands should be given away or otherwise used unless it is clear that those particular lands were wrongly taken. Even then, other settlement options are almost certainly better for Maoris, the public and conservation. When wrongly taken land has later been sold, the Crown is not obliged to buy it back. Why then this government obsession with giving conservation land away?

Most of our conservation lands remain in their wild state precisely because they are remote, or useless for farming or any other productive purpose. Biologists often lament that low, fertile country, with its own special native plants and animals, is greatly underrepresented in the conservation estate. Great amounts of it are higher-altitude country and mountains – scenic, but not biologically, particularly rich. This means that conservation lands were very seldom centres of Maori population before 1840. Ngai Tahu's successful claims before the Tribunal concerned productive coastal and lowland country. Ngai Tahu told the Tribunal that land given in settlement 'should be representative of land lost . . . in character and geographic distribution'.

Most conservation lands are economic liabilities. They are, by definition, not 'productive'. Even if they continued to be dedicated to conservation – which any new owner would doubtless object to – they would make money only if there were significant changes in management – entry charges, at least, and probably much more. Remote lands given to southern Maori by the Landless Natives Act 1906 remain remote and unused. That approach clearly does not work.

If land is to be given to Maoris, then, the obvious answer in many places would be to use the already-developed land of state-owned enterprises, or for the Crown to purchase productive land. State-owned enterprises are owned by the Crown, and their property is still, essentially, that of the Crown. Douglas Graham has said that 'Landcorp farms would be among the most suitable for use in settlement of the Ngai Tahu claim'.[19] Landcorp alone had, in 1995, ninety-seven farms, totalling 78,300 hectares, in Canterbury, Otago and Southland.[20] The Tribunal itself noted that Landcorp, Forestcorp and Electricorp have substantial holdings in Ngai Tahu territory. Yet the Crown, it seems, would prefer to keep these, quite possibly so that it can later sell off those enterprises to some astute overseas bidder.

'Forest and Bird proposals that state-owned exotic forests in Southland be used in exchange for the conservation of Maori-owned native forest were given short shrift by government, despite iwi interest in such a deal. The cutting-rights were sold to overseas-owned forestry giants, leaving the Crown little to trade for the protection of precious forests such as Waitutu.'[21]

The conservation estate is not Crown property in the same way that, say, a surplus office building is. It is legally set aside and dedicated for a particular purpose, and it is in a very real sense the property of us all – including Maoris. Much of it has been saved for posterity only after long public battles against the Crown. The laws which protect it have been arrived at after a century of debates and struggles. They arise from a sound practical knowledge of what works well. Such arrangements should not be altered lightly.

Mr Graham has said that if conservation lands were wrongly taken, 'it is hard to refute the submission "the Crown stole it – give it back".' Yet, even *if* the land claimed had been taken wrongly, which is by no means always the case, Mr Graham's argument surely could also apply to private land. Yet private land is rightly inviolable. Conservation land, although technically 'the Crown's,' is allocated – to the public, and nature – and is therefore more akin to private land than to ordinary unallocated Crown property.

Mr Graham's argument cannot justify giving away validly-acquired conservation land. Yet the Crown is quite prepared to do that, even without a recommendation from the Tribunal. On several occasions in recent years the Crown has shown an outrageous desire to give away sections of the conservation estate without justification. Often these sections are among the most precious lands we have. The Southland Conservation Board embraced with enthusiasm the Tribunal's invalid recommendations that the Crown give away Codfish Island (home to half the world's kakapo, and many other endangered species) and the Crown Titi Islands. (The Tribunal, remember, had found there was no breach of Treaty principles in the Crown's acquisition of these islands.) By five votes to four the Board voted to 'return' the islands to Ngai Tahu. All four board members with Ngai Tahu affiliations voted for the motion; two of them were actually among the claimants. Cabinet has noted that the transfer of these precious islands could be done 'at little cost to the Crown'. The present Ngai Tahu Claims Settlement Bill gives the freehold of the Crown Titi Islands to Ngai Tahu, subject to its being managed *by Ngai Tahu* for nature *and* for muttonbirding; and grants special rights over Codfish also.

In the case of Stephens Island, home to most of the world's tuatara, a Department of Conservation official wrote to Ngati Koata suggesting that they make a claim for the island. Not surprisingly, Ngati Koata did. The tribe did not, it seems, dispute the Crown's purchase of the island. Perhaps the Department was acting under instructions from the then Labour government. Nevertheless, one way or another, the Crown was not actually interested in safeguarding, or even keeping, the conservation estate.

The Tribunal dismissed Ngai Tahu's 'hole-in-the-middle' claim. Yet the Crown, asked by Ngai Tahu, has purchased and proposes to give the tribe three high-country stations beyond Lake Wakatipu, of great recreation and conservation value. This transfer – subject, certainly, to conditions, and to the lease-back of much of it to the conservation estate – is still proposed by the Settlement Bill. The lease-back is declared, at present, to be forever. The Tribunal proposed only that the beds of the Arahura River and its tributaries should be vested in Ngai Tahu, but the Crown proposed to give title to all conservation land in the mountains and foothill watershed. The land is now – again, after much agitation – proposed as a reserve, to be administered by Ngai Tahu.

Without even a claim to or recommendation from the Waitangi Tribunal, the Crown in 1991 took about 3,750 hectares from the Raukumara Forest Park – including the top and the southern side of Mt Hikurangi – and proposed to give it to Ngati Porou. The Maori

Land Court also agreed that nothing required this act of generosity by the Crown. The Conservation Act's procedures were not used; instead Section 436 of the Maori Land Act 1955 was employed. This section says that land acquired for a public purpose may be revested in Maori owners when it is no longer required for that purpose. The fact that the Crown proposed to establish conditions – covenants and easements for conservation and public access – strongly suggests, of course, that the land *was* still required for public purposes. It had also been proposed as an ecological reserve because of its outstanding ecological values. Mt Hikurangi itself is the outstanding feature of the Raukumara Forest Park.

The land has yet to be transferred. Ngati Porou have been stoutly resisting the attempts by DOC to get it to keep its word and allow public access. The process is long and complicated. In early 1998 Ngati Porou announced that they had been obliged by circumstances to charge for access. The entire story is one of incompetence and betrayal by the Crown of the interests of its subjects. What hope does it give us that the Crown would ever act to uphold the covenants promising free public access to the former Lake Wakatipu stations? Ngai Tahu has made it clear it is not happy with the right of the public, to be written into the settlement, to wander at will. Maori MP's on the select committee object to it because they think it is a dangerous precedent for other Maori settlements.

Even if land now part of the conservation estate had been wrongly taken in the past, that land might well then have been a comparatively unimportant part of a larger area. Since then it has been, in a sense, privatised – dedicated to us all. To return it would create fresh injustices – to other New Zealanders, and to a hard-pressed natural world which finds itself in a situation very different from that of 1840. Even the Tribunal pays lip-service to the principle that in remedying one injustice it should not create another.

The Ngai Tahu Claims Settlement Bill proposes to give the tribe a great number of impositions on conservation lands and management. Few, if any, follow naturally from either Ngai Tahu's original statement of claim or the Tribunal's ruling. The Tribunal recommendations simply provided a convenient excuse for the Crown to compromise and negotiate away a large number of public rights.

The bill proposes to give the tribe seats, as of right, on the New Zealand Conservation Authority and conservation boards, the boards of guardians of various southern lakes and the New Zealand Geographic Board. Tribal nominees will be 'statutory advisors' to all fish and game councils. Ngai Tahu are given special exclusive rights – 'nohoanga' – to camp for up to 210 days each year 'so as to have access to waterways for lawful fishing and gathering of other natural resources'. Such nohoanga sites are often on conservation land, to which of course all members of the public have access now. 'Lawful fishing' includes special Maori customary fishing rights.

The bill establishes 'topuni', mainly over mountains – Cook, Aspiring, Earnslaw, and the Takitimu Range – which were freely sold by Maoris last century. These topuni are an addition to existing legal protection of these areas. The 'Ngai Tahu values' of the topuni must thereafter be respected in planning, and any 'specific principles' agreed to by the tribe and Crown for 'avoiding harm to, or the diminishing of' those values, must have action taken by the Department on them.

The bill also provides that the Crown must issue 'protocols' to the tribe about how it will exercise its powers, and how the Department of Conservation 'will on a continuing basis interact with [the tribe] and provide for [its] input into its decision-making process'. These

protocols are issued after consultation with the tribe and 'having particular regard to its views', and thereafter the Department must comply with them. Here is a possible source of immense influence on management of conservation lands and immense potential conflict.

For a long time the public have been involved in managing our national parks and the conservation estate. Their representatives sit on the Conservation Authority and conservation boards, and sat on many earlier boards. They make submissions when policy and legislation are being considered. They have campaigned and lobbied the government successfully on many conservation issues. It must be admitted, however, that the role played by Maoris in conserving our natural lands has not been great. Chief Te Heuheu Tukino, by giving the peaks of the Tongariro mountains to the nation, began our first national park, and the government was very slow in the park's actual establishment. Arawa have made a significant gesture with the gift of a scenic reserve. But Maoris on iwi committees are on the whole much happier with the Forest Service's old 'multiple-use' philosophy than with preservation.

The 1994 Crown proposals 'acknowledge the value of carrying out consultation with the public and non-government organisations . . .' This is not a guarantee of public consultation; nor is it even a definition of it. Two sentences on the subject in a forty-page document is an accurate reflection of the weight the government attaches to it. In the case of the Ngai Tahu settlement, there was virtually none. Occasionally the Minister of Treaty Settlements would give conservation organisations some idea of what was going on; but these scraps of information hardly count as 'consultation'. Certain Maori claimants have ferociously opposed *any* public consultation, using the old argument that their agreement was with 'the Crown' and not 'the people', and that the people have no business showing interest in what is not their affair. This is surely an indication of claimants' future desires for the running of conservation lands where they acquire interests. On at least some occasions during the Ngai Tahu negotiations the Office of Treaty Settlements had to seek Ngai Tahu permission to meet conservation groups at all. And Maori complain about how negative conservation groups are. Settlements are unlikely to last without public support; and that support is less likely if the settlement is reached in secrecy and presented to the public as a *fait accompli*. This grudging attitude of claimants will doubtless continue as people come to dislike Treaty claims more and more. But it does not give us much cause to hope that there will be much valuable consultation in future.

Our wild lands, the bush and mountains, clean rivers and empty beaches, are an important part of our culture and our idea of what it means to be a New Zealander. As our society becomes more racially, culturally and socially diverse, the principle of equality of entitlement to our public lands is becoming more, not less, important. To grant special rights to some New Zealanders is, to that extent, to turn all other New Zealanders into trespassers in the land of their birth.

In South Africa there used to be signs on some beaches and other places, saying 'Whites Only'. Now, on certain pieces of public land in the South Island, will there for most of the year be signs saying 'Ngai Tahu Only'?

Our conservation lands must remain just that – *our* conservation lands. Indeed, if anyone is the true *tangata whenua* of most of them, it would be trampers and mountaineers. Our splendid conservation record is based on Crown ownership – public ownership – public involvement, and the accountability of the lands' public managers to us all. Nothing else will work. Te Heuheu Tukino may well have realised this when he gave the Tongariro peaks to the Crown, and the Taranaki tribes when they gave Mt Egmont. The Tainui Settlement, which did not involve any conservation land, gives hope, although the Ngai Tahu settlement bodes ill for the future.

Claims to plants and animals

Besides these claims to lands, there have been – or are – several attempts by Maoris to obtain control over native plants and animals. The idea of ownership of nature is, quite properly, considered environmentally unsound by most of us. But Waitangi Claim 262, lodged in 1991, claims that *te tino rangatiratanga* 'was and is an absolute authority which . . . incorporates a right of development which permits . . . iwi to conserve, control, utilise and exercise *proprietary and ownership rights over natural resources, including indigenous flora and fauna*'. [22] 'Decision-making authority' over all native plants and animals is also claimed, as well as such other things as 'all rights relating to the protection, control, conservation, management . . . propagation and sale' of flora and fauna. It is also claimed that these rights are so 'absolute' that 'any' exercise of kawanatanga by the Crown (allowed, of course, by the Treaty) is actually a denial of rangatiratanga. Any laws about protection, conservation, etc., are a breach of the Treaty. For the Crown to protect native plants; for the nurseryman to sell them; for a non-Maori gardener to cultivate them; all these are improper.

The claim objects to the introduction of possums – a disaster, certainly – and also objects to the prevention of Maori access to the commercial use, sale and dispersal of native timbers. It is alleged that 'the establishment of scientific reserves, protected areas and other actions or inactions of the Crown which prevent or inhibit Maori access to [the native wood pigeon] is a denial of the right to maintain cultural and spiritual concepts . . .' Since nothing in the law prevents anyone from looking at and admiring pigeons, this clearly refers to the killing and eating of pigeons; and other parts of the claim object to the establishing of protected species.

The claim mentions several species of plant and animal – including kumara (not, of course, a native plant) by name, but nevertheless it is clear that *all* native species are claimed. In the case of the kumara, one must ask: if it was so special, why did Maoris not preserve it themselves? The kumara was in fact abandoned by Maori for potatoes, wheat and other more productive and hardy crops.

The Tribunal has now granted urgency for the hearing of this claim. The claimants have asked the Tribunal 'to have input into the composition of the Tribunal' for the hearing. How fortunate we would be if we could all choose our judges.

Many of us may believe that the Crown could well be doing more for the conservation of our remaining native plants and animals. The underfunding of the Department of Conservation since its establishment has been disgraceful. Allowing uncontrolled exploitation by Maori, however, is hardly the answer.

Many of us may be concerned about the Crown's increasing nonchalance over the accidental introduction of new plant and animal pests. We may well have concerns about genetic engineering. We may think that if rich international corporations make money in one way or another out of our native flora and fauna, we should somehow receive some royalty – although it is hard to see how we could ever enforce such a rule. To the extent to which the claim is motivated by these concerns, we might sympathise with its motives. But to the extent that it is motivated by a desire to own and exploit nature, and exclude all other New Zealanders from any say in the management of their own plants and animals, the claim is racially divisive and environmentally unsound.

There has been another completely separate attempt to obtain for Maoris some special rights over native plants and animals: the controversial 'cultural harvest' proposals. The term 'harvest' is, of course, a loaded term, for it implies that the gathering is a sustainable one; 'harvest' makes us think of fields of grain and orchards, which regularly and reliably produce human food. The word implies, then, that populations of protected native birds and plants can cope with regular human killing of them, but there is plenty of evidence that the opposite is the case.

The original official proposal appeared in a 'discussion paper' published by the New Zealand Conservation Authority in 1994 on 'Maori Customary Use of Native Birds, Plants and Other Traditional Materials'. This document claimed to be prompted by a request from the Minister of Conservation, although the second, slightly less objectionable 1997 Discussion Paper admits that it was the Authority itself that had the idea. The original 1994 paper, only thirteen pages long, was a shoddy and outrageous document, and a disgrace to the Authority. It started off from the completely unestablished premise that all plants and animals belong to Maori. (After all, even the Waitangi Tribunal has not yet made a decision on Claim 262). It ignored completely the parlous state and continued decline of most native bird species and the Maori record of extinctions. For all its claim to be a 'discussion paper', it contained no list of options, with their merits and demerits, but only one future outcome: that of handing over to local Maori groups all decisions about the 'cultural harvest' of protected species, with no input from anyone else.

The entire aim of the paper was not conservation, which never got a look in, but one extreme political option. Nowhere did the document even give a list of species proposed for 'harvest': it was simply a proposal for Maori authority over wildlife. Section 4 of the Act was misinterpreted: it was claimed to mean that 'Treaty principles are given effect to'. Representatives of conservation organisations were in a minority on the subcommittee that produced the document, and a member of the Authority's staff later maintained, in conversation with me, that members of the Authority were not obliged to work *for* conservation, but were rather entitled to 'represent their constituencies' – so conservation organisation people represented conservation, and Maori people represented not conservation, but Maori interests. There is, of course, no justification in the legislation for this point of view.

This discussion paper caused immense outrage – although the Maruia Society found 'little to disagree with' in it. Submissions from the public furiously opposed it, and it was thought that if the Conservation Authority had any sense it would forget the whole thing. Nevertheless, in 1997 the authority produced a rather thicker but only slightly less objectionable second discussion paper.

Even the 1997 paper does not start with the question: 'How can conservation, the purpose of the Conservation Act, be enhanced by Maori "cultural harvest"?' Instead, it still assumes that Maori use is a good thing, and considers questions of conservation only to check that this desirable aim does not harm conservation. The paper contains the usual anti-European bias, dismissing European attitudes very quickly as a 'use ethic' and 'utilitarian'. Not a lot of attention is paid to other, older, European attitudes of sacredness; but that does not stop the paper from disparaging modern environmentalists who recognise some such sacredness and think that nature has rights of it own. It is also surprising that a paper promoting *Maori* use of nature sneers at European attitudes that nature may be used. There is only a reluctant and brief admission of Maori environmental damage. There is a brief admission that many Maori actually oppose 'cultural harvest', but those Maori who want it are represented as Maoridom's authentic voices. There is an assumption that Maori culture is incapable of evolution or change so that it might no longer desire to kill and eat wildlife.

The paper shows a sublime disregard to practicalities. For the Department of Conservation to monitor, in every part of the country, all the populations of all species which might be 'harvested' would cost an enormous amount of money, which the Department does not have and is unlikely to obtain. But these financial questions are ignored. The entire proposal is a financially impossible fantasy.

The paper is not interested or concerned about present Maori poaching, which (it implies) is exaggerated. It does not consider at all the possibility that, once some Maori taking of protected species is allowed, this will break the sanctity that now surrounds those species. When someone now kills a seal, a kiwi or a pigeon, we view that act with horror. If some members of the population may do those things lawfully, that horror will disappear. There will, indeed, be no reason why anyone may not do these things. People will say that the species population is large enough to allow taking – otherwise Maoris would not be allowed to take. Resentment against racial privilege will encourage some non-Maori to kill species just out of bloody-mindedness.

The paper also speaks of the importance of 'New Zealanders' different traditions, values and beliefs, and concepts of the relationships between humans and the natural world'. Yet, surprisingly, it does not consider the cultural significance to European New Zealanders of using native plants and animals. The pioneers logged; they collected birds, ate pigeon and kaka pie, took eels and whitebait, ducks and seals. Cultural sensitivity is a Pandora's box which, once opened, may contain some very unfortunate surprises.

The simple answer is that there is a lot we do not know about nature, and if we take a genuine precautionary approach it is unlikely that any more species should be 'harvested'. Where, now, native species – ducks, whitebait and sea fish – exist in sufficient abundance to harvest, then harvest – by all races – is allowed.

It is often said, in support of 'cultural harvest', that to allow it would merely be to follow the example of overseas countries where it is allowed. The implication is that it would be unreasonable and racist not to follow that example. But those who propose these overseas models as good examples ignore some important differences between them and us. For one thing, Australian Aborigines and North American Indians are, by and large, far less integrated into their societies than are Maori. There is much less intermarriage; many of them live separately, in the outback or in reservations, instead of among the rest of the population. For this reason, also, they may actually rely on such traditional foods. The hunting and taking of those foods, too, is something that has always occurred; it is not, as is the case in New Zealand, a recent revival in order to make a political point. It is widely admitted in New Zealand that the purpose of this harvest is not primarily *practical* for food, shelter and so on, but rather cultural. Let us not forget, too, that many Maoris oppose 'cultural harvest' and consider that, in an age when broiler chickens are plentiful and cheap, killing pigeons is always wrong.

Even more significantly, the biology of the hunted species is different overseas. Salmon and deer, bears and whales, kangaroos and lizards are capable of sustaining more hunting pressure than are our own native bird species, many of which can increase their numbers only comparatively slowly. Maoris have already rendered many birds extinct, and many others are threatened now. Even the most common edible one, the pigeon, is, without hunting, only just maintaining its numbers. These overseas game and hunted species have in most cases lived with predators, of one sort or another, for a very long time. In some cases, too – small whales in North America, for example – there are strict limits on the number that may be taken.

Human beings have also lived in America and Australia for far longer than they have lived here. New Zealand, we must not forget, is the most recently settled of all the world's significant land masses. Maori arrived here only 700–800 years ago, whereas Australia has been inhabited for perhaps 40,000 or 60,000 years. After the Aborigines exterminated the giant herbivores, they gradually developed the use of fire as a tool in land management. The mosaics of vegetation and wildlife have developed for so long with human beings that there is now, many biologists suggest, a need for that management by regular fires to continue, and if it does not, the result will be less diversity of plants and animals and occasional, far more devastating, fires. But this is entirely different from New Zealand's situation. There has been no such co-evolution here. Most native birds are, at best, doing no more than holding their own against introduced predators and ecosystem loss. Any hunting of them will quite clearly lead to a decline in populations, if not extinction.

The Ngai Tahu Claims Settlement Bill lists just about every native bird in the South Island, and many native plants and marine mammals, as 'taonga species', about whose management Ngai Tahu has special rights to consultation. It is difficult not to imagine that Ngai Tahu does not have ambitions for more in the future. Sir Tipene O'Regan, for example, has on various occasions spoken of his hope that native pigeons could again be taken for food.

For a long time New Zealand's conservation movement has been saying that no-one owns the natural world of forests and lakes, birds and seals and whales. They exist in their own right, as part of one amazing and wonderful creation. It is the belief that nature can be owned, and that it is merely matter for us to use, which lies at the root of the environmental crisis. Environmentalists would be racist if, having preached the integrity of nature to European loggers and developers, they did not also preach it to Treatyists and Maori activists. Fortunately our conservation movement is not racist; its share of sentimental one-eyed supporters of the noble savage is very small. New Zealanders should be very grateful to Federated Mountain Clubs and the Royal Forest and Bird Protection Society for their staunch opposition to letting public lands pass into Maori hands. One cannot, regrettably, give the same generous vote of thanks to the Maruia Society, Greenpeace and the World Wide Fund for Nature, even though they do fine work on many other issues. When negotiations began over the most recent settlement of the Ngai Tahu claim, Ngai Tahu made it clear that they expected 'at least' one national park as part of the settlement. The Royal Forest and Bird Protection Society and Federated Mountain Clubs were about the only voices speaking for what most of us believe, and much of the credit for the continued integrity of the conservation estate is owed to them. Those two organisations are almost certainly responsible for the complete absence of conservation land from the latest Tainui settlement – a healthy sign for the future. Treatyists wanting control of conservation lands should remember that it was the Maori chief Te Heuheu Tukino who gave the peaks of the three North Island volcanoes to all New Zealanders, and thus created the beginning of our first national park. He had no objection to public ownership of conservation land. Let us hope that the future is the Tainui sort of settlement, involving no privatisation of conservation land, rather than the Ngai Tahu model of partnership, co-management and special racial interests.

As Aldo Leopold says, we all desperately need a 'land ethic', which would change the role of *Homo sapiens* from conqueror of the land community to plain member or citizen of it.[23] Land is not a commodity that belongs to us; it is a community to which we belong and to which we owe ethical obligations, to use it with love and respect. Our wild lands and our remaining native species should not belong to Maori or to European. They should belong to us all. Or perhaps we should give them to their genuine original inhabitants, the plants and animals themselves. It is time we had a treaty with them.

SEVEN

The Way Ahead

It is no longer possible to label certain issues as the concern of the 'right' or the 'left'. Perhaps, outside a narrow range of arguments between workers and employers, it was never possible. We might, for example, be inclined to suppose that most conservationists are vaguely 'leftish'. Yet even in the United Kingdom, until recently anyway, it was more likely to be Conservatives who were concerned about the beauty of the countryside and the well-being of its animal and plant inhabitants. Labour party supporters were more likely to favour factories and industrial developments. In New Zealand, as in Britain, at least one conservation society enjoys royal patronage. Conservationists are young and old, and of all political leanings.

A good part of European support for Maori protesters and Treaty claimants comes from those who suppose that in offering that support they are furthering the causes of justice, compassion and the brotherhood of man; causes which, for good historical reasons, often attract the label 'left wing'. Yet to suppose that Maoris are fighting for the brotherhood of man, or even for simple justice, is often simply nonsensical. As a basic matter of definition, any claim by one group to some land, resource, or money, which they will then own exclusively, is incompatible with sharing universal brotherhood. To claim that certain New Zealanders have special rights because some of their ancestors arrived 800 years ago is no different from claiming that an Englishman has special rights simply because one of his ancestors came from France with William the Conqueror in 1066. How can the Maori claim be for justice, and the English one be for aristocratic oppression? The conservation estate is run for the benefit of us all. How can human fraternity be advanced by removing parts of the conservation estate from public ownership and giving it to private groups? If, as more misty-eyed Treatyists believe, the Maori ethic is one of 'sharing', why are Maoris not content with all of us sharing the conservation estate now?

There is, moreover, abundant evidence already that all those of Maori descent are not necessarily going to benefit from Treaty settlements. Various Maori voices, Sir Tipene O'Regan's being prominent among them, have declared that just as the Treaty was made with tribes, so settlements must also be made with tribes, and that any person of Maori descent who is unconnected with a tribe is entitled to nothing. Any such entitlements would be regarded as 'suntanned welfarism'. Already, various Maori financial groupings have shown their preference for building up their financial clout rather than paying dividends out to their shareholders. It is ironic that some Maori-allocated fishing quota is harvested by joint ventures using foreign fishermen employed at rates of pay many New Zealanders would regard as exploitative, while individual native Maori fishermen who have historically had access to the resource now find themselves squeezed out. It is no part of justice at all, to take more of our nation's increasingly scarce assets and apply them to foreign capitalists and the creation of a new class of brown capitalists.

It would be insane to suppose that if we are only patient for the next five or ten years, and settle all existing claims 'justly' or even generously, then the present Maori agitation will disappear. Why should it? Since when did giving people things discourage them from asking for more? Now that Maoris realise that claims of wrongs are a satisfactory means of obtaining publicity, popularity in their own circles, and some sort of gift from the state, more claims, not fewer, will follow.

Greed is part of the problem. It is something all of us are prone to, not just Maoris; but they are no exception. We are also in the dangerous position where many Maoris – and non-Maoris – are beginning to believe the radical rhetoric. The belief in grievances, planted in Maori minds by some of their own leaders and by foolish non-Maoris – including not a few schoolteachers – may already be almost ineradicable. As Ireland's unhappy example reminds us, grudges, real or imagined, can be a comfort and companion, a source of support as well as of trouble, for a very long time. The tribal nature of settlements ensures that non-tribal Maoris, those urban, uprooted, alienated Maoris who are often the most needy, will receive nothing from the generosity of the Crown. Their discontent will continue. Moreover, many tribal Maoris have even hinted that the latest settlements with tribes may be only for this generation, so that in thirty years' time the same claims will arise again. And the Court of Appeal has helpfully told us that Treaty principles will evolve from generation to generation.

Maori demands are not only for money, but also for land. Certain Tribunal claimants declare that their policy is to demand an acre of land for every acre unjustly taken. We have considered the justice of such a return of land. It must be said also that the claim for land reveals how claimants are living in the past. Farmers no longer ride on the sheep's back; they have been heading slowly but surely down the road to ruin ever since the heady days of the Korean War, and many have already arrived. We all know this – every magazine has articles about farmers managing to stave off ruin only by diversifying, or getting jobs off the farm. For claimants to desire even farmland (far more productive than, say, conservation land) is not going to benefit anyone. The road to comfort and wealth does not lie in agriculture – more is the pity – it lies in education, ideas, innovation and hard work. All Treaty settlements postpone that painful day when Maoris will have to stop relying on politics for prosperity, and will have to rely on hard work instead.

A New Zealand version of the cargo cult is developing. In other parts of the Pacific, simple tribesmen believe that their prayers will bring aeroplanes full of gifts for them. Here the Treaty is similarly worshipped. But Maoris must, as Sir Tipene O'Regan says, move away from a culture of grievance, claim and battle, and into the modern world. They must, he says, leave 'victimism' and the beneficiary mentality. Some may see a contradiction in this attitude resting on Ngai Tahu's latest generous full and final settlement; but still, in principle, Sir Tipene is correct.

We cannot create jobs for the unemployed simply by abolishing the dole; we cannot starve people into decency. Nor, as a simple matter of brute fact, can we simply abolish overnight all assistance to Maoris and all Treaty generosity, and leave it to Maoris to sink or swim. Over the years, enough money might have already been sent their way, but no state can abandon some of its citizens to poverty and hopelessness without good warnings. But perhaps there have been enough warnings already? Perhaps the fault is that governments reverse each other's policies, always assuring Maoris that 'this is the final arrangement . . .' But it must be made plain, somehow, and very finally, that non-Maoris' patience with Maoris is now wearing very thin, and there will be no more special treatment. Benefits and handouts, although an important safety net, can become a way of life. Let Maoris embrace education, not despise it. Let them abandon tribal approaches that have been outdated for a century.

We cannot blame some of Maori descent, of course, for taking advantage of European gullibility and feebleness of spirit. Who would? If it is clear that large donations of public assets and funds are available, why not ask for them? Since our rulers have, since 1984, been committed to giving away the hard-earned substance of our country for next to nothing, Maoris may as well join the queue.

One must say more. The question has been raised: Why is it permissible for Maori to conquer other Maori, but conquest by Europeans is looked upon as being inadequate to constitute valid ownership? Part of the answer is: that it is Europeans themselves who have created the difference. If New Zealanders had behaved – as for most of our history we have – as if last century's events were in the past, part of the fabric of history, but pointless to revisit, then Maoris would have largely accepted those events, even if unjust, as they have accepted Maori conquests. If the usual practice when, say, we knock someone accidentally is merely to say 'sorry', and nothing more, then those touched soon learn that such little collisions are a minor matter. If, however, someone who accidentally touched another then burst into long, effusive and evidently sincere apologies, the person touched would soon think that here is an opportunity for easy gain. The smiles which apologetic Europeans receive from Maori are not necessarily ones of sincere admiration: they have the contempt of the very Maori they are endowing.

But behind all this lies another more profound reason why Treaty settlements will not stem discontent and anger, especially among younger Maori. No gifts can remedy the fundamental cause of that discontent, which is not so much a sense of injustice for the wrongs of the past, as a discontent with the present harsh and heartless world where one is judged more and more on one's income, employment and possessions. It is a world of unpleasant international corporations who desire us all to be rootless and dissatisfied consumers; where our unthinking consumption will dull the indefinable ache in our hearts and the feeling that there should be more to life and human society than buying more possessions. No-one with

sense can fail to be depressed at the continued disintegration of a once-decent society, the degradation and destruction of the natural world and the way in which our news media, our political institutions and even, inevitably, our thoughts, centre more and more on the insoluble obsession with the economy.

One does not need to be a dangerous radical to be unhappy with the way our world is going. Indeed, conservatism, in the true sense – of conserving the best aspects of the past, its practices and institutions – is just as critical of many aspects of the late twentieth-century lifestyle as radicalism, and may prove in the end to be a more effective enemy.

It is worthwhile noticing that some, perhaps many, Maori radicals are truly conservative in that they turn to the past and maintain that social health lies in restoring some past social order and organisation. It shows, of course, a double standard and inconsistency on the part of many of their liberal supporters that while this proposed return to the past excites nothing but admiration, any suggestion that our European heritage contains many valuable lessons and examples which we can learn from and emulate receives nothing but scorn.

We can never return to the past – to *any* past. Much as we are inspired by the deeds and institutions found in the rich pages of our history, it is still as true that we can never go back. One senses, also, that the Maori past admired by many is historically untrue: without slavery, sexism, warfare, cannibalism, environmental degradation, superstition, harsh lives and early death. Nevertheless, the admiration of a good even if fictitious ideal is commendable, for only by comparing the real with some ideal can we criticise the real and work towards changing it.

There is, anyway, a discontent among many, especially younger Maori, with the whole shape of the world. It is worth noting, also, that substantial Treaty settlements excite no qualms among white captains of industry. Indeed, Hugh Fletcher, in *Maori Sovereignty*, believes that present settlements are not generous enough, and that Maori should be given much more – including conservation land – than offered by the Crown in its recent 'fiscal envelope' proposals. A recent report commissioned by the Business Roundtable proposes that much of the conservation estate should be privatised – inevitably, that privatisation would mean much of the estate in Maori hands, if only because conservation land would then be much more readily available for use in Treaty settlements.

The Business Roundtable has recently published a book by Professor Kenneth Minogue, whose main argument is that the Waitangi process is that of 'a successful society trying to talk itself into a nervous breakdown'.[1] It can only be good for the Roundtable to join the popular side in this battle. Yet this effort of theirs is not convincing evidence that their heart is in the battle. In business, one dollar is the same as another; businesspeople have in the past dealt profitably with worse monsters than radical Maoris, and they will be able to deal profitably with the Business Browntable in future. Their opposition to the Treaty mania is probably cynical, not sincere. If the Business Roundtable is genuinely concerned about racial tensions, it is probably only because it is becoming concerned that those tensions will be bad for business and investment.

It is clear, anyway, that large-scale capitalism does not see any problem with the Treaty industry, presumably because it thinks it can do business with this new tribe of brown capitalists. After all, our governments these days are very ready to accommodate the desires of business. This is yet another reason why we should all be dubious of Treaty settlements; it is also a reason why those settlements will not ease a discontent which actually arises, in part, out of the present economic and social structure of the world.

This economic and social structure makes many of us unhappy. It means the end of the old settled European culture as well as Maori culture. It has no respect for art, learning or religion, unless they make money. It looks upon tradition as an impediment to acquisition, and contentment as an impediment to compulsive shopping. Land is a mere commodity to be bought and sold and used for profit, and human beings are not citizens and brothers and sisters, but only consumers and taxpayers. The proponents of this creed are as much enemies of the common good as any heretics our ancestors may have dealt with. It is one of the great ironies of our time that they have derived assistance from those zealous humane reformers who are all too ready to preach the worthlessness and moral bankruptcy of European civilisation. Maoris have perhaps been fortunate to have the Treaty as a ready-made cure for every ill. If only the Treaty had been kept, they claim, life would be perfect and we would all be happy. European New Zealanders do not possess the same simple antidote and remedy for the problems of the age. But those problems affect us all. In the older, slower, more settled, more traditional, more religious, less commercial societies of our ancestors – European and Maori – there may be many models for the future.

Life, of course, is never perfect, and we are never as happy as we would like to be. We should never expect anything else: perfection is not for this world, and any claim that it is – or that any document, institution, constitution, treaty or anything else, can provide it – is a delusion.

Mike Smith, though he took a chainsaw to One Tree Hill, has a point when he objects to the way in which we – deceived, admittedly, by election promises – have allowed our country to be sold under our noses to foreigners. We all have cause to be grateful to Maoris for the various ways in which they have impeded these sales. But it is not clear that 'Maori sovereignty', whatever that is, will lead to the recovery of our country by New Zealanders – or even by Maori New Zealanders. Many young activist Maoris strongly disapprove of the old tribal way of doing things, a way of comfortable business deals and profitable arrangements for a few. But settlements are often with these tribal entities, and who is to say that they will not be the new force in Maoridom? Many tribal Maoris are not afraid of foreign investment. Sir Tipene O'Regan has said[2] that Ngai Tahu 'have friends in Japan who have dealt with us on a very generous basis, trusting in our capacity to meet our debt obligations', and he is 'convinced that Ngai Tahu will continue to form mutually beneficial relationships with Japanese and other foreign investors who recognise the rangatiratanga of Maori people'. He 'does not think that total economic subservience is a necessary consequence of foreign investment'. All of us, of course, will hope that he is right there. But his dream and Mike Smith's are not the same; Sir Tipene may achieve his dream, but that will not relieve the discontent that the Mike Smiths of this world feel.

Perhaps some of those who agree with what I have written in this book are racist. That cannot be helped. No idea is responsible for its followers; the noblest ideal can be perverted to bad ends. But, for that matter, there are racists among the Treatyists too. Those who maintain that a drop of Maori blood entitles its owner to a privileged status in this country, or gives one a different and superior sensitivity to the land, are also racist. Doubtless Treatyist racists are sincere; so, doubtless, are all racists. But sincerity of belief proves nothing about the soundness of belief. Sincere men and women have died for good and noble causes; they have also died for plenty of stupid ones.

There is an almost wilful blindness about the response of many to the appearance of fascist and neo-Nazi groups. Though we may disapprove of them, their existence is surely clear evidence that in the eyes of some – of a minority, but very possibly a rapidly increasing minority – our racial policies are unpopular and misguided. Society always has malcontents, but the present increase in their number and activity may well be significant. Would it not make good sense to pause and consider, at least, whether there is a grain of truth in this possibility? Moreover, no policy, however wise and enlightened, is a success if it produces immense social tension and anger. Even if the new fascists are unredeemable racists, the fact is that they, just as much as Maori, are here, and will cause increasing trouble if our present racial policies continue. Do we actually want to add increased racial problems to all the other problems we face? Politics is the art of the possible. No matter how wise our present racial policies may be – and that is debatable – they are in fact unwise if they lead to increased and insoluble racial strife.

And who is to say that, in principle, all policies of the new

fascists are actually wrong? The fascists are, of course, their c
worst enemies; swastikas and Nazi salutes are hardly going to win
the hearts of most New Zealanders. But, stripped of the unpleasant
and absurd trappings, some of their policies seem not unreasonable.
We may think that the execution of rapists is excessive, we may disapprove of intolerance of homosexuals,[3] but most New Zealanders,
Maori as well as European, have concerns about immigration, and
most believe that our country should be owned by the people who
live here. It would be unfortunate indeed if the existence of fascist
parties became a pretext for arguing that only such extremists
opposed immigration and foreign ownership.

The fascists, like many Maori activists, are one of the by-
products of the changes of the last fourteen years. They, too, are the
children of Roger Douglas and Ruth Richardson. Since 1984, Labour
and National governments have shared in a terrible attack on a comparatively happy and settled way of life. Government departments,
not always brilliantly run, but at least reliable, serviceable, and
providing many jobs, have been privatised or abolished. Full
employment is now considered an impossible dream – a large 'pool'
of unemployed is openly stated by numerous businessmen to be

**Debate rages as to where the cycle of Maori and Polynesian
offending begins.**

necessary for prosperity. New Zealand used to be a country where everyone was accepted as having a place. This is no longer so. It is not surprising – it is only to be expected – that Maoris, having lost their jobs in the railways or freezing works, and being condemned to unemployment and uselessness for the rest of their lives, should listen to agitators who tell them that they are the victims of great injustices. If we had not had such changes as we have had since 1984, the present wave of Treaty claims and Maori radicalism would probably have been far milder. If one has the particular sense of dignity, self-worth and reward that comes from being gainfully employed, one does not spend one's time on protests. If the costs of Maori claims – and, of course, the costs of the dole, increased health expenditure and all the rest – were included in calculations, the economic success of our new ways of doing things might not be so obvious.

Who are the biggest losers of all in this farce? Young men, and white men in particular. They, and Maoris, are the ones most likely to be unemployed. But unlike Maoris, who can now always expect uncritical shoulders to cry on and a ready audience for any complaint, poor young white men have no-one to love them except their comrades. They can be denigrated, sneered at and despised with impunity, and without any disapproval from self-appointed watchdogs for brotherhood. Poor young white men are totally marginalised and greatly over-represented among our underdogs. The same caring souls who would condemn the merest hint of a slur against any other group readily label them as 'ratbags' and 'scum'. There is no enlightened penal policy for them; no conciliator or commissioner to represent and plead for them. And ironically, some of these pariahs may even have some Maori blood, or at least be indistinguishable in appearance or social status from many Maoris.

Unemployed and despised, it is no wonder that some of them band together for mutual support, and include as their enemies not only (correctly) the new corporate state, but also other victims of the changes who have merely been more successful in getting public support for actions just as predatory. Poor young white men receive very little attention from the professional carers, and not even a modicum of Christian charity. If we had treated them better; if we had shown them a fraction of the interest and compassion we toss around in all other directions, the fascist problem would never have arisen.

What can any healthy, red-blooded young man of any race do in our society? There is hardly a place for them. If there were a war, we would welcome their natural aggression and animal vitality as they threw themselves at the enemy. But in the caring society of everyday New Zealand, they have no place. Their instincts, hormones and messages from the world around them are telling them to get together, to be rowdy, high-spirited and quarrelsome, to drink and party, make love and war and to do exciting and daring things. No coherent society can, of course, allow these instincts to rage unchecked. But our prevailing culture campaigns against so many of their pleasures. It has become hard to do anything vaguely dangerous without the intervention of inspectors, advisers, counsellors and safety experts. I do not defend every bit of young male thuggery, but it does seem that everyone's hand is turned against them. Reformers and economists have combined to do away with the stabilising forces of church, family and community which would once have guided them. Young men, of course, form a good proportion of our new compulsory pool of the unemployed. Even the benefits of civil liberties are denied them. Civil libertarians are often heard defending the freedom to depict gross sexual and violent behaviour – but the suppression of fascist literature, even if it does not mention race at all, is evidently quite acceptable. If freedom of speech means anything, it must mean freedom for other people to say things we disagree with. The American Civil Liberties Union, which actually believes that the freedom to express opinions should extend to *all* opinions, even white racist and black racist ones, is more consistent than our Council for Civil Liberties.

One Christchurch man involved in the neo-fascist movement claimed, perhaps correctly, that the movement enjoyed the support of many who preferred to remain anonymous for fear that publicity might lead to the loss of their jobs. Various caring persons expressed the opinion that, to nip fascism in the bud, it would be perfectly justifiable to dismiss these people from their employment, and that they were therefore wise to remain anonymous. But, as a correspondent to *The Press* pointed out, if we live in a society where people can lose their jobs simply because of the political opinions they hold, then fascism is alive and well here already.

Four young white men who were party to an assault on a young black man in Christchurch in late 1997, but not the actual assailants, were each sentenced to a month's imprisonment. On exactly the same day they were sentenced, a North Island Maori man, who had actually struck an elderly white woman who had allegedly made an (unspecified) racist remark, was fined only $150. (And, of course, a man who almost killed a woman by pushing a crucifix and a piece of wood, up her nose, was this year not even sent to prison at all, because he believed himself to be in the grip of a 'makutu', or Maori curse, placed on him by his mother-in-law.[4]) In a notable attack of double standards, the one-month sentences handed down to the four white men were greeted with glee – it would not be too strong a word – by many of the same people who normally would say that prison and punishment do not solve anything. There was a notable hard-heartedness; perhaps if flogging had still been available, these caring humanists might have thought that worth trying next.

There is most certainly much poverty and disadvantage in Maoridom. But then, there is an increasing number of non-Maoris who are in need. They are the real forgotten people. Obviously, racism and treaty injustice cannot be blamed for their situation. Many European New Zealanders, and their New Zealand ancestors, have been badly treated by employers, banks, government departments, by the system or just by casual predators. What redress are they to be given? Why must racism and treaty injustice be responsible for Maori poverty? By all means let us work to relieve poverty and distress; but we can only do so if first we have correctly identified its causes. The left-wing intellectual and activist Herbert Marcuse once said that 'not every problem which a worker has with his girlfriend is necessarily because of the capitalist mode of production.'[5] The afflictions of the Third World are not necessarily all caused by colonialism, nor are those of Maori all caused by Europeans.

Maoris fail in our system. But so do many Europeans. Let us make the correct diagnosis. The reason is not racism, or Treaty injustice. It is, simply, the system. Having made that diagnosis, we can then apply the correct cure. But no Treaty-worship will cure something not caused by racial injustice. The ways to help human beings do not vary greatly from race to race; the way to help Maori is, *mutatis mutandis*, the same as the way to help anybody else.

Most New Zealanders are democrats. Most of us are prepared, in various ways, to work for or even to fight for that democracy. But democracy is not the same as tribalism, where a few groups, including those anachronistic living fossils – Maori tribes – enjoy a privileged and enriched position. Democracy faces many threats; racial intolerance is only one. The loss of moral standards by those who would tolerate anything (except racism, of course) is one; so is an increasing apathy and cynicism among the people, one which seems increasingly justified by the arrogance of our rulers.

We rejoice at the end of tribalism in Northern Ireland. We deplore its reappearance in the former Yugoslavia, in Rwanda and Burundi and a dozen other places. Why should anyone imagine that the division of this country into Maori tribes and 'tribes' of other races is going to be any sort of improvement?

Tribalism is the negation of the rule of law. 'Tribal identity', whatever that is, and tribal leaders rule. Individuals must submerge their individuality in the tribal ethos. People rule, not law; and our freedom to do what we please, subject to the law, is replaced by the pressure to behave in a tribally-appropriate way.

I suspect that many of those calling for the re-creation of chieftainship and tribal control and law would not be very happy with the result. Communities impose their own laws and regulations, just as the law does. In many respects, social control by communities is more oppressive, as it arises from widely held beliefs (leaving far less scope for individual freedom of thought and action) and often depends very much on the views of the old (a strength in some ways, but also a vexation) or the views or personality of some charismatic and commanding authority.

Maori society of old was not a democracy. Clearly, many of Maori descent do not wish to revert to it, and any restoration of tribal government would be against their will. Even some activists, if forced to make the comparison, might perhaps think in private that by comparison the limits, discomforts and even injustices of our own society are not all that dreadful.

Treatyist dreams of a completely recreated and reorganised society are rather unpleasantly like Pol Pot's regime. They are like the 'utopian social-engineering' that Sir Karl Popper condemns. Treatyists are keen to sweep away all the European past, and to erect in the desert a new, culturally pure society. Their ideal society is not only profoundly anti-democratic, but also denies history. Our laws and institutions should reflect all of our history, not only part of it; and indeed, the pre-1840 history of tribal war offers no sensible constitutional model at all. Any ideals that deny history are, ulti-mately, doomed to failure; although not before a great deal of dam-age can be done by some angry and disordered personalities.

Treatyists are dedicated not to the happiness of people, but to an idea. In this, of course, they resemble the terrible economic theo-rists of the 1980s who have changed our country considerably; and indeed, the keen privatisers in the Treasury and the Business Roundtable would quite possibly be as happy to see formerly pub-lic assets in the hands of Maori capitalists as in the hands of any-one else. Not all Treatyists, of course, have the dreams of the Roundtable, but that may become the model for a time. The Roundtable even favours the privatisation of the conservation estate, and perhaps even of native species; and as far as it is concerned, to give these away to Maori claimants would simply be to kill several birds with the same stone.

Many treatyists and tribalists are no more interested in justice than were their warlike ancestors. Their interest is in advancing the position and privileges of their group. They are merely using new weapons; instead of taiaha and mere, they use and abuse law, de-mocracy and the Treaty.

The European civilisation that was brought here by the pioneers was not perfect – what civilisation is? – but it contained within it the possibilities of progress and renewal. So many Maori at the time rec-ognised this; they eagerly sought education, and encouraged it among their people. It was Maori parents, the evidence is clear, who wanted only English to be taught in schools.[6]

Every age has its strengths and weaknesses; has its virtues, and the defects of those virtues. The perfect human society is not possi-ble, because certain virtues are incompatible with each other. We can dream of a society which has, say, the vigorous democracy of the Athenians, the dedication to the common good of the Roman Republic, the piety of the Middle Ages, the art of the Renaissance, the elegance of the eighteenth century, the entrepreneurial and im-perial vigour of the nineteenth century, and the ecological con-sciousness of the twenty-first century; but entrepreneurial vigour does not always sit well with elegance or environmental concern; democracy and elegance do not go together, and so on. In the same way, it is an impossible dream to have a healthy, sensible, modern Maori society and culture which also displays the warlike vigour and customs of past ages. Nor should this necessarily depress us. Cultures change and adapt, or else they die. European society has changed so much just in this century. Maori who complain of the erosion of their own culture are not alone. The old literate ordered hospitable European culture is under attack from the forces of vulgarity, the profit motive and the lowest common denominator. It is happening to us all; and no recommendation of a Waitangi Tribunal, no Act of Parliament can prevent it. For parliament to try this would indeed be trying to achieve the impossible.

Some cultures die; all, at least, change. We cannot 'preserve' Maori culture, any more than we can preserve any other as it was. The culture of 1840, or 1860, or 1900, cannot leap out of museums and onto the streets.

Maoris cannot have it both ways. If they want to benefit from the comparative peace and plenty which European settlement brought to New Zealand, they must accept that they are the subjects of the Crown, and citizens of one greater polity. There is a fundamental contradiction in demanding integration and acceptance into the wider community, and at the same time demanding exclusivity and self-government. Are we to be one or two peoples? Is it even *possible* to be two peoples . . ?

None of this is to defend every element of the status quo. We could benefit from more diversity – a diversity opposed just as much by Treatyists as by Wellington bureaucrats or free-market capitalists. They are horrified by the idea that, say, the South Island, or all the provinces, have some form of autonomy, since they correctly perceive that those new governments would have little time for political correctness, and would develop a genuine cultural diversity. If the Crown should allow Maoris tribalism and local self-determination, then in justice it should not deny the same thing to European New Zealanders. Democracy and security could be enhanced if we restored those 'little platoons', to use Edmund Burke's phrase – guilds, churches, the self-government of cities and counties – which were destroyed in the zeal for liberty, but which stood between the individual and a state beyond individual control. But clearly, when Treatyists speak of cultural diversity, they usually mean that they want all of us to become more like Maori.

We judge other people by ourselves; we suppose them to be as we are. 'The English,' the Duke of Wellington said, 'are a quiet people'; and we like to think of ourselves as generous, easy-going, trusting and innocent people. This, if it be a fault, is a good fault: excessive generosity is a more noble weakness than meanness. But it is still a weakness. It would be good for our nation if we were rather more cynical and cautious about every claim that someone is a victim or has been wronged; and we are starting to learn this cynicism. It would be good for our nation, also, if we were not as polite to politicians as we are. Such a statement must be made hesitantly, for calm words and rational arguments are surely better, in political debate, than fury, rhetoric and violence. Yet the experience of the last fifteen years shows us that our new breed of politicians is quite prepared to ignore any arguments we put forward, however rational. What is left but to turn to intemperate language, and worse? They leave us no choice. Promise-breaking by political parties strikes at the very roots of democracy. If promises are broken, then elections – where we choose our government by considering their promises – become meaningless. One might as well decide on a government by a toss of a coin. Edward Gibbon described the constitution of the Byzantine Empire as 'autocracy tempered by assassination'. Never would anyone propose anything so extreme as that here in New Zealand; but if our rulers refuse to listen to us – if they make themselves autocrats – then intemperate words and, ultimately, unconstitutional actions may be necessary to recall them to a proper understanding of their duties. Perhaps we well-mannered people must take some of the blame for politicians' arrogance. All of us, from time to time, meet politicians whose policies we disagree with, dislike or even loathe; yet, through courtesy or cowardice, we smile to them, we are charming, if not obsequious, and any criticism we make of their policies is measured and restrained. It would be much better for the country if our feelings were more vigorously expressed. As it is, our civility may well mislead our rulers as to the depth of our feelings. Any decline in civil discourse is to be regretted; but then, politicians themselves have already brought about a decline in rational argument, preferring to fight elections on matters of style rather than substance. Our Victorian ancestors were far more vigorous in their expression than we are; and even if we consider that to return to their vigour from our own namby-pambyism is a regression in standards, it may still be the lesser of two evils.

When will we get some leaders? Why, during the entire Moutua

Gardens occupation, did the government insist that it was not its problem, but purely a matter for the local council? It very clearly was not. If governments – on this and many other issues – keep insisting that their proper function is to do nothing, we may feel entitled to replace them with ones that do something. Why do Maori leaders not condemn extremists? If they do not, are we entitled to assume that they sympathise with them?

Ever since David Lange became a backbencher, he has made some very sensible observations on race relations. He has warned us that 'the whole history of settlements tells you that they can't be [full and final]', and he has suggested that 'grand gestures and generous reparation may in the longer term be fuelling problems rather than mitigating them.'[7] One has to wonder, though, why he did not say those things, or act on them, when his government was in power. (Admittedly, Mr Lange now seems to regret most things that the Labour government did in power.) What happens to politicians, when they gain the Treasury benches, that principle and common sense desert them? The present Minister of Justice said of the 1985 amendment to the Treaty of Waitangi Act – the amendment which gave the Tribunal jurisdiction to investigate claims dating back to 1840 – that it was a 'potential time bomb'. He went on to say, 'When those claims [back to 1840] are received . . . and are taken to the government, what is [the government] to do? Is it to write out a large cheque [from] the taxpayer, or is it to decline the recommendations and refuse to act?. . . I am sure that all New Zealanders want to be as fair as possible in coming to grips with this complex problem; but the answer is not to go back to 1840 to review every government act or omission, including settlements already reached and payments made, and try to decide 150 years later whether prejudice was involved. That will cause greater division that ever . . . I fear the social and economic consequences of the bill, and I ask the House to consider carefully that the legislation might well bring greater trouble to the races than exists at present.'[8] If only we had someone of his good sense as Minister of Justice now.

Instead, Mr Graham floats the idea of 'appointing a marae as a court, presided over by Justices of the Peace who might be Maori', and also the 'idea of a travelling commission to hold talks between the Crown and Maori over the meaning of the Treaty'. John Delamere believes that land occupations are an effective way of bringing Maori issues to the fore, although he deplores violence and intimidation.

Our children learn about the Treaty, but they learn nothing at all about Magna Carta, the English Civil War or many other events in the long history of our government and liberties. Our children are being indoctrinated. Many judges, public servants and parliamentarians seem to have decided that any opinions such as ours are so beyond the pale that they can be safely ignored. Democracy means nothing to them. They betray us now; they will refuse to take responsibility for the racially poisoned world they are busy creating.

It is important to be just and fair. But, when injustices were done long ago, the question of what is just and fair now is, as we have seen, not a simple one. It is important to be compassionate, but not at the expense of others and not at the cost of injuring the common good. There is, moreover, such a thing as 'tough love': the easy solution is, in the long run, not necessarily the kindest or best. We must be compassionate and just, but we must not be fools. God calls on us to be good, not to be gullible.

Yielding to increasingly outrageous demands does not produce racial harmony. It creates resentment in other New Zealanders. In Maoris, it creates expectations that must, sooner or later, be disappointed, resulting in fresh feelings of grievance, unjustified, but real. Some Maoris now quite cheerfully acknowledge that they will receive nothing from Treaty settlements because their leaders will be the only ones to benefit, but many others have absurdly unrealistic expectations of the plenty which they will shortly enjoy, and will only blame European perfidy for its failure to appear. Our reasonableness and generosity over the last decade or so has led neither to an increase in racial harmony nor to a lessening of Maori demands. The policy we are following has ceased to be one of meeting reasonable requests, and has become one of appeasement.

Thirteen percent of New Zealand's population have some Maori blood. By the year 2051, it is said, perhaps 21 percent of the population will have some Maori ancestry.[9] Some time after that, perhaps, all New Zealanders will have some Maori ancestry; maybe then the whole tedious fuss will subside, just as the laws which once governed the relations between Anglo-Saxon and Norman eventually vanished into irrelevance.

If this is so, then we are tearing the country apart now for the sake of an alleged problem which will eventually disappear after many generations. But that will not make the turmoil of the immediate future any less dreadful; it may even prolong the process by several generations.

Our official policies are leading us down the road to apartheid and hatred. South Africa, which knows more about apartheid than we do, has just adopted a new constitution which declares that the state is founded on, among other things, 'the achievement of equality . . . non-racialism . . . a national common voters roll'. Treatyists are leading us away from all these things.

Under apartheid, many dreadful things happened in South Africa. There would seem to be far more justification for something like the Waitangi Tribunal there, where the wrongs were so much worse and recent. But South Africa's Truth and Reconciliation Commission has as its express aim the promotion of national unity and reconciliation in a spirit of understanding. It must grant amnesty to all witnesses who make a full disclosure of the facts. It may recommend appropriate reparation to victims (though parliamentary approval of this is also needed). But the word that is deliberately chosen is 'reparation', not 'compensation'; 'the reparations will be largely symbolic; the nation's way of saying, "We are sorry."' And, after two years of hearings, the Commission has ended its inquiries. South Africa, surely, has chosen the better path.[10]

Civilisation and civil order are delicate things. Prosperity can easily decline and peaceful citizens can easily become depressed, bitter, envious and hate-filled. In Africa and Asia, the former Yugoslavia, and in Ireland we see how easy it can be for a nation to embark on that dreadful course, so difficult to alter, of tearing itself apart. It is not a course we want to follow. The present state of New Zealand – comparatively peaceful, prosperous, educated, and humane – is a rare and precious achievement in human history. It is not, as some seem to suppose, inevitable or indestructible.

Little things can have great consequences. The assassins of Archduke Ferdinand did not want world war, only freedom for Bosnia. Violence is dreadful; and once it begins, it has a life of its own.

It is unhelpful to an already fraught debate when Maori activists threaten extreme terrorism, the burning of forests and the smashing of hydro-electric dams. Tama Iti has said, 'We are going to govern this country.'[11] It is perhaps not surprising that Ministers did not have them prosecuted for sedition; nor that deeply concerned and caring liberals did not care to dwell on matters like this. Far simpler to be outraged only by white peoples' minor racist jokes. For liberty to be defeated, good men need only do nothing.

The fragmentation of our country into homelands and warring states is just a logical step down our present track. Tama Iti, again, claims that 'Maori nationalism calls for the establishment of separate Maori states based on ancestral tribal lands.' In his own state, 'Pakeha would have to adapt to the Tuhoe way of doing things.'[12]

These warnings of partition – like South Africa's 'homelands', although there, of course, they were bad – may seem unduly gloomy. Predictions of violence may seem absurd. Yet Ranginui Walker, as we have seen, has warned that the country may become ungovernable unless a Maori parliamentary veto is established; Wira Gardiner claims that Bosnia is a sort of model for us. Not very long ago, the idea that Maori would forcibly occupy land was absurd, yet we have now seen occupations, not just of public property but private property such as Northland farms. Statues are defaced and other monuments threatened. Racial sympathy sways juries, who acquit or convict, influenced just as much by racial feeling as by law. Maoris with impunity make seditious statements and calls to violence – even to 'kill a white'; any non-Maori saying anything far less inflammatory would at once be prosecuted and condemned. The present Minister of Justice has 'nothing he wants to say' about such seditious calls. The argument is that prosecution will only draw attention to these incendiaries. What is the alternative? To fail to prosecute is a fatal cowardice which merely encourages even more outrageous demands. We are on the path to terrorism, which will create a climate of fear and hatred that will inevitably curse our country for generations to come.

The Crown's policy at present is based on the belief that people are never greedy and always reasonable; that they never seek to take advantage of others. Settle historic grievances, and we will all settle down happily together. Yet Treaty grievances are like the Hydra – dispose of one head, and two spring up in its place.

European New Zealanders are here to stay. They, too, are tangata whenua. This land is theirs, too. Their ancestors, like those of Maoris, were immigrants from beyond the seas. They have made their homes here, and created a new way of life. It would be as unjust to remove them as it would be to send those of Maori descent back to Hawaiki. Indeed, such writers as Michael King believe that 'Pakeha culture is a second indigenous culture, not a transplanted European culture which has been heavily influenced by proximity to Maori things.'[13]

European New Zealanders can no more be removed than can, say, the Protestant Scots planted in Ulster in the seventeenth century. Any Maori movement which denies this fact – by, for example, insisting that Maori are still 'sovereign', and that non-Maori are unwelcome 'visitors' – must be doomed to failure, although this may also be the cause of much unpleasantness. Any movement which even maintains that Maori must enjoy some sort of primacy or superiority as the 'first people' of this country must inevitably cause resentment and irritation. But any Maori movement which does not maintain one or the other of these things runs the risk of being so reasonable and sensible as to have no particularly Maori distinguishing features. A Maori movement which does not claim a special privileged place and special treatment for Maori is hardly a 'Maori' movement at all. We must just hope that reason and good sense are more attractive than grudges and prejudice – but the verdict of history on this question is unclear.

We can remain hopeful if we always remember that the Treaty activists and public figures in Maoridom do not represent all those of Maori descent. At times, Treaty activists remind us piously that 'Maoridom speaks with many voices,' but then they forget that they are only one of those voices. Other Maori voices seem almost silent, but they are there. We all know many of Maori descent who oppose the killing of protected native wildlife and the whole absurd Treaty process. There is no justification for claiming that their voice is any less 'real' or 'authentic' than any other. We must not lose our humanity. We must work towards a society that is just for *all*. At the same time, we should not believe that our refusal to give in to Treaty demands will automatically drive all Maoris into the arms of the radicals.

In its own way, the battle between Treatyists and the rest of us has been a war; and in war, truth is always the first casualty. There have been real wars in our history, though, and in well-kept cemeteries or in nameless desert graves overseas, many young New Zealanders lie, brown and white together, brothers in death. They gave life and joy and everything for the freedom and happiness of their fellow citizens. Let us not betray their trust. Let us stand, like them, for liberty and for what is right; and let our defiance of the Treaty mania be part of our greater stand for a country that is fit for all decent people to live in.

EIGHT

What Should We Do?

There is however a limit at which forbearance ceases
to be a virtue.

– Edmund Burke

History is full of treaties. None of them lasts forever. The Waitangi
Treaty is well past its use-by date. It has become the plaything of
rabble-rousers, foolish or ambitious politicians, and activist judges.
The time has come to treat it in the same way Alamein Kopu treated
her pledge to the Alliance party.

As long as every question, not just of land, but of health, education, environment and everything, becomes Treaty-related, then
racial confrontation must continue. The Treaty's magic status
simply produces division. It is, for activist Maoris, a token, and the
emblem of a cargo cult that has so far been highly successful. Why
would any activist Maori want the claims to stop? But stop they
must. The Treaty's relegation to history would be a great relief to
many, including many Maoris. For – let us remind Treatyists – there
are many voices in Maoridom.

It is difficult to believe that any claim of injustice with any merit
has not already been lodged with the Tribunal. It is thirteen years
since the law was amended to allow the lodging of claims referring
to events back to 1840, and if any action of the Crown has been a
burning, living injustice, thirteen years is long enough for a claimant to lodge a claim. As a first step, then, *the law must be altered so
that no more claims can be made.* Claims already lodged will doubtless cover all cases of historic injustice. If there should be some
present-day or future supposed breach of Treaty principles, Maoris
must seek the redress of their grievances only through the same
channels available to everyone else. After all, even now many Maoris
bring their claims directly to the Crown without consulting the

Tribunal. The Tribunal may then eventually be abolished when it has run out of business.

Amendments to the Treaty of Waitangi Act give the Tribunal the power to make binding recommendations for certain present or former state-owned enterprise land to be given to Maori claimants. *These must be repealed at once.* As already suggested, the mere threat that these powers might be exercised may have greatly influenced governments in the last ten years. The Tribunal is not a court: increasingly it is a lobby group for Maoris. The present Minister of Justice has himself considered such repeal. This would end the agreement made after the 1987 *New Zealand Maori Council* v. *Attorney-General* case. But that decision was essentially a political one, and in any case it was one forced on the Crown only by the lack of foresight of Labour legislators, who believed their Treaty reference would have no greater legal effect than had been given to the social obligation clause in the State-Owned Enterprises Act. It is not for lobbyists to command the redistribution of any public property: it is the Crown that must govern. Not so many years ago Douglas Graham complained that the Waitangi Tribunal 'has enormous powers that it should not have' and maintained that the government, 'which has the final responsibility for resolving grievances [should not] delegate that power to someone else'. Paul East, until recently Attorney-General, described the 1988 Treaty of Waitangi (State Enterprises) Bill as 'dictatorial and totalitarian'.[1]

Claims already lodged, but not yet heard, should undergo some review – some sort of taking of depositions – to see whether a *prima facie* case really has been made out. Members of parliament, and the more politically active judges, would clearly be ineligible for this duty, but among the non-political judges some intelligent decision-making can still be found.

But it is not enough to abolish the Tribunal. In not a few cases, Maori claimants ignore the Tribunal and begin negotiations directly with the Crown. *This, too, must cease.* The Office of Treaty Settlements must also eventually cease to exist.

The abolition of the Tribunal and the Office of Treaty Settlements will prevent no-one from petitioning the Crown. It will not prevent the Crown in future from appointing a commission of inquiry, and even making a settlement with a claimant, should that claimant have put forward a convincing case. But, as observed before, it is difficult to believe that any claim which deserves to succeed has not been lodged already. And it is clear that many claims which do not deserve to succeed have been lodged, and many more will be.

No-one should be eligible to participate in any Treaty settlement or gift without first establishing that he or she has actually suffered an injustice. The simplest and most obvious test – perhaps the only practical one – is that of degrees of blood. If someone has less than, let us say, one-eighth Maori blood, it is unlikely that that person has actually suffered. Any settlement must have as its primary principle, not a simple winding back the clock to the time of some past injustice, but rather the assistance of those people, of sufficient Maori descent, alive today, who have actually suffered as a result of past actions.

The Crown should impose conditions on any money and assets given in Treaty settlements, to ensure that these benefit all who are eligible. Some tribes may object that such conditions are demeaning – but if all would benefit, anyway, then what could be the objection? If similar conditions had been imposed when Third World governments and dictators were borrowing, then more of those loans might actually have benefited those countries' inhabitants. Such conditions are perfectly reasonable; it should not be difficult to find some suitable formula, and one must question the intentions of those who would oppose them.[2]

References to Treaty 'principles' should be removed from our statutes. In particular, Section 4 of the Conservation Act should be repealed. Properly interpreted, it is indeed subservient to the Act's main purpose of conservation. But it has been misused by the courts, and every day its existence is used as a reason for putting Maori interests ahead of the interests of nature and the public.

Conservation land, being dedicated to an increasingly threatened natural world and the use of all the public, is not like some spare office building or empty section somewhere, whose ownership, Crown or private, is immaterial. Apart from the occasional site of special historic significance, *conservation land should not be used in settling Treaty claims, nor should special rights be granted over it to some racially selected members of the public.* Most conservation land cannot be used in an economically productive way without very significant environmentally undesirable changes.

The Crown should not hesitate to prosecute – for disorderly behaviour, sedition, for provoking racial disharmony, for whatever crime – for treason, if necessary – those who break the laws. Europeans are prosecuted now. There cannot be one law for one race and one for another. Judges should also have sufficient courage, common sense and sense of duty to convict and sentence properly.

The Treaty must not be 'enshrined' as part of our constitution. To do that would be to guarantee our present problems would never end. So often, when people insist on their rights, they forget their obligations; and so often, the insistence that one 'right' or another be written into a constitution arises from a distrust of democracy. Power is taken from politicians, and few of us would defend most of our present herd; but power does not just evaporate, it usually just goes somewhere else. It will turn into 'tino rangatiratanga', calls for partnership and all the rest. We should not give power to unaccountable activist judges, generous with other people's money and rights. We should not feed the expectation of Maori corporations and never-to-be-satisfied activists. How often already have we heard politicians and activists maintain that 'valid' Treaty claims, as they perceive them, must be settled regardless of democracy and what the people of our country actually desire?

I do not believe that any written constitution is particularly desirable. It would merely turn more political arguments into quasi-legal debates, and force judges – not that they are all unwilling – to make what are essentially political decisions.

As part of reducing our obsession with the Treaty, *another day, rather than Waitangi Day, should be our national day*. For all its symbolism, the Treaty is not the foundation of our state. It has become so divisive that it should be downplayed. Governments have been wise in deciding not to go to Waitangi itself any longer to be humiliated, abused and assaulted. Perhaps we could revive, and even rename, Dominion Day (26 September). On 7 October we could commemorate the day in 1769 when Captain Cook first sighted our country. Or perhaps we could commemorate 21 May 1840, when British sovereignty was proclaimed and New Zealand became one country instead of a divided land of warring tribes.

We should stop talking about 'biculturalism'. We should talk of the many cultures that have found a foothold here; or, even better, we should keep cultures and their 'rights' out of politics altogether, and dedicate ourselves and our country to caring for and dealing with *people*. The tribal model of New Zealand some Treatyists speak of, where we are all members of 'iwis' - Ngati Pakeha, Ngati Asia, and so on - is absurd and divisive. Our obsession with biculturalism is forced on us by Wellington's obsession with national identy. We should let our national identity emerge by itself; a government that denies itself the right to guide anything else has no business here either. As part of this abandonment of official biculturalism, we should remove the separate Maori agencies within government departments.

What we do not need is more of the same. If more and more New Zealanders are losing patience with the whole Treaty business, it is not because, as the Race Relations Conciliator claims, our understanding is imperfect. On the contrary: we understand only too well. The common sense of the common people sees what the Wellington philosopher-kings do not, that these changes will not improve, but destroy the nation. Dr Prasad is not entitled to imply that we are fools. He is the fool if he thinks that more 'education' about our – or the Crown's – or someone else's – obligations to our 'treaty partner' will do anything except infuriate more people. If those in the race-relations industry exercised their brains as much as they wrung their hands, it might cross their minds that present poor race relations are in part caused by the policies presently being followed. They might actually try to change present racially based policies. Since they do not, we must conclude that they are among the enemies of good race relations. After almost thirty years of Race Relations Conciliators, and thirteen years of Waitangi Tribunal claims dating back to 1840, our race relations are far worse than they have been for most of this century. *The Race Relations Office seems to be little more than a mouthpiece for immigration and Treatyist policies, and should be abolished.*

We should stop or substantially reduce immigration. This of itself will, of course, do nothing to settle arguments between Maoris and non-Maoris. But the recent increase in the number of New Zealanders who are neither Maori nor European is inevitably increasing racial tension. Most Maoris do not want further immigration: it makes them feel increasingly outnumbered, and Asian immigrants, in particular, often come from cultures with very strong racist attitudes. European New Zealanders also feel that the country created by the European pioneers is being lost to their descendants. To save the economy by immigration is based on some very dubious assumptions. Immigration is socially disruptive and environmentally undesirable. Stopping it may not reduce racial tension; but continuing it will certainly increase that tension.

We should not encourage tribalism. Sir Peter Tapsell has written that 'in order to address the . . . problems of . . . employment, education, health, we need new regional organisations where every Maori who now lives in the area has the same rights and responsibilities, irrespective of which canoe brought his ancestors to New Zealand.' Sir Peter has been greatly disappointed by the recent 'secession' to tribalism. Any settlements should aim to benefit Maori people rather than tribes.

We should tell our rulers precisely what we think of them and their policies. We should not mince words. It is with some reluctance that I write this, for the (comparative) peace and politeness of political life in this country is in many ways an excellent ideal. Yet this peace may well disintegrate soon without our help. It is of no benefit to politicians – it actually deceives them – if we are furious in private, yet are courteous and obscure our real feelings when we meet them. Our courtesy does us credit, but for the country's good we should speak our minds. The apathy of the people is more dangerous to democracy than is the tyranny of leaders.

Even if one believes only half the quoted figures about Maori crime, unemployment, health and life expectancy, it is still clear that those of Maori descent are greatly over-represented among the unfortunate in our society. *We must again become a compassionate society which cares for the welfare of all.* At the same time, one does not have to be a member of the Business Roundtable to say that more handouts are not the answer. Sir Peter Tapsell believes that 'indiscriminate handouts have been utterly destructive of Maoridom'. It is a pity that arguments over the social problem are polarised between one side, which would attempt to solve the problem simply by throwing more money at it, and the other side, which would simply cut money off altogether. Neither remedy will work. More money – from the welfare system or the Treaty – is not the answer. Where is it to come from? There are habits of dependence. But neither can people be starved into work and decency. *We must encourage initiative and self-reliance, energy, education, and co-operation.* We must, in the long run, move away from an economic organisation which expresses all of social life in monetary terms and regards human beings merely as isolated individuals performing only economic functions.

Those in need must receive the attention of a caring community and government. It may often be that using Maori organisations, whether organised along tribal or urban lines, is the best way to administer that care. But using those organisations is quite a different matter from administering help by Treaty claims. That is a very imperfect measure. Those most in need may not receive it. Even if they do, gifts may simply encourage the 'hand-out mentality', which even many Maori leaders condemn. Assistance must be given on the basis, not of ancestry, but of need. We may ask the community for a decent basic minimum standard of living; we are not entitled to ask for a fortune.

Our country must be decently governed in the interests of those who live here. We have not seen many governments like this in recent years. If most people who wanted jobs had them; if more and more of our assets were not sold to foreigners; if we all had a modest share in what remains of our prosperity; if national and local government respected the environment and genuinely consulted with people, both Maori and European: if all of this were done, then, in fact, the desires of most Maoris and Europeans would be satisfied and rabble-rousers would have little to work on.

NOTES AND REFERENCES

Chapter One

1. Butler's *Hudibras*. (See Issues 145 and 260 of the *New Internationalist* in particular).
2. Joseph Wood Krutch, *The Modern Temper*, Harcourt, Brace & World Inc., 1929.
3. *National Business Review*, 8 May 1998.
4. Wilson and Yeatman (eds), *Justice and Identity: Antipodean Practices*. Allen & Unwin, 1995, p. 33.
5. *A Study of History*, Abridgement in two volumes by D. C. Somervell, 1957, Oxford University Press.
6. Robert Hughes, *The Culture of Complaint, Lecture 2, Multi-Culti and its Discontents*. In *The Culture of Complaint: The Fraying of America*. Oxford University Press, New York, 1993.
7. Christopher Lasch, *The Revolt of The Elites & the Betrayal of Democracy*, W. W. Norton & Co, New York, London.
8. *A Study of History*, Abridgement in two columes by D. C. Somervell, 1957, Oxford University Press.

Chapter Two

1. e.g. Dr Lockwood Smith, *The Press*, undated.
2. *Dominion*, 30 December 1995.
3. *The Press*, undated,
4. *Maori Sovereignty, The Pakeha Perspective*, p. 99. Hodder Moa Beckett, 1995, Auckland, ed. Carol Archie.
5. *North and South*, February, 1996.
6. *Forest and Bird*, February 1993.
7. *The Press*, 11 September 1995.
8. Under the New Zealand Bill of Rights Act, 1990.
9. The Maori text of the Treaty used 'Nu Tirani', a Maori form of 'New Zealand'. If there had been a genuine Maori name for the whole country, it would obviously have been used in the Treaty.
10. 'Avoiding The Global Guilt Trap', *Independent*, 8 September 1995.
11. *Where The Wasteland Ends*, Chapter 6.
12. *The Disuniting of America, Reflections on a Multicultural Society*, W. W. Norton & Co, 1992, New York.
13. 22 November 1994, *The Press*.

14. There is, therefore, a grain of truth in the insistence of, say, the Business Roundtable, that private property is necessary for freedom. But it does not follow from that, of course, that everything should be held privately, and that there should be no public property. Moreover, if private property is necessary for freedom, then we must have laws ensuring that, in practice, we *all* actually possess property, and limit excessive riches in order that each may share a modest minimum. It is, after all, just as much an interference with one's freedom if one is thrown out on to the street by a private landlord as if one is thrown out by a state landlord. But the right wing does not care for this consequence of its own theory.

15. David Chandler, *The Independent*, 21 July 1995.

16. *The Principle of Partnership and the Treaty*, PANZ Monograph, 1993.

17. 1990 statement of the New Zealand Catholic Bishops Conference.

18. *Hudibras*, Pt 1, Canto 1.

19. A letter in *The Press*, 6 February 1997, from J. S. Fisher and others, 'affirm[s] the right of all people to hold *informed* views . . .' (emphasis added)

20. Their account is published in *Maori Sovereignty: The Pakeha Perspective*, Hodder Moa Beckett, 1995, Auckland, ed. Carol Archie.

Chapter Three

1. Ngai Tahu have claimed on various occasions that their actual losses have been about $20 billion. This sum would just about be enough to make every single person of Ngai Tahu descent a millionaire. For them to accept anything less would be generosity on their part but not justice.

2. Sandra Lee, MP, says that to offer Maori only 'settlements that are politically sustainable and which the public will accept' is 'unacceptable'. 'Maori should not have to constrain their negotiations in some way that is politically correct or acceptable to the public. It is the government's responsibility to negotiate without regard for how the public will react.' *Maori Sovereignty, The Maori Perspective*, pp.122-123

3. Robin Mitchell, in *The Treaty and the Act* (Cadsonbury Publications, 1990) argues in his 1998 submission to the Maori Affairs Select Committee on the Ngai Tahu Claims Settlement Bill that so few Ngai Tahu could not, even by the Maori law of *ahi ka* (the lit, domestic fire, and therefore occupation) be considered to be occupiers and owners of so great an area, and it would probably be more realistic and accurate to consider much of the South Island as the 'public lands' of the tribe, like the public lands the state and the community now have, rather than as 'private' lands.

4. Since 1823 (4 Geo. IV c.96.2) the Supreme Court of New South Wales had had jurisdiction over offences committed by British subjects living 'in the [then independent] islands of New Zealand'.

5. *The Press*, 10 August 1998.

6. Tim Flannery, *The Future Eaters*, Reed, 1994, Chapter 23.

7. IA 1 1845/1310, National Archives, Wellington; Correspondence to the Colonial Secretary from C. B. Robinson, Police Office, Akaroa, 30 June 1845.

8. Sir John Harington, *Epigrams; Of Treason*.

9. Norman Smith, *Maori Land Law*, Wellington, A. H. & A. W. Reed, 1960, pp. 94–95.

10. '. . . if Pomare wished to give a feast, he would have five or six children served up at it. At Te Raki fifty people were cooked at once . . .' E. C. Richards, *The Chatham Islands*.

11. By the Te Runanga o Ngai Tahu Act 1996

12. *The Press*, 4 March 1993.

13. Tony Simpson, *Te Riri Pakeha*, 1979, Alister Taylor, Martinborough; ch. 5.

14. *Ngai Tahu's Tangled Web*, Alan Everton, *The Free Radical*, Issue No. 26, August 1997, p.5..

15. *The Press*, 22 August 1997.

16. Clause 8 – the Deed of Settlement means the Deed 'as from time to time amended'.

17. 'When you settle for 2% or 3% of what you lost you can't also say "This is full and final . . ." That seems to me to be a perversion of justice' – Maori claimant lawyer Joe Williams, quoted in the *Sunday Star-Times*, 31 August 1997.

   The reporter quotes the Waitangi Tribunal as saying in 1995, 'Maori should not be required to sign a full and final release for compensation. How tribes can legally sign for a fraction of their just entitlement is beyond us.'

   Sir Robert Mahuta, who signed a full and final settlement with the government in 1995, says, 'You tell me any government that can bind any future government with their policies. Does that work? Of course not . . . It's just a whole lot of rhetoric.' *Sunday Star-Times*, 31 August 1997.

18. *Press*, 2 May 1995.

19. Owen McShane, *Press*, 27 March 1995.

20. This section was contributed by Mr David Garrett, BA, LLB (Hons) (Canterbury), Barrister and Solicitor of the High Court.

21. Page 312.

22. Alexander Mackay, Compendium of Official Documents relative to Native Affairs in the South Island, 1872, Vol. II, p. 148.

23. Submission to Maori Affairs Select Committee on the Ngai Tahu

Claims Settlement Bill, 1998, NTS/17 and 17a.

24. Kenneth Cumberland, *Landmarks,* Reader's Digest Books, Surry Hills, NSW, 1981.
25. John Laurie *N.Z. Herald,* 2 June 1998.
26. John Laurie, *NZ Herald,* 2 June 1998.
27. In *Civilisation,* BBC & John Murray, London, 1969, Chapter 13.

Chapter Four

1. As explained in Chapter 5, the law is that the Treaty, insofar as it purported to cede sovereignty, was 'a simple nullity' (the words of Prendergast C.J. in *Wi Parata* v *Bishop of Wellington*). No body politic existed capable of ceding sovereignty. But nevertheless the words of the Treaty, which Maori chiefs agreed to, spoke of such a cession of sovereignty.
2. The *contra proferentem* rule ('against the profiting party') means that where a treaty exists in different versions, the interpretation which should be preferred is that which favours the weaker or disadvantaged party.
3. Reprinted in Claudia Orange, *The Treaty of Waitangi,* p. 265.
4. Even the word 'taonga', defined now as 'treasures', and taken to mean practically anything, was defined in Thomas Kendall's 1820 *Grammar and Vocabulary* as 'property procured by the spear, &c; name of a person', and an 1844 edition of the same work still defines the word as 'property'.
5. Muriwhenua Fishing Report 1988, pp.186-7.
6. I have heard some Treatyists claim that Maoris considered that a kawana's powers were limited because the 'kawana' they were most familiar with was Pontius Pilate, the Roman governor of Judaea, and that he (they claim) had very limited powers, not even being able to impose the death penalty. It is indeed true that many Maoris were familiar with the idea of Roman governors; but it is absolutely clear, from the gospels, that the powers of those governors were very great. In fact, they alone had the power to impose the death sentence. The Jewish Sanhedrin could not. That is precisely why Jesus was sent to Pilate. Maoris familiar with the Bible would have had a good general idea of a governor's powers, and of the vast ultimate authority resting in a far-away monarch.
7. Professor Kawharu's translation.
8. James Belich, *Making Peoples*, Allen Lane/The Penguin Press, 1996, Chapter 8.
9. *Maori Sovereignty, The Maori Perspective* ed. Hineani Melbourne, Hodder Moa Beckett, Auckland 1995.
10. Moana Jackson's *Culture Houses Model for a Positive Future,* distrib-

uted at a Wairarapa Polytech staff session by Irihapeti Ramsden.

11. *Press,* 3 October 1995.
12. TV3, The Ralston Rort, 13.4.1994.
13. A summary offered by Wira Gardner in *Maori Sovereignty* – to which book, as noted above, Iti himself does not contribute.
14. *Press,* undated.
15. *Maori Sovereignty, The Maori Perspective,* p. 103.
16. *Maori Sovereignty, The Maori Perspective,* p.122.
17. *Maori Sovereignty, The Maori Perspective,* pp.136-137.
18. *Maori Sovereignty, The Maori Perspective,* p.38.
19. *Maori Sovereignty, The Maori Perspective,* p. 32.

Chapter Five

1. 1878 3 N.Z. Jur (N.S.) S.C. 72.
2. 'against the profiting party': see also footnote 2, Chapter 4.
3. James Belich, *Making Peoples.*
4. *The Press,* 20 September 1996: Dame Sylvia Cartwright is reported as saying, 'To ignore poverty in our own country is like suggesting the police should concentrate only on violence in the streets. Poverty in New Zealand, like violence in the privacy of our own homes, must be brought into the open and acknowledged before solutions can be found and put in place.'

    She said a disproportionately high number of households in poverty are headed by women and that 'child poverty is almost always associated with women's poverty'.

    She urged political leaders to recognise that poverty does exist, especially as 'New Zealand women must be able to show the rest of the world that true equality for women and girls can be achieved'.

    On 23 September *The Press* reported that the High Court judge accused of straying into politics with her comments on poverty appears to be ducking the risk of further controversy. Dame Sylvia Cartwright did not turn up to make a scheduled speech at a women's suffrage celebration brunch at an Auckland hotel yesterday . . . one of the organisers told the gathering that Dame Sylvia thought the best way to deal with the controversy was to make no further statements.

    An editorial in the *New Zealand Law Journal* [1996] p. 362 observed of her speech: 'The long-term damage is the most insidious. If a Labour/Alliance government now promotes Justice Cartwright to the Court of Appeal or to be Chief Justice, then, irrespective of her merits, it will be impossible to avoid the feeling that this was an appointment made on political grounds. It would also send a message that the path to promotion is not sound judging but political activism, a reason why the tradition of non-promotion should itself be adhered to. The result would be the undermining of judicial independence, again playing into the hands of those who do not believe in it anyway.'

5. *Finnigan* v. *N.Z. Rugby Football Union* [1985] 2 NZLR 181.
6. See Roger Kerr, [1997] NZLJ 361.
7. [1997] 1 NZLR 513.
8. [1994] 3 NZLR 385.
9. *The Law of Torts in New Zealand* 2nd edition, p.1023.
10. See footnote 6, Chapter 2.
11. [1991] NZLJ 316.
12. Resource Management Law Reform Working Paper No. 27, 1988.
13. (1989) 19 VUWLR 335.
14. R. P. Boast, [1987] NZLJ 244.
15. (1995) *Public Law 59*.
16. According to a letter to the Minister of Justice from the United Party.
17. Section 5, Law Commission Act 1985.
18. (1989) 19 VUWLR 347.
19. 'The Law Commission recognises the Treaty as the founding document of New Zealand' – Issue 1 of its newsletter. The Treaty 'gives Parliament the authority to make statutes, and the judiciary [its] authority' – issue 6. Law Commission Paper 11 on legal education believes that 'Maori academic staff are best placed to present material on the Treaty and Maori cultural issues . . .' Writing in 1990, Professor Ken Keith, then a Law Commissioner, contemplated without difficulty the possibility that the courts might 'review fully the meaning given by statutory decision-makers to the principles [of the Treaty], or the relevant weighting of aspects of the principles, or their application to a particular situation.' Is this any part of a court's proper function?
20. There is an intellectual fashion these days to claim that fundamental constitutional changes are often not consciously made by particular statutes for example but instead somehow mysteriously evolve and happen while we sleep. So New Zealand's independence from the United Kingdom, it is said, was achieved not by particular statutes – although there were various – but just *happened*. Some Treatyists make this argument — that it has just 'become' our supreme law, without anyone lifting a finger.

There may be occasions when this is the only way to explain some slow profound constitutional change. But as a general rule, as Lord Chief Justice Mansfield said, 'If it is law, it will be found in our books. If it is not found there, it is not law.' The idea of basic legal changes just happening without anyone's purposeful action (and indeed contrary to the wishes of a majority of the population) is fundamentally undemocratic. But of course, democracy has never been Treatyists' long suit.

21. (1910) 30 NZLR 343.

22. [1987] 2 NZLR 188.

23. [1987] 1 NZLR 641.

24. *Tainui Maori Trust Board* v. *Attorney-General* [1989] 2 NZLR 513.

25. *Te Runanga o Muriwhenua Inc. Society* v. *Attorney-General* [1990] 2 NZLR 641.

26. The fee tail was a device for 'entailing' a landed estate, so that it would remain forever in a family. The heir in each generation would have no more than a life interest. Although the fee tail was a proper lawfully-recognised fee, the common law preferred the fee simple, the ordinary sort of land ownership known to us today, and the law recognised various devices which would in effect turn a fee tail into a fee simple. A 'fee' is simply a heritable estate in land.

27. (1989) 19 VUWLR 335 at 345.

28. *The Principle of 'Partnership' and the Treaty;* PANZ Monograph No. 6.

29. (1990) 14 NZULR 5.

30. [1989] 2 NZLR 513.

31. Section 6(2).

32. *A State Servant looks at the Treaty,* (1990) 14 NZULR 82.

33. *Attorney-General* v. *New Zealand Maori Council (No. 1)* [1991] 2 NZLR 129, *Attorney-General* v. *New Zealand Maori Council (No. 2)* [1991] 2 NZLR 147.

34. [1994] 1 All ER 623.

35. *N.Z. Maori Council* v. *Attorney-General* [1989] 2 NZLR 142.

36. [1994] 2 NZLR 20.

37. A143/97.

38. [1991] NZLJ 228.

39. *The Press,* 25 March 1997.

40. P.651.

41. Dick Scott, *Ask That Mountain,* Heinemann/Southern Cross, Auckland, 1975.

42. The Race Relations Conciliator has already decided that this phrase – as intemperate a piece of racist invective as one could surely ever find – is not objectionable under the Race Relations Act.

43. [1993] NZLJ 229.

44. *Tahora 2F2 Block* v. *Waiora District Council,* 4 March 1997.

45. [1986] 1 NZLR 680.

46. Urban Maori authorities have complained to the Human Rights Commission that the Fisheries Commission refuses to employ urban Maoris, and that this is discrimination 'on the basis of race, colour and ethnic origin'.

47. *North and South,* March 1998.

Chapter Six

1. *The Future Eaters*, p. 55.
2. Jared Diamond, in *The Rise and Fall of the Third Chimpanzee* (Vintage, London, 1992), gives the figure of 28; Carolyn King, in *Immigrant Killers* (Oxford University Press, Auckland, 1984), gives 35.
3. See the tables at the end of *Immigrant Killers*.
4. The evidence suggests that the Polynesian rat, the kiore, was introduced to New Zealand perhaps almost 2,000 years ago, presumably by wandering human voyagers. It still seems, however, that the first permanent human settlement was by Maoris only about 800 years ago.
5. Barney Brewster, 1987, *Te Moa: the life and death of New Zealand's unique bird*. Nikau Press, Nelson.
6. *The Future Eaters*, pp. 246–47.
7. Geoff Park, 1995 *Nga Uruora: the groves of life*. Victoria University Press, Wellington.
8. *Otago Daily Times*, 19 June 1997.
9. Pigeon poaching is not restricted to Northland. 'Dr Margaret Mutu, a [then] member of the New Zealand Conservation Authority, has encouraged iwi at public meetings to exercise their right to harvest native wildlife. She asserts that harvest in forests such as Herekino in her tribal territory is sustainable, although she has done no scientific assessment . . . To deny a Maori [pigeon], says Mutu, is no different from denying Pakeha bread. [Pigeon] are part of the staple diet. They are part of what I expect to see on the table when I go to the local marae.' Other activists insist that the right to harvest is inalienable even if the birds go extinct in the process. *Forest & Bird*, November 1995.
10. *Press*, 21 June 1988.
11. A claim implicitly denied by the Waitangi Tribunal, which has criticised the Resource Management Act, and claimed that it is 'fatally flawed', because it makes 'sustainable management' its guiding principles, and not the Treaty (Ngawha Geothermal Report, Wai 304).
12. Ngawha Geothermal Report.
13. References in the Act to Maori interests oblige every local body to perform regular meaningless homage. The Canterbury Regional Council's Draft Natural Resources Regional Plan (Part A: Air, Christchurch), pp. 17–18, describes the effect of air pollution on 'tangata whenua values' thus: 'Poor ambient air quality also detracts from the value of clean air as taonga to tangata whenua. Air is significant to tangata whenua because of its interrelationship with other resources (e.g. water, flora and fauna) and its life-supporting capacity. The Regional Council is committed to establishing a rela-

tionship with tangata whenua in Canterbury which recognises the principle of rangatiratanga in respect of their resources and other taonga while maintaining the Council's own authority and responsibility to control discharges to air. Consultation in previous years has identified that tangata whenua want "all harmful contaminants removed from air discharges" and the cessation of all harmful discharges into air which threaten the life-supporting capacity of air, land and water. It is important that the physical, amenity, aesthetic and life-supporting qualities of clean air as taonga be maintained. Reducing the adverse health effects of air pollution will assist the health status of Maori people, particularly for those with respiratory complaints.' Does this sort of waffle tell us anything more than that Maoris, just like everyone else, dislike air pollution and want a healthy environment?

14. *Nelson Mail,* 23 March 1998.
15. *EDS and Tai Tokerau District Maori Council* v. *Mangonui County Council* (1989) 13 NZTPA 197.
16. *Otago Daily Times,* 6 September 1997.
17. [1995] 3 NZLR 553.
18. Hugh Barr, pers.comm.
19. *Otago Daily Times,* 24 March 1993.
20. According to a paper prepared by Bruce Mason, Public Access New Zealand researcher.
21. *Forest & Bird,* February 1994.
22. An amended statement of claim dated 31 July 1998 makes it explicit that 'this claim is about te tino rangatiratanga'.
23. Aldo Leopold, *A Sand County Almanac,* Oxford University Press, New York, 1949.

Chapter Seven

1. Kenneth Minogue, *Waitangi: Morality and Reality,* New Zealand Business Roundtable, 1998.
2. *New Internationalist,* May 1992.
3. A recent neo-fascist poster in Christchurch called for the death penalty for rapists and child molesters as well as murderers. For some reason Mr Mike Moore, M.P., considered this poster 'racist'. We might well apply other adjectives to it, but 'racist' does seem to be the wrong one.
4. *The Press,* 24 March, 1998.
5. This is a principle similar to Freud's 'There are times when a cigar is only a cigar'.
6. See correspondence in *The Press* in May 1995, citing requests from Maori elders and the petition to Parliament of Wi Te Hakiro in 1876.
7. *The Press,* 11 February 1997.

8. *Hansard,* 18 December 1985.
9. *The Press,* undated, report on Statistics New Zealand figures.
10. The quotation is from the Commission's own explanatory pamphlet. Article 25 of the Constitution does, after generally guaranteeing the safety of property, allow its expropriation in certain circumstances, subject to the payment of compensation. This expropriation is, however, just as much for the purposes of land reform, and bringing about equitable access to resources, as for the remedying of past confiscations. The confiscations, in any case, are far more recent: they can date back no later than 1913, and most will actually be in living memory.
11. *The Press,* 4 May 1995.
12. *The Press,* 23 September 1997.
13. *N.Z. Education Review,* 25 October 1996.

Chapter Eight

1. Quoted in the *National Business Review,* 11 April 1997.
2. David Lange (*Press,* 11 February 1997): 'The government shouldn't hand out public money without being sure exactly what it will get for it. Maori agencies shouldn't take public money unless they are willing and able to account to the public at large for their spending of it.'

INDEX